From Apology
To Protest:

The Black American Novel

From Apology To Protest:

The Black American Novel

Noel Schraufnagel

EVERETT / EDWARDS, inc.

POST OFFICE BOX 1060
DELAND, FLORIDA 32720

)

Library of Congress Catalog Card Number 72-95180
Standard Book Number 0-912112-02-6
Everett/Edwards, inc., DeLand, Florida 32720
©1973 by Noel Schraufnagel
All Rights Reserved
Published 1973
Printed in the United States of America

To Darlene, Darcy, and Dana.

CONTENTS

Introduction

The birth of the modern Negro novel is marked by the publication of Richard Wright's *Native Son* in 1940, in the same way that the modern English novel is dated by the 1740 edition of Samuel Richardson's *Pamela*. Both authors changed the course of fiction in their respective eras. Before the appearance of *Native Son* most of the novels of black Americans either avoided racial issues, or were in the apologetic tradition, which portrayed heroic Negro characters who were physically victimized by white racists. Wright began a new trend in protest literature by presenting a character who is psychologically thwarted by racism. The example of *Native Son* evoked the production of similar novels during the forties. The evolution of this movement into the militant protest novel of the sixties, as well as the reaction of overt forms of social protest, is the subject of this study. The major novels of the period between 1940 and 1970 will be discussed. Minor literary streams, such as science fiction and detective stories, are excluded, primarily because they are not directly related to the mainstream of black fiction.

The psychological impact of racism presented in *Native Son* and the Wrightian protest novels of the forties depicted the Negro as a depraved victim of American society. Protest fiction eventually changed, however, and the *apologetic novel* came into vogue following World War II. This trend depicts an exemplary black protagonist who is physically challenged by bigoted whites. At about the same time apologetic protest emerged, a reaction against protest was launched. The result was the rise of the *accommodationist novel.* This type of fiction does not avoid racial issues but deals more specifically with the development of an individual black character as he struggles to adjust to white society. This tendency of the characters to accommodate themselves to white America, rather than to fight it, was carried over into another fictional movement. The *assimilationist novel*, dealing primarily with white characters, became popular in the fifties as black novelists attempted to escape the shadow of *Native Son*. The protagonist of Wright's novel, though, could not be ignored and he eventually evolved into the revolutionist of the *militant protest novel*. The latter trend depicts blacks in an organized retaliation against whites.

The covert form of white oppression portrayed in *Native Son* dehumanized the black protagonist. The ghetto inhabitant therefore retaliated with acts of violence that satisfied his sense of helplessness, and thus emerged as a symbol of rebellion against a racist American society. He served as a prototype for the characters that appeared in other novels in the years following the publication of *Native Son*. Wright himself, after achieving international fame, acted the role of a rebel by becoming an expatriate. From his self-imposed exile in Europe he enjoyed a brief but influential reign in the realm of the Negro novel. The Wrightian style of psychological protest was prevalent in the forties. With Bigger Thomas as a pattern, black authors such as Ann Petry and Chester Himes presented oppressed figures who were denied the opportunity to develop as individuals. The characters had no ambitions or dreams comparable to those of whites, as a racist atmosphere tended to produce people with inferiority complexes, or some other form of emotional instability. These social misfits, judged from the white point of view, were shown to be the inevitable result of the American society.

After World War II, however, the Wrightian protest novel was replaced by several distinct literary trends. The fiction patterned after *Native Son* began to disappear as black authors revealed a preference to depict the diversity of Negro life. Racial protest remained popular, but it was treated in different ways. One approach was the revival of the apologetic protest novel by Willard Savoy and William Gardner Smith. In this type of fiction, a talented black protagonist attempts to advance socially, or to oppose the white power structure, and is subsequently victimized by prejudiced whites. This direct confrontation with white authority is in contrast to the method used by Wright and his followers. Rather than portraying the psychological effects of racism, the apologetic writers attempted to show that the blacks who are fortunate enough to escape the ghetto are nevertheless doomed if they try to assert themselves as human beings. Physical retaliation is the primary method of depriving Negroes of their rights.

As the apologetic protest movement was struggling to fill the gap left by the decline of the Wrightian novel in the late forties, a different fictional trend made an appearance. Protest elements were relegated to a position of secondary importance by novelists who were more concerned with revealing the individual problems of black characters striving to enter the mainstream of American life. In these accommodationist novels the protagonists do not directly challenge the authority of the whites. They merely attempt to adjust to the special problems created by a hostile world. One of the primary goals is to find a relatively comfortable place in life without altering the society that is controlled by whites. Social aspects are not ignored but they are not the primary emphasis as in the protest novels. Such writers as William Demby, J. Saunders Redding, Ralph Ellison, and James Baldwin reacted to the overtly propagandistic novels of the era by concentrating on the diversity of the black experience in America. By stressing the unique problems of individuals rather than the evils of racism, the accommodationist authors were generally able to be more objective in their work. Consequently, such prominent novels as Ellison's *Invisible Man* and Baldwin's *Go Tell It on the Mountain* dominated the early fifties.

While this type of fiction was the major challenge to protest literature, some black authors abandoned racial material completely in an effort to obtain objectivity. The assimilationist novelists, then, by concentrating on white characters, attempted to avoid the label of propagandists. They preferred to become a part of the American literary tradition rather than to become spokesmen for the Negro. From an artistic point of view, assimilationism theoretically allowed the author freedom to explore his subject matter without producing a tract. He could portray American life from the viewpoint of a detached observer instead of an embittered victim. The assimilationist novel came into vogue in the fifties as former protest and accommodationist writers such as Ann Petry, William Gardner Smith, Chester Himes, and James Baldwin experimented in the area; however these same writers entered the protest realm with later novels. The movement towards a renewed interest in racial pride evolved from the civil rights activities that gained impetus with the growing fame of Martin Luther King. On almost a reverse ratio the assimilationist trend declined and was virtually abandoned in the sixties.

The death of assimilationism was accompanied by the rebirth of militant protest. In 1954, the year the Supreme Court began a new era in civil rights by ruling against segregated schools, John Oliver Killens and William Gardner Smith started a new trend in fiction. The militant protest novel depicts blacks in an organized effort to resist white oppression. Unlike Wrightian protest, in which the protagonist strikes out blindly in an individual act of violence, a planned retaliatory measure is perpetrated. This type of protest novel was first produced by Sutton Griggs. His *Imperium In Imperio* (1899) related how a secret organization of blacks attempted to take over the state of Texas. The novel was met with disfavor, however, and militancy was abandoned, with a few exceptions, until its revival by Killens and Smith. The former's *Youngblood* (1954) depicted the rebellion begun by a black laborer in the South who refused, finally, to be cheated by his white employer. Smith's *South Street* (1954) revealed the need for an armed Negro organization to combat white violence in the streets of Philadelphia.

It was not until the sixties, though, when the American scene was shaken by many violent racial confrontations, that the militant protest novel became popular. The passive tactics of Martin Luther King not only challenged the discriminatory practices of much of the country, but evoked the emergence of such radical leaders as Malcolm X. The latter figure emerged as the archetype of the militant protagonist in the fiction of John A. Williams, Ronald Fair, James Baldwin, and Sam Greenlee. The militant novels of the period portray violence as a necessary means of shocking whites into realizing that blacks are demanding immediate enactment of their rights, and an end of institutionalized racism. Force is regarded as the only answer to racial oppression in a country that has continually failed to fulfill its obligations to minority groups. The armed revolution depicted in Greenlee's *The Spook Who Sat by the Door* (1969) is the ultimate threat to white racism in the militant novel, as well as a gruesome prophecy for the United States.

Along with the emergence of the militant protest novel as a major factor in Negro fiction of the sixties, apologetic protest developed into a more respectable art form. Young writers such as John A. Williams and Ernest J. Gaines gave new life to the trend by presenting protagonists who were less idealized than the typical characters of an earlier era. Rather than dealing with romantic individuals who are destroyed by a white mob, apologetic novelists of the sixties depicted Negroes who merely tried to escape from poverty and injustice. In rebelling from the denial of their human dignity, they were not the victims of violence, but of the more subtle types of racism. These characters struggled against oppression on an individual basis with a definite goal in mind. Thus they represent a middle ground between the Wrightian rebels, who commit blind acts of violence, and the organized groups of the militants.

Despite the prevalence of protest fiction in the sixties the accommodationist trend also continued to thrive. The number of Negro novels increased greatly during this period and not all of the authors embraced militancy or individual rebellion. As in the previous decade when Ellison and Baldwin led the revolt against protest, accommodationist writers continued to depict the efforts of Negroes to adjust to the middle-class way of life. The typical protagonist, epitomized in Kristin Hunter's *God Bless the Child* (1964), is concerned with moving up the social ladder—in escaping the deprivations of the ghetto. One of the major themes is the quest for an identity within the culture dominated by whites. The movement toward racial pride, so prevalent in protest fiction, is subordinated to the attainment of a relatively comfortable and secure place in American life. Discrimination makes this goal difficult but all the more coveted. The movement towards equality, then, is made within the established rules of conduct rather than through violence or another form of overt challenge to white authority.

The three decades of the Negro novel under consideration here consist essentially of three types of protest fiction, as well as accommodationism and assimilationism. James Baldwin's career is perhaps best representative of the novelistic tendencies of the period. He violently objected to the propagandistic intent of *Native Son* and produced *Go Tell It on the Mountain* (1953) as an example of the direction black writers should take. He later changed his attitude by forsaking accommodationism and writing *Giovanni's Room* (1956), a novel with white characters which propagandized for the cause of homosexuality. In the sixties Baldwin entered the realm of racial protest with *Another Country* (1962), an apologetic novel that revealed how a Negro was destroyed by systematic racism. This was followed by a militant book, *Tell Me How Long the Train's Been Gone* (1968). The increasing social commitment of Baldwin, the country's most famous black writer, is indicative of the general mood of black novelists. Once the aesthetic reaction to the pattern protest novel receded, the tendency to concentrate on an exposition of American racist practices ensued. However, the writers have shown, over the years, an ability to combine artistic elements with a social message. The result is that *Native Son,* despite its influence, is no longer the single novel by an Afro-American to be widely read in this country. Some of the significant American novels since 1950 have been produced by black authors.

About the Author

The author is a native of Abbotsford, Wisconsin, graduating from the local high school in 1957. After several years as a factory worker he enrolled at the University of Wisconsin - River Falls, winning the Chisholm Award (1966) and receiving a B.A. in 1967. He received an NDEA Fellowship, and subsequently a Ph.D., from the University of Nebraska. Currently he is an Associate Professor of English at Alcorn A.&M. College in Lorman, Mississippi. He is married and the father of twin daughters.

CHAPTER I

Before *Native Son*

It was not until the middle of the twentieth century that novels by American Negroes became numerous. However, since the publication of William Wells Brown's *Clotel, or the President's Daughter* (1853) the dominant theme in the Negro novel is the problem black people face by living in a racist society. Black novelists in the United States have responded to white oppression by exposing it in their fiction either in an overtly propagandistic manner or by subjugating the protest elements to aesthetic principles in a method that nevertheless covertly condemns discriminatory practices. But the question of what it means to be a Negro in a country that has institutionalized racial discrimination persists regardless of the style or talent of the author.

The conditions under which blacks were forced to live in the nineteenth century were conducive to the writing of protest fiction but there were few Negroes who had the freedom, the education or the time to write. Beginning in the late eighteenth century, though, there were several white writers who produced anti-slavery novels. Hugh Henry Brackenridge's *Modern Chivalry* (1792-1815), *The Oriental Philanthropist* (1800) by Henry Sherburne, *The Algerine Captive* (1797) by Royall Tyler, *The Slave, or Memoirs of Archy Moore* (1836) by Richard Hildreth, and *Recollections of a Southern Matron* (1836) by Caroline Howard Gilman fit into this category. But it remained for Harriet Beecher Stowe's *Uncle Tom's Cabin* (1852) to catch the imagination of much of the nation. The novel is designed to emphasize the inhumanity of the people who profit from the slave trade as

1

contrasted with the Christian humility of Uncle Tom. In her depiction of Tom and the Harris family, Mrs. Stowe attempts to destroy the myth of the domestic tranquility of the plantation.

Uncle Tom's Cabin attacked not only the conditions of slavery but the type of fiction known as the plantation tradition. Produced primarily by white Southerners to defend slavery, the plantation tradition created stereotypes of Negroes in an effort to prove that they were naturally inferior, and content only under the protection of the white master on the plantation. Sterling Brown sums up the tradition in his study first published in 1937:

> The pattern seldom varied: scenes of bliss on the plantation alternated with scenes of squalor in the free North. The contented slave, the clown and the wretched freedman are the Negro stereotypes, ... A plantation with a kindly master was basis for generalizing about all plantations, of whatever type, in whatever sections. A pampered house-servant, who refuses uncertain freedom for a comparatively easy place, becomes 'the' Negro slave; a poor unemployed wretch becomes 'the' freedman.
>
> The intractable, the ironic, the abused Negro is nowhere on these plantations . . . runaways in these books are generally flighty creatures and half-wits, and even they finally steal back to the South. Judicial records might be filled of instances of brutality, but the occasional whippings are shown to be for due cause such as stealing a ham from a poor woman who could not spare it. Miscegenation is missing in spite of the proofs walking about in the great houses or in the fields or the slavepens. Slavery is shown as a beneficent guardianship, never as a system of cheap and abundant labor that furnished the basis of a few large fortunes (and assured an impoverished, disfranchised class of poor whites).[1]

Given impetus by such early nineteenth century novelists as George Tucker, John Pendleton Kennedy, William Gilmore Simms, and Nathaniel Beverly Tucker, the plantation tradition became a fixture in American literature. It grew to its greatest strength after the publication of *Uncle Tom's Cabin*. Against this literary background, William Wells Brown, an ex-slave who fled to England with the help of a Quaker family, produced *Clotel* (1853). Published in London, the novel is a propagandistic condemnation of slavery designed to advance the Abolitionist cause. The plot is interspersed with tales of the inhumanity practiced by whites against slaves. In addition the author inserts his own comments on the evils of slavery in an effort to contradict the plantation tradition as thoroughly as possible.

The plot of *Clotel, or the President's Daughter* revolves around a mulatto woman and her two daughters who are sold as slaves after the mother has been discarded by her white lover. The separate careers of the three women are traced but the emphasis is on one of the daughters, Clotel, who finally ends her tragic life by drowning in the Potomac River as she is being pursued by a gang of whites. The fact that she dies within sight of the White House, occupied by Thomas Jefferson, is more than a coincidence, as the title of the novel suggests. Brown comments on the suicide of Clotel by stating that it

> should be an evidence wherever it should be known, of the inconquerable love of liberty the heart may inherit; as well as a fresh admonition to the slave dealer, of the cruelty and enormity of his crime.[2]

Brown reiterates this thesis throughout the book. Although it adds nothing to the literary value of *Clotel*, the patent propagandistic approach indicates the author's basic concern. He is interested only in exposing the evils of slavery and in refuting the claims of the plantation tradition. Primarily because of the inclusion of Jefferson in the reprobation of the American system of slavery, though, *Clotel* was not published in the United States until 1867. The American edition Is in a revised form in which an anonymous senator is substituted for the President. Reference to the President was also deleted from the title.

The first novel by an American Negro published in this country is Frank Webb's *The Garies and Their Friends* (1857). It deals with a woman of Negro ancestry who passes for white. She marries a white man and lives peacefully in Philadelphia until the secret of her lineage is discovered. The result is mob violence in which Mr. Garie, her husband, is killed. As in the case of *Clotel*, Webb's novel exposes the effects of racism without showing much concern for literature as art.

Before the Civil War the only other long piece of fiction published by a black was Martin Delany's "Blake, or the Huts of America." A fragment of a novel, "Blake" (1859) appeared in the *Anglo-African Magazine*. The twenty-six extant chapters extol the virtues of the black characters, including their intelligence and beauty. The protagonist is a runaway slave who travels throughout the South in an effort to organize slave uprisings. The fragment is filled with the horrors of slavery and is modeled to a large degree on *Uncle Tom's Cabin*, the major differences being that the Christian symbol of Uncle Tom is replaced by a militant figure resembling Stowe's George Harris.

Black American fiction, then, was born in the protest tradition established by the white Abolitionists. Both William Wells Brown and Martin Delany borrow freely from the model provided by *Uncle Tom's Cabin*. The ingredients for this type of anti-slavery novel included

> The separation of husbands from their wives and parents from their children ... the cruelties of overseers; the hair-breadth escapes of fugitives from their wicked pursuers; the insincerity of pro-slavery clergymen; the demoralizing influence of the slave system as a whole upon the white people of the South, ...[3]

and the glorification of black characters in response to the crude stereotypes illustrated by the plantation tradition. The antithetical stereotypes that appeared in the Abolitionist fiction were just as grotesque. They reveal the fact that Negro characters were used essentially as devices to argue for or against slavery.

Frank Webb's *The Garies and Their Friends*, though, indicated that there was more at stake than slavery. Freedom did not eliminate racial prejudice and discrimination. After the Civil War the battle of the books continued to reveal the furor created by the presence of blacks in a white country. The plantation tradition insisted upon the contented existence of the slave and the wretched life of the freedman. Thomas Nelson Page emerged as the most prominent white writer from the South to assert the validity of the Southern system of treating blacks as inferiors. He was aided in his propagandistic program by such compatriots as Grace Elizabeth King, Ruth McEnery Stuart, James Lane Allen, Maurice Thompson, Harry Stillwell Edwards, Joel Chandler Harris, Walter Hines Page, and F. Hopkinson Smith. As the Abolitionist cause subsided, many white novelists from the North imitated the Southern image of the Negro. Theodore L. Gross states that

> In the 1880's such Northern writers as Frank Stockton, Harriet Spofford, and Constance Fenimore Woolson accepted the Southern version of the Reconstruction; the admirable freedman of Reconstruction was the devoted Negro who recalled his contented existence before the war and who voluntarily remained faithful to his past masters. The favorite formula of Reconstruction authors—Northern and Southern—was one in which the Negro alleviated his ex-master's poverty.[4]

The plantation tradition in the late nineteenth century insisted upon the subjugation of the Negro to his white superiors. The proper role of a black after the legal abolishment of slavery was that of a servant. The faithful retainer was contrasted with the wretched freedman who had neither the inclination nor the intelligence to make a living for himself. Under the guidance of benevolent whites, however, the blacks could be expected to regain the happiness they enjoyed as slaves when they sang and danced on the plantation.

The vast majority of American Negroes were too busy struggling for an existence during the Reconstruction to produce a significant amount of literature. In the absence of black novelists, and in the decline of the Abolitionist works fashioned after Harriet Beecher Stowe, other white writers took up the battle in behalf of a more reasonable presentation of black characters in fiction. Earlier, Herman Melville had displayed a tendency towards the creation of fictional Negroes who were individuals rather than types. After the Civil War the novels of Albion W. Tourgée, Mark Twain, and George Washington Cable most effectively combated the image created by the plantation tradition.

Tourgée, a former Union soldier who lived in post-bellum North Carolina, wrote several novels in whch he championed the Negro cause, the best known being *A Fool's Errand* (1879) and *Brick's Without Straw* (1880). Tourgée tends, however, to idealize the freedman of the Reconstruction, in a direct assault on the Southern stereotype, rather than to create individual black characters. Cable remedied this situation to some extent in *The Grandissimes* (1880), his famous novel of race relations in the South. The legendary story of Bras Coupé, the heroic black African prince who refuses to become a slave, is repeated by various characters throughout the novel. It provides an ironic contrast to the miserable life of Honore Grandissime, "free man of color," who cannot escape from the stigma of possessing Negro blood in the hypocritical Creole society of New Orleans at the time of the Louisiana Purchase.

Perhaps only *Huckleberry Finn* presents a more interesting portrayal of a black character than *The Grandissimes* in nineteenth century American literature. Although Jim is exploited as a stereotype at the beginning and end of the novel, Twain's humanistic depiction of the black man, who desires the freedom of himself and his family, is one of the high points of the book. The emphasis is on Jim as a singular human being, and it is to this that Huck responds, rather than to the concept of race. Twain is much less successful in *Pudd'nhead Wilson*, in which he deals with ideas relating to race and environment more than with individual characters.

By the last decade of the nineteenth century black writers began to enter the novelistic arena themselves as a Negro middle class started to emerge. The emphasis in most of the novels produced at this time is on the creation of counter-stereotypes to combat the degrading images projected by the Southerners. Frances Harper's *Iola Leroy* (1886), "helped to establish the precedent of developing well-mannered, educated colored characters to offset the stock-characters of the plantation tradition."[5] *Appointed* (1894), a novel by Walter Stowers and William H. Anderson, dealt with a systematic program of oppression as applied by whites. *Hearts of Gold* (1896), by J. McHenry Jones, revealed the injustices practiced against Negroes, while it praised the black upper classes as models of decorum. Pauline E. Hopkins, in *Contending Forces* (1900), followed the example of Jones in "placing the case of worthy but oppressed Negroes before the bar of American justice."[6]

It remained for Sutton Griggs, though, to sound the note of militancy that was not to be matched for over half a century. His first novel, *Imperium in Imperio* (1889), a forerunner of such militant protest novels as *Sons of Darkness, Sons of Light* (1969) and *The Spook Who Sat by the Door* (1969), reveals a plan to take the state of Texas by force under the direction of a secret Negro organization. The novel begins as a farce when two black youths, Belton Piedmont and Bernard Belgrave, vie for academic honors in a prep school in the South. Both boys are extremely intelligent, but as they go their separate ways after graduation they discover that being black is a handicap that cannot be easily overcome. Belton is actually lynched for helping a white girl find the right page in her hymn book in church and escapes only by feigning death when the whites cut down the rope too soon.

After a number of years of discrimination, Belton becomes part of the Imperium in Imperio, a black organization that acts as a secret governmental force for the protection of Negro rights throughout the United States. When Bernard, Belton's old rival, is initiated into the Imperium, he sways many of the members into a militant position. When a Negro is lynched because of his appointment to the position of postmaster, Bernard proposes his militant plan to form a separate Negro nation in Texas. Belton objects by preaching moderation and patriotism, but he is executed for refusing to cooperate with the cause of the organization. Only the betrayal of one of the moderate members of the Imperium keeps Bernard's plan of vengeance from being put into action.

There was not much of a market for militant protest at the turn of the century, however, and Griggs turned to writing apologetic fiction in his later work, which included *Overshadowed* (1901), *Unfettered* (1902), *The Hindered Hand* (1905) and *Pointing the Way* (1908). Unlike the racial protest novels of the 1940's which explore the psychological effects of racial prejudice, the earlier protests against racism concentrated primarily on physical results in the manner of the anti-slavery novels such as *Uncle Tom's Cabin* or *Clotel*. Sterling Brown defines an apologist novel as a form of protest against the plantation tradition in which Negro characters are presented as models of decorum.

> The heroines are modest and beautiful, frequently octoroon; the heroes are handsome and priggish, frequently black. . . . The villains are too often poor-whites. The incidents are romantic and often fantastic. The injuries of the Negro are seldom conveyed with full power; like the abolitionists, these novelists thought that listing would make up for rendering. The race problem, at the core of their work, turns their novels into tracts. Acceptance of certain traits as racial, such as optimism, loyalty and faith, and underestimation of the Negro masses invalidate much of their discussion.[7]

The concept of apologizing for a race was not especially conducive to exploring the depths of the black experience. J. Saunders Redding suggests that if a black writer, at the beginning of the twentieth century, wanted an audience he had to conform to the accepted standards of Negro behavior or dissemble completely by writing of white characters.[8] This meant, in the absence of a novelist skilled or independent enough to depict the essence of Negro life, that a black novelist wrote either in opposition to the plantation tradition, by portraying counter-stereotypes, or that he ignored Negroes entirely. Grigg's *Imperium in Imperio* conforms partially to the former pattern, but its militancy violated the code of decorum and the novel achieved little popularity. More to the liking of the white audience was the work of Paul Laurence Dunbar. A popular poet who catered to the tastes of white America, Dunbar wrote four novels which were published around the turn of the century. The first of these, *The Uncalled* (1898), is a relatively competent novel of a white youth who becomes a minister, under the stern guidance of his guardian, only to discover that love is of more consequence than a God of vengeance. Reminiscent of Harold Frederic's famous study of the psychological destruction of a strict Calvinist in *The Damnation of Theron Ware* (1896), *The Uncalled* revealed a potential that was never fulfilled, as Dunbar turned to melodramatic romance in his later works. *The Love of Landry* (1900) and *The Fanatics* (1901) deal with white lovers who are separated because of class barriers and political differences. Dunbar wrote of black characters in *The Sport of the Gods* (1902) but his thesis corresponds to that of the plantation tradition. In this novel he echoed the philosophy of Booker T. Washington by urging the black masses to remain in the South to provide a labor force for white industry. However, his argument is weakened by the use of the plantation concepts of the wretched freedman and the faithful retainer. Dunbar even resorted to didactic passages about the wicked influence of the urban North on poor and uneducated blacks in an effort to convince his audience that the South was the proper home of Negroes.

Dunbar, though, was not typical of the black author of his time. Patronized by William Dean Howells, he sought to become popular rather than to retain the racial and literary integrity he possessed as a young man. Charles W. Chesnutt sounded the note of racial protest, still basically apologetic, that dominated the black fiction early in the twentieth century. His first novel, *House Behind the Cedars* (1900), deals with the theme of "passing." Rena Walden, reared in a house provided by her mother's white lover, in the colored section of the town, decides to pass for white and to marry her white suitor. Her deception is discovered and Rena spends the rest of her short life in obscurity. A change of heart by the Southern lawyer, who had dismissed her after he learned of her Negro blood, comes too late, as the young woman dies before he can confess his love for her.

While *The House Behind the Cedars*, despite its melodrama, is perhaps Chesnutt's best novel, in his two later efforts he deals more directly with the problem of conflict between the white and black races. In *The Marrow of Tradition* (1901) he bases the plot on the riots that occurred in Wilmington, North Carolina in 1898 when Negroes tried to vote. Dr. Miller, the black protagonist, is a moderate on the issue of retaliation until his son is killed in the rioting. He is tempted to change his position and commit himself in favor of violent retaliation until his professional ethics enter the picture. He performs an operation which saves the life of a white boy and in the process decides that violence is not the answer to white oppression.

In his third novel, *The Colonel's Dream* (1905), Chesnutt exposes the Southern system of exploiting black labor. The tone of the novel is conciliatory, however, as Colonel French, the white protagonist, designs a plan which will provide blacks with adequate opportunities in the labor market. The novel deals with race relations in a practical manner, but Chesnutt is more concerned with stating his argument than in writing good fiction.

Chesnutt's fiction suffers as a result of his propagandistic purposes. His novels indicate a desire to combat the discrimination typical of his own life, as well as to offset the image of the Negro as projected by white writers. At the time that Chesnutt was writing, a relatively new concept of black depravity was presented to the public. The stereotypes of the plantation tradition were joined by the image of the brute Negro that emerged from the work of Hinton Helper, Thomas Nelson Page, and Charles Carroll. The supreme white racist, however, was the Reverend Thomas Dixon who, in his *Trilogy of Reconstruction*, attempted to retain the old tradition of the South by appealing to the baser emotions of humanity. *The Leopard's Spots* (1902), *The Clansman* (1905) and *The Traitor* (1907) are defenses of the terrorist tactics of the Ku Klux Klan. The Negro, in the propaganda of Dixon, is displayed as a primitive savage who will commit any crime in his lust for white flesh. In *The Clansman*, from which the infamous 1916 movie *The Birth of a Nation* was created, a brute Negro rapes a white woman only to be identified when it is discovered that his image has been imprinted on the cornea of the dead victim. Negroes, according to Dixon, corrupt everything "white" that they come in contact with and therefore the Klan is eulogized as the preserver of Aryan culture and the protector of white womanhood.

The literary advent of the brute Negro did not dramatically change the fiction produced by the apologetic black writers. W. E. B. DuBois and James Weldon Johnson did publish novels which tend to approach the racial protest novels of the 1940's in their systematic and intrinsic condemnation of white oppression, but they are still of the old school of apologetic protest which aggrandizes black characters without getting to the core of the consequences of racism. DuBois, the famous sociologist, tried his hand at fiction in *The Quest of the Silver Fleece* (1911).

The book is an attempt to expose the economic roots of racial discrimination. The black protagonists, Bles and Zora, are robbed of their cotton crop by a Southern landowner. As a result they move from the South to Washington, D.C., where they attempt to put political pressure on the plantation system. Failing to accomplish much, they return to the South to organize black sharecroppers into a cooperative system. The ultimate goal is to join the poor blacks with the poor whites to combat the cotton trust.

Despite his knowledge of social and economic conditions, DuBois, as David Littlejohn states,

> indulged in the literary excesses of his era to a voluptuous degree. ... His two Negro heroes are sublimely heroic fantasy creatures. ... The villains, to balance, are diabolically villainous. The morally biased cosmetic high color of both high life and low life; the crude caricatures of outsiders; the constant 'high blood pressure' effect of his frenziedly artificial events—one either winces at all this excess, or (a common effect of good melodrama) is ashamed of giving in.[9]

The failings of DuBois are only partially remedied in James Weldon Johnson's *The Autobiography of an Ex-Coloured Man* (1912). Published anonymously, the novel, despite its concern with the overworked theme of passing, its pedantic discussions of race relations, and its digressions, presents a panoramic view of Negro life and the color problem. Johnson presents most of his insights into black-white relationships in the reflections of the narrator rather than through the action itself; nevertheless he analyzes many of the major race problems to a greater extent than any other novelist of his era.

The narrator, a talented and educated man of Negro ancestry, who is presumably relating his autobiography, decides to pass for white after observing a multitude of harrowing experiences of racial prejudice. In watching a black man being burned to death by a mob of whites, he concludes that he does not want to be branded as an inferior simply because of a small percentage of "Negro Blood." He tries to rationalize his decision to become a member of the white race by convincing himself that the greater opportunities inherent in being white, and the fear of being lynched, are not the basic factors. He later realizes that his choice is a cowardly one, but he cannot make the move that will transform him into a "nigger."

From his advantageous position as a white man, the narrator has the opportunity to observe various facets of both races in their relationship to each other. He is aware that black people are forced to look on all things not only from the aspect of an individual citizen but from the viewpoint of a "nigger." They have to perform the role that white people expect of them. Johnson's hero reflects on this situation:

> This gives to every coloured man, in proportion to his intellectuality, a sort of dual personality; there is one phase of him which is disclosed only in the free-masonry of his own race. I have often watched with interest and sometimes with amazement even ignorant coloured men under cover of broad grins and minstrel antics maintain this dualism in the presence of white men.[10]

This dual personality is basically a defense mechanism, but it also allows Negroes to understand more about the white race than the whites know about their darker counterparts. Blinded by their prejudice, the whites see only what they want to in connection with Negroes. If a grinning minstrel satisfies a white bigot, that is what the Negro shows him. While this is far from an ideal situation, it is reason enough for the narrator of the novel to be slightly optimistic about the plight of the Negro,

> for it indicates that the main difficulty of the race question does not lie so much in the actual condition of the blacks as it does in the mental attitude of the whites; and a mental attitude, especially one not based on truth, can be changed more easily than actual conditions.[11]

The primary need of the blacks is an opportunity to compete for social, economic, and political positions that are not closed simply by the blind hatred of the majority of whites. One of the major impediments to the attainment of equal opportunities, according to the narrator, is the literary image of the Negro projected by white writers. He states that

> log cabins and plantations and dialect-speaking 'darkies' are perhaps better known in American literature than any other single picture of our national life. Indeed, they form an ideal and exclusive literary concept of the American Negro to such an extent that it is almost impossible to get the reading public to recognize him in any other setting; ... This generally accepted literary ideal of the American Negro constitutes what is really an obstacle in the way of the thoughtful and progressive element of the race. His character has been established as a happy-go-lucky, laughing, shuffling, banjo-picking being, and the reading public has not yet been prevailed upon to take him seriously. His efforts to elevate himself socially are looked upon as a sort of absurd caricature of 'white civilization.'[12]

Johnson, through his fictional representative, calls for a new tradition in literature which will depict the various aspects of

Negro life, especially the attempts of black people to break away from the limitations set by white society. The novel itself takes a step in this direction, but it is basically a catalog of grievances against the racial policies of the American society. It resembles an essay more than a work of fiction. Yet, in its depiction of Negro folk culture, in its analysis of the color problem in American life, and in its suggestions for improved racial relationships, *The Autobiography of an Ex-Coloured Man* is one of the important novels of the early twentieth century.

The black population of the United States, the vast majority still subsisting at a poverty level in an urban ghetto or a depressed rural area in the South, did not yet, however, produce the literary figures to answer Johnson's plea, and it was again the white novelists who created the popular literary image of the black man after World War I. With the continued migration of Negroes to the North, such places as Harlem seethed with people looking for a release from the restrictions of life in the ghetto. Marcus Garvey and his "Back to Africa" movement became popular for a while, but his dream died when he was arrested for mail fraud in 1925. With most Negroes resigned to existing in a ghetto, one of the major attractions for them was the night life. The bistros of Harlem enticed white people, as well as black, and one of the results of the white influx was the belief that Negroes were naturally less inhibited.

In fiction this concept became the cult of the primitive in which blacks were depicted as people who obeyed their instincts, regardless of the cost, presumably as a result of their savage African background. At the same time, their intellectual capabilities were virtually ignored. New stereotypes were created as Eugene O'Neill, Sherwood Anderson, Dubose Heyward, and Carl Van Vechten popularized the primitive Negro who lived for the moment. In Anderson's *Dark Laughter* (1925), the uninhibited sexual activity of blacks is glorified. In the same year, Heyward's *Porgy* stressed the gambling, sexual and drinking habits of a black community. The merits of the novel, and some of the characters, became matters of secondary importance as Sportin' Life emerged as the stereotype of the "typical nigger," especially in the dramatization of the popular story.

It became obvious that the primitive Negro was in vogue as a literary figure when Carl Van Vechten's *Nigger Heaven* (1926) appeared. The thin plot of the novel is merely an excuse to portray life in the gin mills of the ghetto. Hugh M. Gloster contends that:

> Van Vechten undeniably took particular delight in emphasizing—even exaggerating and distorting—the primitive aspects of Harlem. To him the cabaret was a transplanted jungle, and Negroes were creatures of impulse and emotion, yearning for animalistic exhibitions of Africa.[13]

The success of *Nigger Heaven* inspired such black writers as Claude McKay and Wallace Thurman to produce novels in the Van Vechten vogue. McKay's *Home to Harlem* (1928) presents Jake, a typical primitive black, who lives the life of physical pleasure in Harlem. A sequel, *Banjo* (1929), implies that the uninhibited life of the Negro is superior to European culture. Wallace Thurman's *The Blacker the Berry* (1929) attempts to deal with the theme of black pride, but the romantic view of the ghetto tends to undermine the serious intent of the novel. The stereotyped Negro made prevalent by Van Vechten is as unrepresentative as are the concepts of the contented slave, wretched freedman, or brute Negro of an earlier period, and the work of McKay and Thurman suffers from the primitivistic element they incorporated.

This, however, was only one aspect of the Harlem Renaissance. The outbreak of black writing during the twenties, as an intelligentsia began to emerge from the black bourgeoisie, took several forms. The emphasis is on white racism, though, in virtually all of the fiction of the period. One of the most interesting books is Jean Toomer's *Cane* (1923). It is a potpourri of stories, poetry, and drama that treats racial matters in a relatively objective manner while at the same time illustrating the problem of retaining a black identity in a country dominated by white values.

Perhaps stimulated by the writing of Toomer, Rudolph Fisher, in *The Walls of Jericho* (1928), and Countee Cullen, in *One Way to Heaven* (1932), both satirize the higher class of blacks who imitate many of the questionable conventions of their white counterparts. Fisher, especially, ridicules the exoticism associated with Harlem, but also explores the various aspects of black life on several levels of society in a realistic manner. In contrast to the narrow view of Harlem presented by Van Vechten, these novelists attempt to reveal a diversified picture of the ghetto. The primitivistic aspects are placed in perspective. It is primarily the false values which many Negroes adhere to that Fisher and Cullen are interested in. But they also depict blacks who are concerned with race pride. As a result, *The Walls of Jericho* and *One Way to Heaven* surpass the literature of the Van Vechten vogue by presenting a more comprehensive view of the black experience in America, although neither is an outstanding literary achievement.

Most of the novels produced by blacks put a greater stress on racial themes, and the Renaissance had its share of these too. Walter White, Jessie Fauset, and Nella Larsen all wrote novels of passing in which they try to indicate that life on the darker side of the color line is preferable, despite the discrimination that accompanies it. White's *Flight* (1926) deals with a heroine of mixed blood who marries a white man only to return to the black community when she grows tired of her husband's empty life. Fauset's *Plum Bun* (1929) and *Comedy American Style* (1933) both present Negro women who unsuccessfully try to find happiness in the white world. In *Quicksand* (1928) and *Passing* (1929), Nella Larsen also depicts heroines who strive for success in white society, but who are thwarted by a discovery of their Negro ancestry.

Robert A. Bone contends that the derogatory treatment of passing presented by White, Fauset, and Larsen represents a version of racial loyalty. These authors are pointing out the necessity of accepting one's racial identity—a manifestation of Renaissance nationalism that demands the continued struggle of blacks to win their rights through pride and determination in the face of resistance by white America.[14] The tendency towards black nationalism also revealed itself in the apologist novels of the period. The tendency to protest against white oppression by presenting heroic blacks who are physically destroyed by white bigots is a popular form of fictional propaganda.

Walter White's *The Fire in the Flint* (1924) is a protest against a form of racism, based largely on sexual mythology, that prevents a talented Negro doctor from practicing his trade, and that allows a mob of whites to kill his brother when he defends a black girl from mistreatment by white boys. In the Jim Crow environment of a Georgia town Negroes are forced to play the roles of clowns or servants in order to survive. Those who step out of their place by trying to assert their humanity, as do the dignified Harper brothers, are destroyed by the defenders of the status quo, the Ku Klux Klan. White, however, is not satisfied with the condemnation of the Klan that is implict in the novel. He intrudes into the narrative to state that

> They had been duped so long by demogogues, deluded generation after generation into believing their sole hope of existence depended on oppression and suppression of the Negro, that the chains of ignorance and suppression they sought to fasten on their Negro neighbors had subtly bound them in unbreakable fashion, ... It is a system based on stark, abject fear—fear that he whom they termed inferior might, with opportunity, prove himself not inferior.[15]

The overt censuring of discriminatory systems and the glorification of blacks in the face of such handicaps are the common elements of this type of fiction, despite the example of Johnson's *The Autobiography of an Ex-Coloured Man*. White's Negro characters exhibit all the heroic virtues that the white ones lack in his melodramatic exposure of injustice in the South. Jessie Fauset's *There is Confusion* (1924) illustrates that aspiring Negroes of the North are confronted with racial prejudice which is just as devastating as that endured in the South. W. E. B. DuBois' second novel, *Dark Princess* (1928), exhibits a panoramic view of racial discrimination and political fraudulence. The primary victims are a black medical student, who is denied an opportunity to become a doctor, and Kautilya, the dark Princess of Bwodpur, who plans with him to organize non-white people on an international basis in an effort to fight oppression.

The emphasis on racial themes in which blacks emerge as valiant warriors against injustices is also evident in several historical novels by Negro writers. Still fighting the plantation tradition, such novelists as John H. Paynter, John H. Hill, and Arna Bontemps drew their versions of what happened during the time of slavery. Paynter's *Fugitives of the Pearl* (1930) describes the attempted escape of slaves. Although this plan is unsuccessful, the author displays how one family of blacks manages to obtain its freedom. The image of the contented slave is further attacked in Bontemps' *Black Thunder* (1936). The novel is a comprehensive fictional portrayal of the slave insurrection of Gabriel Prosser in 1800. It stresses the great love of freedom possessed by the vast majority of the slaves.

Bontemps, whose first novel, *God Sends Sunday* (1931), was in the Van Vechten vogue, tried the historical approach again in *Drums at Dusk* (1939). This publication records the Negro quest for freedom in Haiti under the famous historical figure,

Toussaint L'Ouverture. Bontemps, however, tends to be overly melodramatic in his portrait of heroism. This weakness is even more blatant in John H. Hill's *Princess Malah* (1933). The heroine is the daughter of George Washington's brother. She also has both Indian and Negro ancestry. Despite the romantic tendencies of the plot, Hill tries to present a more realistic picture of the relationship between master and slave than is done in the plantation tradition. In a similar vein, George Schuyler's *Slaves Today* (1931) exposes the persecution of Liberians by the white ruling class in twentieth century Africa.

The novels of these black writers did not match the popularity of the white plantation tradition in the thirties, however. Stark Young's *So Red The Rose* (1934), a fine novel in some respects, but containing the old Negro stereotypes, and Margaret Mitchell's *Gone With the Wind* (1936) emerged as two of the most widely read books of the period. In addition, the popular regional novels of Julia Peterkin depicted blacks in the old primitivistic stereotype, and such humorists as Irwin Cobb and Octavus Roy Cohen tried to keep the minstrel tradition alive. Their work was partially offset, though, by the more realistic presentation of T. S. Stribling, Erskine Caldwell, William Faulkner, and Hamilton Basso.

Black writers in the thirties, as indicated by the historical fiction of Bontemps, Paynter, and Hill, continued to stress racial themes illustrating white oppression. There are, however, a few exceptions. *Ollie Miss* (1935) by George Wylie Henderson is about black sharecroppers in Alabama who exist in an isolated world. The novel emphasizes the folk customs of the rural Negroes. In a pastoral setting, Ollie, a young woman who works the land as well as most men, renounces an unsatisfactory love affair. Despite her pregnancy, she looks forward to nurturing the green things of her own farm without her former lover. The absence of white people in the novel allows Henderson to concentrate on Ollie Miss, who learns through suffering and moral awareness the value of being honest with herself.

Zora Neale Hurston's two novels of the thirties also make use of Negro folklore in settings conspicuous for the absence of whites. *Jonah's Gourd Vine* (1934) is the story of a mulatto preacher whose illicit love affairs lead to self-destruction. Although the characterization is not impressive, the author vividly depicts certain phases of Negro life in Alabama and Florida.

Social problems are not stressed as the blacks are resigned to their inferior status. *Their Eyes Were Watching God* (1937) presents the tempestuous life of Janie Starks in the black community of Eatonville, Florida. Janie stands up to the scorn of her neighbors in an effort to find happiness with Tea Cake, a penniless gambler and drifter. She comes to understand the meaning of love in her wanderings through the villages of the Everglades. When Tea Cake dies she returns to Eatonville, convinced that she has experienced life at its best. She is thus oblivious to the gossip of the townspeople.

Racial discrimination is simply taken for granted in *Their Eyes Were Watching God*. After a severe hurricane, for instance, the bodies of white people are buried in coffins while black bodies are merely rolled into shallow depressions. Problems develop, though, when a number of badly damaged bodies cannot be identified as to race. This ironical situation is the extent of Hurston's racial protest. William Attaway, in *Let Me Breathe Thunder* (1939) also avoids direct racial confrontations to a large extent, but by presenting white characters instead of black. In its treatment of migrant workers it is typical of the proletarian novels of the time, although hardly comparable on a literary level to Steinbeck's *The Grapes of Wrath* (1939).

Despite the presence of writers like Henderson, Hurston, and Attaway, there is a growing tendency in the Negro novels of the thirties, though, to deal primarily with racial attitudes and practices. Perhaps no novel illustrates the ridiculous aspects of racial prejudice better than George Schuyler's *Black No More* (1931). This farcical book relates how a black doctor discovers a product that will make Negroes white. The frustration and confusion of having no black people to discriminate against reaches majestic proportions as the Negro race virtually disappears. However, it is discovered that Caucasians are actually a little darker than the bleached Negroes. Thereafter the racial bigots take pride in the darkness of their skin and learn to hate anyone that looks especially white.

Langston Hughes, a great believer in the social responsibility of the black writer, wrote two novels in his long literary career. In *Not Without Laughter* (1930), he attempted to illustrate the difficulties facing a black youth growing up in a small Kansas town early in the century. While the novel concentrates mainly on the struggles of a black family to make a living and provide their son with an education, many instances of discrimination

17

are inserted, indicating that racism is an integral part of black life. It is the special destiny of the young protagonist to overcome the handicap of color and to receive an education that will allow him to help the entire black race in the fashion of W. E. B. DuBois. Hughes himself, though, was disenchanted with his crude depiction of racial chauvinism and did not publish another novel until *Tambourines to Glory* (1958).

Victor Daly's *Not Only War* (1932) attempts to reveal race prejudice during World War I. A white officer from the South, who has a black concubine back home, objects vehemently when a black soldier dates a French girl. It is only in combat that their differences are forgotten and they recognize each other as individuals. The fact that they are both killed is apparently the author's comment on the improbability of the disappearance of racial prejudice in America. Also in the apologist tradition is *Greater Need Below* (1936) by O'Wendell Shaw. It exposes the unfavorable conditions imposed by whites on a typical Southern tax-supported school for Negroes—through the use, however, of idealized characters and a weak plot.

The folly involved in clinging to illusions of white superiority is the theme of *Aunt Sara's Wooden God* (1938) by Mercedes Gilbert. Aunt Sara is the mulatto mistress of a white aristocrat and the wife of a black man. She has a son by each but she favors the "wooden god" of the white and aristocratic line. Her black son, recognizing his mother's preference, sacrifices himself by serving a prison term for a crime committed by his half brother. Aunt Sara continues to worship whiteness, then, as she does not realize the treachery of her wooden god.

The tendency of creating heroic black characters who withstand the perils of racist environments is also evident in W. E. Turpin's first novel. *These Low Grounds* (1937) traces three generations of a black family as it experiences the inevitable social and economic difficulties that overcome many of the Negroes who try to make a better life for themselves through legitimate means. The novel concludes with the protagonist determined to keep on teaching black people, even after he has failed to arouse a reaction to the tyranny of a white lynch mob. *O Canaan!* (1939) is also a Negro family chronicle but the portrayal of white racism displayed in the earlier novel is not duplicated. Turpin concentrates more on the personal problems of the individuals, although the white society looms menacingly in the background, indirectly affecting the lives of the black protagonists.

River George (1937), a novel by George Lee, presents a Negro character who, as an educated sharecropper, does not fit into the pattern of life in the South. He attempts to organize black farmers and his action results in a fight with a white man. The protagonist is forced to flee after he kills the man and he eventually becomes known as the legendary River George. When he returns to the scene of the fight years later, however, he is promptly lynched by the local whites, who never forget or forgive a militant Negro.

One of the characteristics of the early protest, or the apologetic, novel is the optimism of the main characters in regard to achieving racial equality. Novels such as *Imperium in Imperio*, *The Fire in the Flint*, and Lee's melodramatic *River George*, all of which depict black men who strike back at white authority, also present protagonists who believe in a moderate, legalistic approach to fighting white oppression. The fact that these protagonists are murdered indicates that the authors themselves do not necessarily share the opinion that equality can be won by peaceful means. The alternative of violence, however, is never really expounded on in a serious manner except in *Imperium in Imperio*, one of the rare militant novels before 1960.

On the other hand, the protest novels of the forties, modeled after Richard Wright's *Native Son* (1940), are seldom concerned with the winning of civil rights, for the reason that they deal primarily with individuals who are trying merely to assert themselves as human beings. The only recourse that is open to them is violence. Because of the psychological conditioning imposed by the ghetto environment they accept defeat. At a given point, though, the protagonists realize that their lives are worthless, and, since they have little to lose, they attempt to express themselves in the only way that seems possible. The psychological exploration of these violence-prone people is the major difference between the protest novel and the apologist novel, in which exceptional Negroes are physically destroyed. Sterling Brown's distinction between listing and rendering is significant, as the protest writers of the forties attempt to reveal the long range effects of racism rather than just to show individual examples of racist activities. They try to depict oppression as a way of life rather than as isolated incidents.

If black novelists before 1940 did not reveal a great deal of technical skill it is because it takes time to develop writers.

Eighteenth century America produced virtually no novels, although the genre was thriving in England and elsewhere. The problem of survival was prevalent—and this was the concern of most Negroes following the Civil War. Another reason for the scarcity of first rate Negro novels before 1940 is that the concern with protesting against living conditions and the black stereotypes of the plantation tradition was greater than the desire to produce art. The professional black artist did not really emerge until the middle of the twentieth century. By that time Richard Wright had created an art form out of the protest novel and triggered a new era in the realm of black fiction.

CHAPTER II

Wright and the Protest Novel

In a volume of short stories entitled *Uncle Tom's Children* (1938), Richard Wright violently protests against the Jim Crow system of the South. The mythical descendants of Uncle Tom who are presented in these stories are not at all like Mrs. Stowe's popular character. They are victims of economic exploitation, racist myths, and mob violence. Opportunities for retaliation are rare and the victims tend to nurse a hatred for their oppressors, as a wrong move invariably results in a lynching party. In these early stories Wright shows that racism in the South is a life style that destroys, psychologically and morally, both blacks and whites.

"Big Boy Leaves Home," the outstanding production of the book, exposes one of the basic myths connected with racism. Set in the South, the story depicts four Negro youths who are discovered by a white woman while they are swimming in the nude. Her companion, an armed and uniformed soldier, promptly shoots, killing two of them before the remaining two charge him. In the ensuing struggle, the white man is killed. Big Boy and Bobo attempt to escape to the North, fearing the inevitable mob violence. Bobo is caught, however, and as Big Boy watches from his hiding place, the whites burn and mutilate him. The murder of Bobo is a festive occasion for the white townspeople, who regard it as a community entertainment. Women and children joyfully watch the enactment of Southern justice, the women breaking out in song as the body is engulfed in flames. The men, who were in a hurry to burn the youth before it rained,

21

vie for dismembered parts of the corpse. Liquor is passed around and jokes are made until the rain comes to put an end to the party.

Although the young Negroes killed the white officer in self-defense, the question of their guilt or innocence is not the point: their real "crime" was to be seen naked by a white woman. Frightened, or fascinated, the blond beauty, the epitome of Southern womanhood, refused to leave the place where the boys had left their clothing, despite their pleas. Dan McCall contends that the woman's failure to move

> is part of the general pattern in the story which embodies the racial confrontation in sexual terms. The behavior of the woman is composed of sexual come-on and paralyzing fear. And the Southern fantasy is itself a compound of such ambivalence; presumed Negro sexual superiority is a function of the Southern white community's own fantasies of guilt.[1]

The myth of Negro sexual superiority is linked with the myth that every black male desires a white woman. Together they work to create the fear and hatred revealed in "Big Boy Leaves Home." The fear of being sexually inferior produces jealousy and the necessity for vengeance in the white men. The act of burning and mutilating the black youth is basically an act of sexual revenge. Concomitant with the fear of rape held by the white women is sexual desire and curiosity. The burning of the Negro is a vicarious sexual experience for the women who watch. Thus, the story depicts some of the basic sexual fears and taboos of white feelings that contribute to the formation of racist attitudes, or that stem from previously accepted opinions in regard to racial characteristics.

In 1940 Big Boy was transformed into Bigger Thomas and *Native Son* made Richard Wright an international literary figure. In presenting the same sexual taboos that appeared in "Big Boy Leaves Home," Wright helped to assure the popular success of the novel, and significantly influenced the direction of black literature. With the aid of sexual myths *Native Son* exposes the psychological effects of years of racism as applied to the life of a Negro youth from a Chicago ghetto. Irving Howe has remarked that the novel changed American culture by exposing, as no one had done before, the dangers of racial discrimination.[2]

The exposure of the racial hatred, fear and prejudice of the country in a popular novel by a young black writer did not cause the market to be flooded by similar books, but it did instigate a trend that dominated the fiction of blacks in the decade of the forties. *Native Son* differs from the apologetic protest of its predecessors in several respects, all of which tend to make it a more effective form of protest. Wright does not employ a protagonist of exceptional abilities and education who heroically struggles for his rights against villainous whites. He does not list a series of discriminatory events designed to harm the hero economically or physically. He does not write of tragic love affairs or of unfulfilled destinies.

The racial protest novel, in Wright's hands, emphasizes the psychological condition of the protagonist. The thoughts and the emotions of the character are revealed as he moves through a daily routine in a world in which the primary elements are confinement and lack of opportunity. The depravity of a life limited by racial policies eventually leads to an explosive situation. The protagonist strikes back at an oppressive and unjust society through an act of violence, which tends to provide a satisfaction that was otherwise lacking. The physical rebellion is the only logical alternative for a person who views the world as a barren and hostile place. To remain passive is to accept one's unhappy fate. To act is to assert one's humanity and individuality. If the immediate environment offers nothing else, violence serves a valuable purpose.

In *Native Son* the spark that sets off the explosion in Bigger Thomas is provided by the taboo that is associated with a relationship between a black male and a white female. Bigger's knowledge of the taboo against being seen in the company of a white girl precipitates a series of catastrophic events. However, he discovers that violence gives him a feeling of completeness that he had never before experienced. This in itself is an indictment of the society that produced Bigger, but Wright presents a lengthy trial scene which explains the existence of a Bigger Thomas. The author's purpose is to reveal how the life of the black youth is limited and conditioned by his environment. Through this explanation white America is exposed in terms of its hypocrisy and its racial practices.

Wright, in "The Literature of the Negro in the United States," suggests that as long as racial prejudice exists it will be reflected in the literature of the Negro to the virtual exclusion of other themes.[3] In *Native Son* he gives a prime example of what he means. In the opening pages of the novel Wright illustrates how the Thomas family lives, as well as the debilitating effects of these circumstances on Bigger, an unemployed black youth. Bigger shares a one-room flat with his mother, brother, and sister. In embarrassingly going through the morning ritual of getting dressed under crowded conditions, they are interrupted by the appearance of a large rat. Bigger, after several unsuccessful attempts, finally kills the rodent with a skillet. The battle with the rat upsets Mrs. Thomas. Her life is difficult enough without having Bigger wreck what serves as their home. She begins to torment her eldest son about his shortcomings as a provider for the destitute family and for his inclination to spend his time with his equally worthless cohorts. During the course of this tirade the author presents Bigger's frame of mind.

> He hated his family because he knew they were suffering and that he was powerless to help them. He knew that the moment he allowed himself to feel to its fullness how they lived, the shame and misery of their lives, he would be swept out of himself with fear and despair. So he held toward them an attitude of iron reserve; he lived with them, but behind a wall, a curtain. And toward himself he was even more exacting. He knew that the moment he allowed what his life meant to enter fully into his consciousness, he would either kill himself or someone else. So he denied himself and acted tough.[4]

Besides foreshadowing the later actions of Bigger, Wright in the scene with the rat and its immediate aftermath, reveals him to be a prototype of the black youth of a Northern ghetto. He lives in a crowded apartment with a fatherless family. He has no job and few prospects. Bigger compensates for the harsh realities of ghetto life by withdrawing into a hard shell of apathy. He associates with a gang which gains its strength from a communal hatred of the white world. By acting the role of a braggadocio, he keeps his tendency towards violence precariously in check. Bigger is a victim of what Horace R. Cayton refers to as the fear-hate-fear-syndrome. As a result of his mere existence in a world dominated by whites, he has a fear of being persecuted. This leads to a hatred of whites, but at the same time, the knowledge that this hatred will lead to punishment, if discovered, tends to compound the original fear.[5]

Bigger's fear of the white world is revealed in a conversation with Gus, one of the members of the gang. As the young men watch an airplane sail through the sky they realize that their own lives are barren in comparison with those of the white people. Bigger comments on the difference in the two worlds.

... I just can't get used to it. ... I swear to God I can't. I know
I oughtn't think about it, but I can't help it. Everytime I think about
it I feel like somebody's poking a red-hot iron down my throat. God-
damnit, look! We live here and they live there. We black and they
white. They got things we ain't. They do things and we can't. It's
just like living in jail. Half the time I feel like I'm on the outside
of the world peeping in through a knot-hole in the fence.'[6]

Bigger, an outsider in his native country, has a premonition
that something is going to happen to him that will be completely
out of his control. Wright brings this vague idea to reality in
the person of Mary Dalton. Hired in a menial capacity by the
rich Dalton family, Bigger comes into contact with the white
girl and her boy friend Jan, who is involved with a Marxist
organization. The two young white people attempt to treat Bigger
as an equal in the hope of winning his political favor, but the
black youth is confused and embarrassed by their crude efforts.
After a wild night out on the town, in which Bigger is forced
to forsake his role of chauffeur for the position of companion
on equal grounds with Mary and Jan, it becomes necessary for
Bigger to help the girl to her room because of her drunkenness.
In the process he encounters the blind Mrs. Dalton. Afraid of
being discovered with the white girl, Bigger accidentally
smothers Mary in an effort to keep her quiet.

The actions of the protagonist are based on his knowledge
of the rules against sexual intimacy with white females. Expect-
ing to be punished for being in the girl's room, Bigger is paralyzed
with fear and he presses down too hard and too long on the
pillow with which he is stifling Mary Dalton. Yet the death of
the white girl, and the subsequent need to dispose of the body,
produces in the black youth a certain sense of accomplishment.
Once the horror of what has happened wears off, Bigger is filled
with a feeling of importance. In disposing of the body in the
furnace of the Dalton house, which necessitates the dismember-
ment of the girl, he is performing an act of vengeance on the
society that has denied him so much.

In "Fear," the first section of the novel, Bigger succumbs to
his emotions. However, his acceptance of the death of Mary
Dalton has a stabilizing effect on him, and he learns to use
his fear to his advantage. In "Flight" the author reveals how
Bigger acknowledges the consequences of his action for the
first time in his life. He forgets about blaming his condition on
the white society and decides to take his·fate into his own

hands. He cannot deny the fear of being apprehended by the law, but instead of waiting for the police to come he makes some moves of his own. First he tries to throw suspicion on Jan who, Bigger realizes, is hated almost as much as himself by the American people because of his political beliefs. Bigger then tries to collect ransom for the missing Mary, who is assumed to be kidnapped.

When the bones of the girl are discovered in the furnace, though, the young Negro realizes that he is in trouble. Accompanied by Bessie Mears, his black mistress, he flees to an abandoned building in the ghetto. Bigger decides that Bessie is a threat to his safety, however, and he beats her to death with a brick. The brutal act completed, he reflects on the course his life has taken. What is most impressive is that

> there remained to him a queer sense of power. *He* had done this. *He* had brought all this about. In all of his life these two murders were the most meaningful things that had ever happened to him. He was living, truly and deeply, no matter what others might think, looking at him with their blind eyes. Never had he the chance to live out the consequences of his actions; never had his will been so free as in this night and day of fear and murder and flight.[7]

Bigger does not fully understand the implications of his freedom, but he does know that he is in an exhilarating life and death struggle with the white world. The newspaper accounts of Mary Dalton's death arouse the populace of Chicago, who suspect that the girl was raped before she was thrust into the furnace. Drawing on sexual mythology, the press paints vivid images of the bestiality of the already condemned black youth. In the minds of the white bigots, Bigger is the brute Negro incarnate who should be eradicated in any way possible, preferably by lynching. He finally is captured by a white mob but is saved from violence by the presence of the police and a multitude of newsmen.

Wright created "Fate," the third and final section of *Native Son*, in order to explain in more precise terms the reasons for the existence of Bigger Thomas. The validity of the psychological portrait of the youth is argued through the voice of Boris Max, a communist lawyer. The trial gives the lawyer an opportunity to condemn the American system that produced such a grotesque character as the defendant. He explains that their existence in a ghetto, outside the mainstream of American life, tends to form a spirit of rebellion in many blacks. They reject the mores of the dominant culture and, in their place, adopt a value system that is in many ways opposite to the norms of white society. To the defendant, the action that resulted in the deaths of the two girls was creative—a violent rebellion against the laws of an alien world. Max informs the jury that

'Everytime he comes in contact with us he kills! It is a physiological and psychological reaction, embedded in his being. Every thought he thinks is potential murder. Excluded from, and unassimilated in our society, yet longing to gratify impulses akin to our own but denied the objects and channels evolved through long centuries of their socialized expression, every sunrise and sunset make him guilty of subversive actions. Every movement of his body is an unconscious protest. Every desire, every dream . . . is a plot or a conspiracy. Every hope is a plan for insurrection. Every glance of the eye is a threat. *His very existence is a crime against the state!*[8]

The systematized oppression applied by the white populace is designed to keep black people from advancing economically and from attaining their fullest potentialities. Max points out that many whites practice a lethal brand of discrimination without even realizing it. Mr. Dalton, Bigger's employer, is an example. The rich white man thought he was doing the Negro a favor by giving him a job. But at the same time, as a real estate operator, Dalton is largely responsible for keeping blacks within the confines of the ghetto. He makes his living by exploiting poor black people and then tries to assuage his guilt by assuming the role of a philanthropist. Dalton does not even recognize the hate and fear contained in a young Negro such as Bigger Thomas. The blindness of Mrs. Dalton is also extended to her husband in racial matters. Bigger becomes visible to him only when the shock of his daughter's death forces a negative response.

Max has little hope of convincing the jury of their communal guilt in the defendant's crimes. He asks instead that they merely give Bigger a chance by passing a sentence of life imprisonment instead of death. In prison, Max argues, Bigger will have an identity, a freedom that he could find in the ghetto only through violence and rebellion.

'He would have for the first time an openly designated relationship with the world. The very building in which he would spend the rest of his natural life would be the best he has ever known. Sending him to prison would be the first recognition of his personality he has ever had. The long black empty years ahead would constitute for his mind and feelings the only certain and durable object around which he could build a meaning for his life. The other inmates would be the first men with whom he could associate with a feeling of

27

equality. Steel bars between him and the society he offended would
provide a refuge from hate and fear.'[9]

Max assumes that, even though his client is a victim of society,
there is little hope for any penalty less than the death sentence.
Despite the lucidity of his argument and his modest final plea
to the jury, the words of the defending attorney fall on deaf
ears for the most part. It is the prosecutor, in his fiery plea for
law and order, who speaks for the majority. There is no room
for sentimentality or sociological facts in his philosophy, especially when dealing with a "nigger." He calls for the death of
Bigger in order to protect American society. There was never
any doubt among most of the people of Chicago that the defendant would be electrocuted, and their lust for blood is satisfied
by the verdict of the court.

Bigger accepts his fate philosophically. He rejects the solace
offered to him by religion and makes peace with himself instead,
with the realization that the acts he committed were justifiable
answers to the series of denials that had constituted his life.
The deaths of the girls give him the satisfaction that is generally
reserved for the achievement of a major goal in life. Bigger did
not graduate from college or become rich, but he did retaliate
against the white racists by committing a crime of diabolical
proportions. The beheading and burning of Mary Dalton is a
violation of white womanhood — a sexual act comparable to
the rape that is assumed, but that never took place. The murder
of Bessie Mears, on the other hand, is due to Bigger's awakening
sense of power and the belief that the laws of the white world
mean nothing to him. Bigger finally comes to the realization
that he did not kill Bessie merely to keep her quiet. As the day
of his execution approaches Bigger tells Boris Max that he did
not want to kill but that he could not control himself. It was
something he had to do.

> 'What I killed for must've been good! . . . It must have been good!
> When a man kills, it's for something . . . . I didn't know I was really
> alive in this world until I felt things hard enough to kill for 'em.
> . . . It's the truth, Mr. Max. I can say it now, 'cause I'm going to
> die. I know what I'm saying real good and I know how it sounds.
> But I'm all right. I feel all right when I look at it that way. . . .'[10]

Only through violence can Bigger Thomas attain a sense of
accomplishment. Death is easier to face for the youth, with the
recognition that he has broken out of his shell and asserted
his individuality in the only way that he knew how.

The fact that *Native Son* is melodramatic does not detract too much from its effectiveness as propaganda. In the manner of *Uncle Tom's Cabin*, it affects the emotions of the readers by making them aware of the plight of a protagonist who is the victim of a cruel system of oppression. Wright, however, reverses the formula by presenting a monster rather than a heroic figure. Bigger is a grotesque character who rises out of the ghetto to strike a futile blow at the system that had held him in check. Thus he fulfills the role of a brute Negro, and at the same time is used as a stereotype to condemn the society that produced him.

Wright's protagonist is more than a victim of racial exploitation. He is the unique creation of a life style based on this racism. Once he is awakened to the sense of power that results from the use of violence, Bigger emerges as a rebel who, in his own ineffectual way, tries to destroy the society that surrounds him. Edward Margolies suggests that there are three types of revolutionism presented in *Native Son*. The Marxism represented by Boris Max and Jan Erlone is not an integral part of Bigger's life since it is forced on him from the distant perspective of whites who are primarily interested in political causes rather than in individual humanity. Black nationalism is a part of Bigger's character, in the sense that his hatred of white people in general tends to give him a feeling of solidarity with most of the black people in the ghetto. However, there is no attempt at organizing blacks into a coalition to be used against oppression, and Bigger stands alone against his enemies—a condition that he finally accepts. It is as a metaphysical revolutionary, then, that the black youth is most prominent.[11]

Albert Camus defines metaphysical rebellion as the movement by which an individual protests against the condition he finds himself in. It is a protest against being a part of a created universe which is unjust and chaotic. Frustrated by the state of society, and by the inadequacy of his own life, the metaphysical rebel attempts to apply his own version of justice to the world. The original desire of establishing justice, if met with resistance, may create in the rebel an avidity for injustice to match that which is prevalent in his society. The recognition of the need to revolt, and the act of revolting, represent moments of freedom to the individual. He becomes aware of his potentialities and of his worth as a human being. As a metaphysical rebel, he demands

29

respect for himself and clarity and unity for the world. The alternative is chaos.[12]

Bigger Thomas, in the role of a metaphysical rebel, finds an identity that is meaningful. Denied by society, he turns to a violent form of revolt in which murder becomes a creative act. Though Bigger begins his rebellion as a result of an accident, the taboo against his association with Mary Dalton was indirectly the cause of her death and the new life of the protagonist. It was only a matter of time until a person so alienated from the values and customs of the community became a revolutionary. Bigger is the germ of the black militants of the 1960's as he acts out violently the same kind of murder that the white bigots do in a quiet and legal way. His career is ended before he has a chance to develop into a militant challenger to racial injustice, though, and he has to be content with the knowledge of his personal accomplishments.

Wright's protagonist, conditioned by his environment to both fear and hate the white world and its values, is a symbol of the oppressed people of the world. He stands as a warning to American society, as Boris Max realizes when he asks: "Who knows when some slight shock, disturbing the delicate balance between the social order and thirsty aspiration, shall send the skyscrapers in our cities toppling?"[13] Bigger discovers by chance what some of the black militants have since taken for granted—that violence is a potential answer to the problems of the black man in the United States.

The figure of Bigger makes *Native Son* a significant novel, but not a great one from a literary standpoint. The obvious propagandistic intentions of Wright are not integrated completely into the fictional form. The third section of the novel, "Fate," resembles an essay that has been supplied to elucidate the sociological and psychological aspects of Bigger's life, and much of the eloquence of Boris Max is superfluous. Wright had already made his points in the action described in the first two parts of the book. Even these earlier scenes are interspersed with documentation and authorial comments designed to illustrate that Bigger's fate is predetermined. The naturalistic framework is also stretched to allow for the development of melodramatic situations.

James Baldwin, in "Many Thousand Gone," complains that scenes such as the beheading of the Dalton girl tend only to

30

provoke the mania for the sensational and to substantiate the American image of the depravity of the Negro. Bigger, according to Baldwin, emerges as a subhuman who is not representative of a way of life that can be comprehended by most white people. There is little of the realities of Negro life revealed in the novel as Wright, in his effort to create a social symbol, concentrates on the fantastic adventures of Bigger.[14] Wright is not interested in drawing from the depth of the black experience, according to Baldwin. He also fails to concern himself with the authenticity of particular events in his novel. In "How Bigger Was Born" he confesses that he prefers to create scenes that will emotionally affect a reader rather than to depict reality or plausibility.[15] He is more interested in shaping the reaction of the audience through exaggeration and sensationalism than by adhering to the realistic facts of the exploitation of ghetto inhabitants. Thus, Wright, in revealing an extreme form of depravity, stresses the potential threat to white society that exists in a person such as Bigger Thomas. This is, in essence, Wright's answer to Baldwin, although it does not invalidate the latter's criticism.

The concern with social propaganda is reflected in the characterization. With the exception of the protagonist, the characters of *Native Son* are not portrayed in depth. They tend instead to represent standard responses of social classes or special groups in regard to the race question. Mr. and Mrs. Dalton, the self-aggrandizing white liberals who personify the upper strata of society, attempt to fulfill their moral obligations by hiring Bigger in a menial capacity. Typically, they see only a black person in a chauffeur's uniform rather than a person who has hates, fears, and dreams of his own. Visibility comes to the blind Mrs. Dalton and her imperceptive husband only when tragedy strikes. Mary Dalton and Jan Erlone, idealistic young radicals, try to lure Bigger into accepting their concept of universal brotherhood, and, at the same time, show their prejudices concerning Negroes. Boris Max, despite his sincerity, exploits the plight of the young Negro for the benefit of Marxist ideology. The prosecutor, the voice of the reactionary majority, calls for the death of the defendant as the only means of protecting white society. His primary purpose for the plea, though, is his own political advancement. By catering to the prejudice of the public he hopes to make a name for himself at the expense of Bigger.

While these figures merely stand for certain segments of the population they do serve Wright's propagandistic purposes. They all consider Bigger as someone to manipulate, without recognizing his unique human qualities. The lack of recognition is the primary reason for his rebellion. Wright created Bigger as a warning to people who categorize all blacks as "niggers" rather than acknowledge them as individual entities. The unchaining of the passion lurking beneath the surface of Bigger's apathetic exterior tends to reveal the potential for violence that exists in the black community. Wright's protagonist is especially relevant to the tempestuous race relations that have developed since the publication of *Native Son* in 1940. Bigger Thomas is no longer an exception who exists in a social or literary vacuum: he walks the streets under the banner of the Black Panthers; he exists, multiplied many times, in the novels of black militancy of the sixties.

The literary legacy of Bigger Thomas had more immediate effects in the novels of blacks. The Wright school of protest that emerged in the forties marked the end of the period in which black writers entertained white audiences by depicting primitivistic or sentimental aspects of Negro life. The denial of an individual identity and the continued discriminatory practices of the white power structure tended to produce a resentment in black novelists that evolved into the creation of the metaphysical rebel, a protagonist whose mode of expression was violence.

CHAPTER III

The Protest Tradition in the Forties

Most of the black novelists of the forties who wrote about Negro life tended to stress the adverse effects of white oppression. Wright's publication of *Native Son* in 1940 had presented the sinister side of segregation in the North in an impressive manner, and before long other black novelists began to explore the problems of the urban Negro. Not even the challenge made in the late forties by several proponents of "pure literature" deterred the steady, if somewhat sparse, production of propagandistic novels. The pressures of living in predominantly white America were not conducive to the creation of Negro fiction that was concerned primarily with art. Literature, for the Negro, has traditionally been a means of telling the truth about American history in regard to racial matters. Richard Wright told a sordid version of the truth about ghetto life as it had never been told before, and, in the process, helped to break down the invisible wall that white society had built between the two worlds. The struggle for racial equality began to be reflected in the metaphysical rebels created by the protest novelists.

Carl Offord's *The White Face* (1943), deals with a familiar problem of the Negro experience in the United States. The novel relates the unhappy adventures of black sharecroppers who leave the South in an attempt to find a brighter future in the North. The migration to Harlem proves disastrous for Chris and Nella Woods. Chris, unable to find employment in the city, is relegated to attending to his sickly child while his wife works as a maid. The death of the baby increases the desperation of

Chris and when he is introduced to a fascist-oriented black nationalist organization he is easily persuaded to join its ranks. As a member of the militant group he becomes more race conscious and learns to hate all whites. He also grows alienated from his wife because she works for Jews, the most detested of the whites according to the organizational policy. The pressures of ghetto life and the influence of the black militants eventually leads to an eruption of violence on the part of Woods. He consequently becomes a pawn in the power struggle between the black fascists and the Colored Congress, a group resembling the NAACP.

Offord's novel emphasizes the many hardships that await a poor family of black people who migrate to a ghetto. The promise of the North usually turns out to be a false basis for hope for Negroes, but the protagonist of *The White Face* has little choice in the matter. A fast trip to the supposed safety of the North becomes almost mandatory for Woods. When Harris, the white overseer of the plantation tries to cheat Chris out of his money, and then, revealing the cruelty of a Simon Legree, begins to whip him when he objects, the Negro sharecropper breaks one of the taboos of the South by striking a white man. His rebellion against his designated role as a "white man's nigger" necessitates the new role of a fugitive. He escapes the white mob and, with his wife, the child, and a teenage nephew, manages to reach Harlem, where problems of a different kind arise.

The kind of incident that precipitates the protagonist's flight from Georgia was already something of a stock device in protest fiction. However, Offord is more inventive in the larger portion of the novel that deals with Harlem. Chris Woods, demoralized by the vicious life of the city, is greatly impressed by Manny, one of the black militants. Manny tells him of his early experience in the South when he helped to subdue the Ku Klux Klan. With Chris listening in amazement, he goes on to say that the fascism that the Germans are practicing in their country is also the answer to racial discrimination in the United States. Through force and brutality, he states, freedom can be won. Manny's organization, backed by strategic white power factions, intends to start its revolution by attempting to destroy American Jews. The black fascist tries to convince Chris of the validity of the movement by arguing that

'The black man's been brutalized. Every nigger you meet is a walking streak of vengeance. He's a walking killer. The white man made him that way and he's itching for a chance to get back at the white man. . . . We got to turn Hitler's slogan upsidedown. Instead of Strength through Joy it's going to be Strength through Fear. How that sound?'[1]

To the rejuvenated ex-sharecropper it sounds good. He puts himself at Manny's disposal without understanding anything but the opportunity to gain a measure of revenge for the life he has been forced to lead. The dormant streak of vengeance is awakened and transformed into action as Chris Woods becomes another Bigger Thomas. He severely beats a Jewish lawyer, the son of his wife's employer, and is captured by the police after a wild chase. The black fascists try to exploit the situation by claiming that Chris was merely protecting his wife, who had been raped by the lawyer. However, while in prison, Chris is also charged with the murder of Harris, who died shortly after Chris left the South.

Although her life is threatened by Manny, Nella Woods denies that she was raped. Instead she decides to fight for her husband through the litigious channels of the Colored Congress. Nella and her friends win the battle in court, but she can not save Chris from the philosophy that the militants have implanted in him. When she visits the prison, where he is to remain in custody for five days while the governor reviews the case, with freedom, however, almost assured, Chris explodes into a rage and calls her a "lousy white-man bitch." He wants no help from the white people who have denied him the basic rights of humanity. His days in prison have given him a chance to reflect on the way his life has been manipulated by Jim Crow ethics. The result is a form of madness that is only intensified by Nella's visit, with her story of the peaceful triumph of justice. He has discovered that hatred gives him the incentive to live—hatred for the white face of oppression that haunts his memory.

His black life had been put into a pattern by the white face to suit the purposes of the white face and he had no control whatever over it. The white face owned the land. The white face had stolen him from Africa and brought him here to work the land and be governed by it. Never to govern it. . . . When they cried out the white face lynched them.

So his spirit lashed out during the black nights of anguish. That he should die within this pattern made for him by the white face! That he should live and die by it, without smashing it, without crack-

35

ing it, without even bruising it! His helplessness! His total nothing-
ness in the world of the white face! The sneering whipping snarling
lynching denial of the power of man in him![2]

The need to assert himself—to indicate that he has some control over his life—is so great that Chris Woods attempts to escape.
However, he is shot down by the guards, his lust for violence
satiated at last. In the North he has learned that being black
is as great a disadvantage as it is in the South. His hopes dashed,
he finds a savior in Manny, who preaches that violent social
action is the answer to racial problems. The hopelessness of
this solution, however, is illustrated by the rational behavior of
Nella, who is able to win a legal battle while her husband only
nurses his anger in jail.

Offord makes it clear, though, that the logical and legalistic
way of gaining freedom will not appeal to those poor and
uneducated blacks who have discovered that violence works
much faster and provides a degree of satisfaction that is not
attainable in the process of litigation. The years of abuse suffered
by the protagonist, climaxed by the atrocities of Harlem, have
destroyed his patience and his faith in justice. The black militants
know how to exploit this situation for their own benefit. The
victory of Nella and the Colored Congress is a hollow one. It
cannot restore one's humanity after a lifetime of oppression has
worked to "brutalize" an individual. A comprehensive change
in the attitude of white society is necessary in order for an organization like the Colored Congress to do much good, and, of
course, the time necessary to make any strides in this direction
will not have much effect on people who have run out of patience
and time. Chris Woods, painfully aware of the injustices of his
world, tries to change it through anarchy. Like Bigger Thomas,
he unconsciously fulfills the role of a metaphysical rebel.
However, Woods never comes to terms with his role. Under
Manny's direction he has been provoked to the point that vengeance against the white face has become an obsession. He
is a rebel with a cause, but his limited vision is too great a
handicap. It leads, in essence, to self-destruction.

The White Face vividly portrays the evils inherent in a racist
form of capitalism. But it suffers from some of the characteristic
failings of propagandistic fiction. The melodrama of the plot
is matched by the stereotyping of the characters. Woods, in
his deterioration into a brute Negro, is contrasted to his wife,

a black matriarch who is strength and goodness personified. The forces of evil are represented by Manny. He is an eloquent spokesman for the black militants, but his association with fascism tends to negate any positive influence he may have extended to Woods. There is no middle ground for the protagonist. He is transformed into a beast as an indication that the effects of racism are more potent than any particular point that can be won in a court decision. Nella survives only because she has the strength, and the faith, that are usually drained from a black male over the years. Offord, however, conveys his message largely through sensationalism.

The unrelieved racial tension of *The White Face* is echoed in *If He Hollers Let Him Go* (1945), Chester Himes' first novel. It differs from Offord's work and from *Native Son* in the sense that the protagonist is not an unemployed inhabitant of a ghetto, but an intelligent Negro who possesses a good job. But racial prejudice works in many ways and Himes merely reveals another aspect of it. He, too, presents a metaphysical rebel who hastens his own ruination in the process of self-expression.

If He Hollers is set in California during World War II. Bob Jones, a foreman at the Atlas Shipyard, is obsessed with the knowledge that his position is in jeopardy because of the color of his skin. His extreme race consciousness, and the prejudice of many of the laborers, produces a great deal of pressure. An intense young man who is anxious to succeed, Jones develops a neurotic condition that is destined to lead to a catastrophe.

The problem of race first comes to the attention of the protagonist through a traumatic experience when the war breaks out. One of his Japanese friends is imprisoned in a concentration camp without the benefit of a trial or the formality of a charge. The previous discriminations against Jones take on a significance that he had not thought of before. He realizes that bigotry exists everywhere, and reflects on the possibility that it could explode into violence against him.

> It was the look in the white people's faces when I walked down the streets. It was that crazy, wild-eyed unleashed hatred that the first Jap bomb on Pearl Harbor let loose in a flood. All the tight, crazy feeling of race as thick in the street as gas fumes. Every time I stepped outside I saw a challenge I had to accept or ignore. Every day I had to make one decision a thousand times: Is it now? Is now the time?[3]

The times of crisis come often for Jones, who is always on

the verge of exploding into a defensive rage. Even his dreams, filled with crippled men and tethered dogs, tend to reveal his fear of oppression and the concomitant feeling of impotency. Edward Margolies contends that the protagonist is psychologically emasculated as a result of systematic racism. In being constantly reminded that he is a "nigger," Jones suffers from castration fears that rob him of self-esteem. In compensation he lives fast and is antagonistic to nearly everyone. Despite his intellectual awareness of what is happening to him, he does not have the strength to correct his situation.[4]

Jones refuses to leave his destructive route, losing his composure at the least hint of a racial reference. His days at work are periods of agony and frustration as he awaits the incident of discrimination. When he is not working, Jones methodically hurts the few people who are close to him. Suspicious of his girl when she introduces him to one of her associates, a white man, Jones takes the opportunity to reveal his militant racial attitude, knowing that it will cause Alice a great deal of embarrassment. He proposes that a revolution is the only solution of the "Negro problem," as force is the only thing that whites respect.

A chance to put this philosophy into action is presented when Jones is hit from behind by a white man in an altercation during a dice game. He decides to kill the man but twice passes up the opportunity. Instead Jones revels in the power he feels in having the life of a white man in his control. The discrimination and hate which is directed against him at the shipyard cannot detract from the pleasure of the vengeance he is planning. However, in recognizing the fear that the intended victim is living with, Jones decides the murder isn't necessary. To have a white man afraid of him is even a better use of power than actual violence. The protagonist describes his emotions as the frightened bully walks away from him.

> I turned and watched for a moment, feeling good, feeling fine, loose, free. I had gotten over the notion; I had spit the white folks out of my mouth. There wasn't anything they could do to me now, I told myself; nothing they could say to me that would hurt.[5]

But Jones doesn't take into consideration the power of white womanhood. The apparent solution to his problems is completely nullified by Madge, a white hussy from Texas, who has a personal grudge against him. Aware of the taboo whites enforce in regard to interracial sexual encounters, Madge frames Jones, who had previously refused to satisfy her amatory desires, on a charge of rape. A death sentence could be no more lethal. Jones is nearly beaten to death by the inevitable "lynch mob," consisting of his fellow workers at the shipyard. Recuperating from his multiple injuries in a hospital, before the trial, Jones has a chance to reflect on the fate that awaits him.

> But now I was scared in a different way. Not of the violence. Not of the mob. Not of physical hurt. But of America, of American justice. The jury and the judge. The people themselves. Of the inexorability of one conclusion—that I was guilty. In that one brief flash I could see myself trying to prove my innocence and nobody believing it. A white woman yelling, 'Rape,' and a Negro caught locked in the room. The whole structure of American thought was against me; American tradition had convicted me a hundred years before. And standing there in an American courtroom through all the phony formality of an American trial, having to take it, knowing that I was innocent and that I didn't have a chance.[6]

In a bizarre ending the protagonist is consigned to the army, as Madge apparently confesses to her macabre ruse. The judge decides that Jones must be punished anyway, for having the nerve to consort with a white woman. Wanting only to be a man, the defendant is forced to play the role of a humble Negro to satisfy the judge's distorted sense of justice. It hardly matters by this time, though, as Bob Jones has been physically and mentally beaten to the point that he has resigned his claim as an individual human being. White society has triumphed, and he merely fulfills his destiny by passively accepting his designated role as a pawn in the white power structure. Jones has learned that a black man cannot fight the system by directly and pugnaciously opposing it. There are too many pitfalls awaiting the bold Negro, and to avoid one trap is merely to be unprepared for another. The result of fighting is to be victimized by a continual emasculating process. The chances of surviving as a complete individual are very bad.

Like Bigger Thomas and Chris Woods, Bob Jones experiences a measure of satisfaction from life only by resorting to violence, or the fear that it evokes. He asserts his own reign of terror on the white world by frightening a man who is representative of the entire system of oppression. In controlling the destiny of this person, the protagonist assumes he has found the key to his own life. His singular rebellion is doomed to failure, though, as the omnipotent codes of the oppressors are too prevalent to bend to the blows of a contentious but guileless individual.

Himes makes the point that the advantages that his protagonist possesses, in relation to many blacks, do not make him immune from the psychological and physical effects of racism. Although the multitude of injustices committed against Jones, and his emotional reactions to them, tend to become rather tedious, the author achieves his propagandistic goals more successfully than Offord. Melodrama is not avoided, but stereotyping is kept to a minimum as Himes focuses on the internal struggle of Bob Jones rather than on the stock characters generally found in protest fiction. Jones responds more to a gesture, or a word, that signifies an alien world than to another person. The inner conflict of the protagonist is not resolved with any great insights concerning the nature of the problem, but Himes does suggest the hopelessness of Jones' situation in the grotesque ending of the novel. This is perhaps all Himes is capable of doing. Few novelists, though, have explored the psychology of race with greater discernment.

The tendency towards violence is the primary aspect of the Wright school of protest. In *The Street*, Ann Petry indicates that a black woman may also be a potential candidate for the role of a metaphysical rebel, who, through an act of violence, attempts to assert herself in opposition to the power structure of the dominant society. The energy used to battle oppression over a long period of time can, if it is diverted, produce a condition conducive to revolt. With the limited means of expression that are available in a ghetto, the result of an outburst of emotion is often catastrophic.

The Street (1946) indicates how a ghetto shapes the lives of its inhabitants into a rigid framework of poverty and hopelessness. Owned by white men, who are concerned only with the profit it brings, 116th Street in Harlem is the last refuge of those people who have nowhere else to go. The legitimate opportunities to make a comfortable living are extremely rare, especially for a single woman burdened with a young son.

The plight of Lutie Johnson is a familiar one. Separated from her husband, Jim, the young black woman struggles to support herself and Bub, a child about eight years old. While it is easy for a Negro woman to find a low-paying job in the area around Harlem, the problems of providing for a boy and maintaining self-respect in an overcrowded human zoo are momentous.

Forced to pay a high rent for a couple of rooms in a dilapidated tenement, Lutie is also unable to protect her son from the influences of the street while she is at work. Lutie herself, still an attractive woman, is a prime target for the hustlers and pimps that inhabit the ghetto, including Jones, the lustful building superintendent, and Junto, the white owner of a good deal of the street, and some of its women. Lutie longs to escape from 116th Street but she realizes it isn't just the street, or the city, that is at the root of her troubles. It is the white people who divide the city into enemy camps, giving to the Negroes a limited amount of space and a minimum of light and air. Imprisoned in Harlem, she begins to hate the white people who hold her captive, and the black people who try to take advantage of her.

An opportunity is presented to Lutie, however, in the person of Boots Smith. The Negro musician gives her a chance to sing with his band. The success of her performance, though, is marred by her discovery that she is merely a piece of property in this role also. In financial trouble as a result of being exploited by a white lawyer, Lutie appeals to Smith for help. He informs her that Junto controls the band and that the white man intends to possess her as well. The black bandleader decides to beat Junto in at least one way and attempts to seduce her. It is at this point that Lutie rebels in the only feasible way. She resorts to violence, the language of the ghetto, in an effort to defend herself not only from Smith but from the entire world that has misused her. Grabbing an iron candlestick, she strikes at the nearest representative of that world with a fury that is out of control.

> A lifetime of pent-up resentment went into the blows. Even after he lay motionless, she kept striking him, not even seeing him. First she was venting her rage against the dirty, crowded street. . . .
> Then the limp figure on the sofa became in turn, Jim and the slender girl she'd found him with; became the insult in the moist-eyed glances of white men on the subway; became the unconcealed hostility in the eyes of white women; became the greasy lecherous man at the Crosse School for Singers; became the gaunt Super pulling her down, down into the basement.
> Finally, and the blows were heavier, faster now she was striking at the white world which thrust black people into a walled enclosure from which there was no escape; . . .[7]

Using the street in Harlem on which Lutie Johnson lives as a symbol of the oppression of an entire race, Ann Petry reveals what the effects of economic, social, and psychological discrimination can do to even the strongest of people. Jim Johnson, Lutie's husband, had been destroyed much sooner under the emasculating pressures of unemployment and disrespect. He turned to other women as an element of escape, and to bolster his ego. Lutie, a black matriarch in the mold of Nella Woods, tries to reshape her life and what remains of her family. However, a lifetime of frustration, of working and bowing for white people, is triggered into an explosion by Boots Smith, an agent of Junto and the white power structure.

Thus Lutie Johnson takes a place with Bigger Thomas, Chris Woods, and Bob Jones as a protagonist who discovers that violence is the key to asserting the self—of performing a creative and fulfilling act of self-expression. Lutie differs from the others, though, in realizing that what she did is foreign to her nature. It was a temporary release of pent-up emotions. After she gains control of herself, instead of taking satisfaction in her act, she is repulsed by it. Lutie flees from Harlem, not wanting her son to know that she is a murderer.

While Lutie, then, is not a typical metaphysical rebel since she does not decide to use force to alter her way of life, or society, she is a personification of the potential for violence that is produced by conditions in a ghetto. The environment is the controlling factor of the novel. *The Street* proposes the question of whether a Negro can maintain his humanity in a place like Harlem, which is the result of a racist society. The answer leans toward the negative, as the case of Lutie Johnson reveals.

The melodramatic conclusion, which the author employs to emphasize her point, is also the basic weakness of the novel. The main body of *The Street* is concerned with realistically illustrating the effects of environment and oppression on an individual. Petry does this almost as well as Wright, and the novel fails only when it tries to emulate the sensationalism of *Native Son*. The tragic nature of the protagonist's struggle to retain her dignity in the face of great odds is revealed with restraint throughout the novel, but the author, in an effort to cater to the public, creates a scene replete with blood and lust. While the depiction of violence is an integral part of *The Street*, the artificial situation invented in the end tends more to fulfill the requirements of popular pulp fiction than to conclude a fine novel adequately. The novel would have been more honest if

Lutie had, with premeditation, killed either herself or Smith upon the discovery that she was being used in her role as an entertainer in much the same way in which she had been taken advantage of as a domestic or a secretary. The necessity of self-defense merely excuses Lutie's actions when no excuses are needed. She is being psychologically destroyed throughout the novel and the portrayal of a mental breakdown does not demand the threat of a physical assault. Nor does a conscious choice, based on hopelessness, need any further provocation to be enacted. An acceptance of an act of violence, rather than an apology for it, would be in order, given the set of circumstances presented by the author in the major portion of *The Street*.

In revealing the fallibility of the black matriarch, Ann Petry was, in a sense, destroying a myth. There is, after all, a limit to endurance. Curtis Lucas' novel *Third Ward Newark* (1946) explores the nature of a more prevalent myth concerning black womanhood. One of the common fictions, especially among white Southerners, that grew out of slavery is that no such thing as the rape of a Negro woman is possible.[8] The implications are that they are sexually promiscuous, a role that correlates with their status as subhuman. Against a background of economic and social exploitation, Lucas' novel suggests that black girls are susceptible to lack of respect, which often has serious psychological effects.

Lucas, in an earlier book, *Flour Is Dusty* (1943), had limited himself to the conventions of the mystery story, spiced by a romantic subplot and social commentary. *Third Ward Newark*, however, is a much more serious endeavor. The novel illustrates how the life of Wonnie, a black girl, is marred by a physical assault and the aftermaths. An orphan who escapes from a state farm for girls, Wonnie and a friend are raped by two white men. The friend is killed but Wonnie recovers and attempts to press charges, but her bid to convict the rapists fails because of lack of evidence. Wonnie becomes obsessed with the idea of revenge, a passion that is fed by her continual sense of degradation arising from her traumatic experience. She is finally murdered by one of the white rapists, who fears the threat to his safety that Wonnie represents.

The problems that the girl faces in regard to inadequate housing and economic exploitation in the ghetto of Newark are secondary to the neurotic tendencies from which she suffers.

43

The greatest burden that Wonnie carries is the knowledge that as a black woman she does not have the esteem and status of white women, and more importantly, is not protected by law. The self-rejection that many Negro women feel due to their history as receptacles of the lust of white men, and the national promotion of white standards of beauty, is compounded in Wonnie by her personal experiences. An early victim of a passionate crime, she lives for the purpose of extracting vengeance but again is cut down by an act of violence. In between, her life is plagued by racial discrimination and a tortured sense of personal worth that impels her to hate both herself and her tormentors. Wonnie has the temperament of a Bigger Thomas, rather than a Lutie Johnson, but she lacks the opportunity to take advantage of her tendencies toward violence. A frustrated rebel, she dies, like Chris Woods, unfulfilled in her desire to wreak havoc on the white world.

Lucas handles his topic with integrity but the novel suffers from its rather awkward attempt to combine the environmental and naturalistic elements with a psychological case study. This is basically Wright's pattern in *Native Son*, but Lucas depends even more on sensationalism and the evocation of pity than did his predecessor. The environment is important in the formation of the psychology of the protagonist, but as much damage is done by the physical assault as by the more subtle pressures applied by white society. Again, however, it is the nature of the protest novel to exploit the sensational, but Lucas, in following the tradition, nevertheless explores an important problem. To this extent, *Third Ward Newark* is a valuable novel.

The Wright school of protest is primarily limited to the depiction of racial exploitation. One popular novel by a black American during the decade, though, was Willard Motley's *Knock on Any Door* (1947). A protest novel in the tradition of Wright, it has one major difference. The characters, with a few minor exceptions, are white. The pattern of the protest novel has been changed little, however, and Motley has even been accused of stealing the plot from *Native Son*.

Knock on Any Door presents Nick Romano as the Italian version of Bigger Thomas. Writing in the naturalistic style of Dreiser, Farrell, and Wright, the author makes it clear that the protagonist is a victim of society. The real villain of the novel is the environment of the Chicago slums. Born in poverty and ignorance,

44

Romano drifts into a life of corruption and crime and dies in an electric chair at the age of twenty-one. Contributing to the making of this hoodlum are such factors as parental neglect, police brutality, the failure of the church to relate to modern life, and the indifference of an industrialized society. The streets of Denver and Chicago in which Nick is reared are permeated with the attitude that crime pays and that respectability lies in financial success, regardless of the way in which the money is earned.

A sensitive youth who is designated by his parents to become a priest, Nick grows up in Denver during the Depression. The misfortunes of the family coincide with Nick's involvement with the law for petty crimes. He is finally sent to reform school, where he meets experienced young hoodlums. By the time he is released and joins his parents, who have been forced to seek employment in Chicago, the young Italian is ripe for the opportunities that the larger city presents in regard to crime. A subsequent jail sentence, an unsuccessful marriage, and several fruitless attempts to maintain a steady job, tend to persuade Romano to return to his lawless ways. He finally kills a policeman, who had formerly beaten Nick mercilessly in applying the typical method of obtaining information, and is tried for murder.

At the trial, after Nick has confessed to the crime, his lawyer attempts to convince the jury that they are responsible for the crime of the youth. The people of the American society brutalized and murdered the boy by assigning him to be reared in the poverty and the slums of a big city, by sending him to reform school and to jail where criminals are produced instead of redeemed. The lawyer states that Nick

'is any boy anywhere in the world conditioned and influenced as he has been conditioned and influenced. He is your son or brother or mine. We are, all of us, the result of everything that has happened to us and that surrounds us.'[9]

Knock on any door of the streets of Chicago or any large American city, he is saying, and you will find another Nick Romano, or the potential for one.

While the story of the depravity of the Italian youth is analogous to the plight of Bigger Thomas, Knock on Any Door is different in the sense that Romano is not surrounded by the aura of inferiority associated with the Negro. He is not branded by his color as a person to be despised and exploited. There are no myths that attest to his inherent worthlessness that can match those applied to a black boy. Romano's environment is conducive to a life of crime, his experiences tend to alienate him from respectable society, but much of his trouble is the result of his own ignorance and pride. Women love him and he has influential friends, but Nick rejects them all rather than lose his reputation for toughness. He wills his own death as a final act of defiance.

The rebellion of Nick Romano, then, is not the rebellion of Bigger Thomas: the Italian's battle is only in part with a hostile society. In essence, he rebels from everyone—from those who have helped him as well as those who have hurt him. His rebellion is in his choice of a life of crime and in his confession to the charge of murder. This is his way of asserting himself, but it is a negative assertion made by a youth to whom life is no longer desirable. The killing of the policeman is an act of destruction rather than of creation, and the confession to the act fulfills the unconscious aspirations for his own death. Unlike Bigger Thomas, who is just discovering himself and the meaning of his life at the time of his execution, Romano has known for too long what he is, and the truth sickens him. While Bigger develops into a metaphysical rebel, Nick lives as a weak facsimile of one until the futility of it becomes too much.

The difference between the two protagonists is basically that of color. Bigger's only choice in attaining self-respect is through violence. Nick, with the benefit of a white skin, has several options before him but chooses the easiest course, partly to gain revenge on his parents, who are incapable of expressing their love in any but a domineering way. Once he starts on his unmarked road to rebellion, he does not have the strength or the inclination to change his route. He fits too easily into the value system of the lower-class toughs who reject much of the middle-class morality. But the trouble with this kind of rebellion is that it flounders on the contradictions of the debasement of the self and self-aggrandizement. There is no central goal to strive for, and efforts to disrupt society are based largely on economic necessity and ego-building compulsions. A black rebel, if he can control his fury, is likely to have more direction to his actions, and, while survival is perhaps even less sure, life is apt to be more exhilarating while it lasts.

Although the character of Nick Romano is an interesting psychological study, the novel itself is rather weak. Motley repeats most of the faults of Wright and Dreiser. The journalistic style is redundant as the author tries to evoke sympathy for the protagonist. The plot is contrived and the trial scene is long and tedious without possessing the profound social insights of *Native Son*. The minor characters are more flat than round. The lack of originality is obvious. The sensational elements that assured the popularity of *Knock on Any Door* are not really necessary in the development of Nick Romano. Still, the complexity of the protagonist, the portrayal of his relationship to society, to his family, to the women of his life, to the odd assortment of people that are attracted to him, saves the novel from being a complete artistic failure.

During the last years of the decade the protest tradition changed under the influence of William Gardner Smith and Willard Savoy. These two novelists revived the apologetic protest novel, a trend popular before the appearance of *Native Son*. Apologetic fiction depicts a talented Negro who is physically thwarted in his ambitions by white bigots. The rebels of Wright, Offord, Himes, and Lucas, with their potential for violence, do not play major roles in either Smith's *Last of the Conquerers* (1948) or Savoy's *Alien Land* (1949). Smith presents a sophisticated rebel who tries to fight the system within the confines of the American Army. Savoy, on the other hand, takes a different direction by returning to the old theme of "passing."

Last of the Conquerors is a story of American troops in occupation of Germany shortly after World War II. The idyllic love affair between Hayes Dawkins, a black soldier, and Ilse, a German girl, is eventually interrupted by the presence of white Americans who bring their prejudices across the Atlantic with them. Dawkins, however, has discovered what it is like to be a free man in a country that had only recently produced a Hitler. The German paradise fades only when the black soldiers are transferred from Berlin to Wildsdorf, where Captain Polke, a white Southerner, does his best to make life miserable for them. The discriminatory practices, especially against those Negroes who date white girls, are climaxed by a movement to eliminate half of the blacks in Germany with a dishonorable discharge. Dawkins is sent back to the United States through the manipulations of Captain Polke, who considers him dangerous. Dawkins has intelligence and integrity—in other words he refuses to be a "white man's nigger"—and Polke does not want him to hinder his systematized

47

racist policies by acting as an inspiration to other Negroes. The implication is that in the United States Dawkins will be "kept in his place."

There is, of course, justification for Polke's worries. Dawkins, who has been beaten and badgered at every attempt to resume his relationship with Ilse, nurses a quiet hatred for his white tormentors. He attempts to thwart Captain Polke's activities by keeping his fellow blacks informed of what is being done to them. As a typist in Polke's office he has access to information, but his role as a spy is not a very satisfactory one as there is not much the black soldier can do except desert. When one of them goes berserk, however, Dawkins gets a chance to do something more concrete. The Negro, after shooting several whites, is on the verge of being captured, but Dawkins helps him to escape. As a result, though, Polke begins to suspect his typist and the latter's days in Germany are numbered.

Although he is relatively ineffectual as a foil to military racism, Dawkins is representative of a new kind of rebel. Educated and intelligent, he does not resort to an outburst of violence. He is able to withstand the pressures of racial discrimination and, at the same time, work quietly behind the scenes at challenging the system. Dawkins is a forerunner of the civil rights activists that came into prominence in the fifties.

Last of the Conquerors exploits the racial situation in America for its propagandistic value. The United States is compared very unfavorably to Germany. The Germans who appear in the novel treat the black soldiers with respect, but the white Americans systematically set out to destroy the military careers, and even the lives, of their Negro compatriots. Although Smith tends to overstate his case, he exposes some of the old wrongs in a relatively original manner. The tone of anguish and rage, a common feature of the protest novel, is balanced here by the tranquility of the German landscape as viewed through the eyes of the lovers, and also by the cool and calculated actions of the protagonist. However, the brilliance of individual passages is not maintained throughout the novel. The propagandistic elements, delivered in a bitter tone, enter the plot to a degree that detracts from the total effect of the work.

While Smith expanded the protest novel by employing a European setting and a new type of protagonist, Willard Savoy transforms an old thematic device into a vehicle for devastating social commentary. Unlike earlier writers such as Charles Chesnutt, Jessie Fauset, and Nella Larsen who popularized the novel of passing in which disillusioned Negroes return to the black side of the color line, Savoy presents a protagonist who elects to "remain white." The reasons for his choice are well documented, for in *Alien Land* the author imparts a panoramic view of racism in the United States.

Kern Roberts, the son of a famous Negro civil rights lawyer, grows up in Washington, D.C., where he is confronted with the usual amount of discrimination, alleviated only mildly by his father's fame. His boyhood is highlighted by a trial in which he testifies against a black rapist. Because of his part in the conviction of the Negro, and because of the whiteness of his skin, Kern is treated as an outcast by black people, as well as by most whites. It is only when he goes to school in the South that he begins to understand why the Negroes turned against him. The brutal discriminatory practices that Kern encounters in Alabama awaken him to the fact that racism is more than just an inconvenience. His Negro relatives are murdered by Bill Noble, the stereotype of the cruel Southern sheriff, for merely standing up for their rights. It is obvious, then, that black people have no rights in the South. Kern himself is forced to submit to the absolute authority of the sheriff before he is sent back home with the warning to forget about school, as it only gives "niggers" foolish notions.

It is in the process of his flight from the horrors of Alabama that Kern Roberts makes his decision to pass for white. He makes up his mind to enter into the world of opportunity and freedom merely by ceasing to identify himself as a member of the Negro race—even if it means alienation from his father. The problems attached to being socially designated as an inferior creature, because of an undetermined amount of "black blood," are too much for him to bear as long as the white world is within his grasp. Kern eventually becomes relatively satisfied in his role as a white man, an accomplishment made easier by a reconciliation with his father, but the solution to racism that he chooses is indicative of the insanity of the problem. The implication is that the problem of race is an insurmountable barrier to the promise of America. For most black people the country is indeed an alien land in which they are doomed to be outsiders.

Savoy's novel does not progress much beyond the protest

49

elements, however, since the protagonist is presented as basically a victim. He is so profoundly influenced by discrimination that he takes the easy way out. Even after making his peace with his white wife and his black father, though, Roberts must live with the fear of being exposed as an imposter. Apparently this form of bondage is preferable to being a Negro. Savoy, especially in his section on Alabama, does everything in his power to convince the reader that the protagonist does what he has to do; but in the process Savoy exploits the racial aspects of violence and sex to the point that the novel loses all claim to objectivity. The minor characters are stereotypes used to support the author's proposals. The father and son conflict, which tends to add a note of authenticity, is not explored to any great depths. *Alien Land*, then, which does not stand very well by itself, does not add anything of significance to the protest tradition either. It does indicate, however, a trend away from the Wright school of protest.

It is the spirit of Wright's Bigger Thomas, though, that dominates the decade. The Wrightian protest novel is not the only type of black fiction to be produced in this period, but *Native Son* is the most important novel of the forties. Its influence can be seen in the work of Offord, Himes, Lucas, Petry, and Motley. Yet, Smith and Savoy indicate that this influence is waning somewhat at the end of the decade. This is borne out by the revolt against protest that began to take shape in the forties under the direction of people such as Ann Petry, who temporarily abandoned the protest tradition, William Attaway, Zora Neale Hurston, and Dorothy West. These writers, and other black novelists of the decade, indicate a growing distaste for the pattern, or Wrightian, novel and its tendency towards stereotyping ghetto inhabitants.

CHAPTER IV

The Revolt Against Wright

Despite the popular success of the Wright school in the forties there were many black novelists who did not follow Wright's lead. While no pattern or movement comparable to that initiated by *Native Son* appeared, three general trends are discernible. Proletarian fiction, dealing with the plight of the working class, is one of these minor categories. The accommodationist novel, which illustrates the attempts by blacks to adjust to white society, comes into prominence in this decade. A third category is the assimilationist novel, which presents a white cast of characters. Much of the work in these areas is of little significance, but several fine writers emerged. William Attaway, Ann Petry, Zora Neale Hurston, and Dorothy West produced novels of merit. Although the fiction of these writers is not in the Wrightian protest vein, the effects of racism are not necessarily excluded. However, racial themes are generally subjugated to broader topics, or they are handled in a manner that is distinct from the tradition of *Native Son.*

The proletarian novel, popular in American literature in the previous decade, attempts to expose the injustices and economic inequalities endured by laborers. Steinbeck's *The Grapes of Wrath* (1939) is probably the most famous of the novels illustrating the problems of the working class. Black proletarian novelists tend to combine racial themes with economic and labor exploitation. The goal of proletarian fiction is to promote corrective social action, basically the aim of the racial protest novel except that racism here is of secondary importance. The villain

51

is only indirectly the white man. The protest is directed toward industry under the capitalistic system.

William Attaway's *Blood on the Forge* (1941) remains one of the most comprehensive interpretations of the economic exploitation of the Southern blacks who migrated to the industrial centers of the North. Earlier, in *Let Me Breathe Thunder* (1939), an assimilationist proletarian novel, Attaway presented two white migratory farm workers who are as much adventurers as they are victims. *Blood on the Forge*, though, deals with Negroes from Kentucky who are forced to migrate. They make their way to the Pennsylvania steel mills where the working conditions tend to rob the men of their humanity.

The three Moss brothers, sharecroppers on a Kentucky farm, flee from the South after one of them has struck a white man. Although this key incident is a stock device of racial protest fiction, the emphasis shifts to more universal human concerns as the novel progresses. In the industrial environment of Pennsylvania, the Negroes, along with the Irish, Italians, Slovaks, and Ukranians, must struggle to survive, and to maintain self-respect. Not all of them do. In the end, the Moss brothers are destroyed by the steel and the machines. Chinatown and Melody Moss, after many dehumanizing experiences, are both seriously injured in mill accidents. Big Mat Moss, reduced to little more than an animal by the conditions under which he lives and works, regains a measure of his former dignity by becoming a strikebreaker. His chance to vent his frustrations in violence comes to an end, though, when a union sympathizer beats him to death in a battle between the two labor factions.

In their flight from the South the Moss brothers seek to escape from an old system of oppression based largely on racism. But life in the steel mills of the North is even more difficult for them. Industrialization tends to detract from their communion with the land and to rob them of their sense of accomplishment. They are forced to live in crowded quarters among people who are foreign to them. The blast furnaces and the machines provide physical and psychological challenges that men of the soil are not equipped to deal with. Their troubles are increased by the fact that they are in competition with white men for employment.

Attaway, though, is as concerned with the destructive effects of the machine, and its concomitant evils, on the individual and on the land, as he is in depicting racial and economic discrimination. It is a combination of forces that destroys the men of the steel mills, but being black is an added handicap for the Moss brothers, for they are assigned to the most difficult jobs and are rejected by some of their white compatriots. *Blood on the Forge* insists on three major necessities in American life: the rape of the land by the machine must be stopped, working conditions must be regulated to provide more conveniences for the laborer, and that old bugaboo of racial discrimination must somehow be combated.

The major resemblance between Attaway's novel and *Native Son* is that Big Mat achieves a measure of satisfaction through violence before he is himself killed in battle. Big Mat, however, is merely asking for a bit of revenge before his imminent death, while Bigger Thomas is discovering the way to a meaningful existence. Big Mat submits to his fate in the steel mills and Bigger scorns the limited version of life offered by the ghetto. While both are victims of oppression, Wright's protagonist, although psychologically perverted, according to white standards, refuses to surrender his humanity. Big Mat is broken by the machine and only under the auspices of his role as a scab does he take out his remaining fury on the whites.

Attaway's novel deals essentially with the problems of working men. The fact that they are black intensifies their problems, but it is of secondary importance to their status as members of a class that is exploited by a cruel capitalistic system. The influence of Faulkner and Steinbeck is more apparent than that of Wright as the author stresses the unhappy fate of the virgin land and the inhumane conditions of the mills. The argument for humanitarian corrective measures is primarily implicit in the action, but Attaway abandons his objective stance near the end of the novel and borders on didacticism by attempting belatedly to attach significance to Big Mat's death, a contradictory maneuver that detracts from an otherwise impressive literary performance.

The black proletarian novel did not achieve much success. Steinbeck's *The Grapes of Wrath* (1939) was probably the last popular novel of this type. However.Alden Bland kept the tradition alive with his production of *Behold a Cry* (1947). It stresses the problems of the working class in Chicago during the race riots and labor troubles of 1918. The book presents a black protagonist who tries to find some semblance of order in the tumultuous

53

city. Because of the labor dispute that is being waged, though, and the personal difficulties that emerge from obtaining employment, and from being black, the protagonist fails miserably.

Ed Tyler, another Negro who has left the South to seek employment in the promised land of the North, runs into a roadblock when he attempts to fight organized labor. During a strike Tyler becomes a scab and he is badly beaten by the striking union members. The protagonist also gets into trouble at home as his wife discovers his adultery. He eventually deserts her for a woman who convinces him that love is more important than marital responsibilities. Tyler uses his sexual escapades as an escape from the realities of his unhappy existence. As in the case of Bob Jones in Himes's *If He Hollers Let Him Go*, he compensates for the bleakness of the labor and racial situation by turning to a variety of women in an effort to prove his manhood.

While Bland builds a relatively strong foundation on which to express his ideas on race and labor problems, he concentrates too much on the sexual exploits of the protagonist to comment very poignantly on the social milieu. He provides brief glimpses of Ed Tyler trying to explain the meaning behind the race riots, and what it is to be black in America, to his two sons; but most of the time Tyler is depicted in his amatory pursuits. There is too little correlation between these activities and the difficulties Tyler faces in taking a job vacated by a striking union member who hates scabs, especially if they are Negroes. Although the novel reflects the absurdity of existence in Chicago during World War I, as internal strife threatens to destroy the city, it does not explore the situation to any great depths.

During the thirties Marxism exerted an influence on many American writers. For a while, communism appealed to many who sought answers to urgent social problems, and people such as James T. Farrell, John Dos Passos, Theodore Dreiser, and Richard Wright embraced Marxist doctrines to some extent in their writings. In the forties some of these same people denounced their radical views, as "the god that failed" became one of the popular literary themes. *In Lonely Crusade* (1947), Chester Himes discusses some of the attractions that the Communist party had for Negroes who were interested in advancing their cause, both racially and economically, through labor unions. Himes, however, rejects this approach to salvation for the Negro.

The second of Himes' novels, *Lonely Crusade* presents a black protagonist who becomes involved with Communists in his role as a union organizer. At first enthralled with the prospects of unity in the labor ranks, Lee Gordon discovers that his Marxist friends are interested only in promoting their ideology. His dream of organizing workers of all races, shattered when he is betrayed by racist motivations within the ranks of the Communists, is again tenable when the union and his white employer come to his rescue. Gordon indicates his new hope by rescuing the union banner from a tiring colleague during a parade and marching proudly down the street, resolved to keep the labor organization free from communistic influences.

The individual rebellion of Lee Gordon, who had sworn to distrust all whites after his unfortunate experiences with the Communists, is halted at the point where he becomes dependent on organized labor and a benevolent white man to combat the evils of Marxism and industrialization. Gordon is able to see beyond the racial aspects of his existence, but Himes is not convincing in his depiction of the protagonist's convictions. The changes in the union man's views are the result of a contrived set of circumstances rather than a logical sequence of events. Himes is intent on displaying anti-communist propaganda, which is not as comprehensive as the author's attack on racism in *If He Hollers Let Him Go*, published two years earlier.

The proletarian novels of Attaway, Bland, and Himes, while not primarily concerned with racism, do not avoid the presentation of discriminatory practices. The accommodationist novels published in the forties, dealing with various aspects of Negro life, also portray racism in one form or another without, however, concentrating on it exclusively. There are no patterns or formulas as in the racial protest novel. Rather, a particular phase of black experience is depicted in regard to the relatively common pursuit of adjusting to the dictates of white society.

House of Fury (1941), by Felice Swados, deals with a prison for women. The lives of the inmates are very difficult; the author stresses conditions that need improvement before the institution can meet minimum standards of humane treatment. The major emphasis is on the efforts of the black prisoners to accommodate themselves to the cruel conditions. The white women receive favors that are denied to the blacks, a situation that produces severe racial tensions. The novel offers no solution, though, and the final implication is that the situation will become more serious. Each inmate possesses her own fears, hates, and prejudices that are only increased by imprisonment. The author's main concern is to indicate that a prison headed by untrained and bigoted people produces criminality rather than preventing or correcting it. While an objective position is maintained in this respect, the novel suffers from weak characterization and a tendency to present sordid personal experiences of the prisoners that are not relevant to the plot. They tend instead to contribute to the sensationalism and melodrama of the book, elements that exist in abundance.

Picketing Hell (1942) is a satirical treatment of black religion by Adam Clayton Powell, Sr. The novel reveals the hypocrisy that is prevalent in a Negro congregation. But at the same time Powell points out the need for an updating of church policy and also implies some of the reasons why a great number of Negroes, misused by the outside world, seek a refuge in religion. The author traces the career of Tom Tern, a minister who rises to great heights among the black population of New England. Tern, after migrating from the South where he was known as a great liar, is converted to the ministry. Refusing to accept the program offered by the deacons of the church, he puts his own into operation and becomes extremely popular. Tern eventually climaxes his career by attending a conference of churches in Europe, where he predicts the downfall of Hitler before he dies in the pulpit.

Powell exposes many of the hypocritical tendencies of the people connected with the church. The women's auxiliary prospers primarily because of the sexual attractiveness of the protagonist, who does nothing to discourage the attentions he receives from his female parishioners. The sins of some of the most active members of the church are revealed, although the people themselves never abandon their pious poses. Even Reverend Tern is shown to be insincere about his religion on numerous occasions. However, the minister is quick to attack many of the weaknesses and inconsistencies of the existing syllabus on church policy while at the same time replacing them with improved practices and theories that he is able to enforce because of his popularity, especially with the women. The church is depicted as one place in a hostile environment where Tern, and other blacks, can rise to a position of prominence.

Despite the humor of the novel, it tends to read like a sermon on church reform. The satire becomes buried under the mass of material on the business of the church. Powell fails to combine his preaching and his fiction into a cogent whole. He does, to be sure, inject enough comedy into the book to keep it from becoming a tract, but the narrow aspect of Negro life recorded in *Picketing Hell* is even more limited by the failure to depict the influence of the white world, except in a patronizing manner near the end of the book.

Lewis Caldwell's *Policy King* (1945) reveals the effects of organized gambling on a Negro family. It indicates that gambling is one of the few available opportunities for young men to escape from the poverty of the ghetto. It also warns of the dangers involved in the gambling life. An alternative solution is offered which consists of hard work and moral fortitude in the pursuit of a career that is acceptable to the moral codes of white America. There is an inherent contradiction in the book, though, that is never resolved.

Caldwell's novel is a chronicle of a black family in Chicago. Reverend Marshall tries to instill his idea of morality in his children. His two sons turn instead to the policy racket that thrives in a ghetto environment. They eventually come to their downfall, as one is killed in gang warfare and the other is sent to prison. The minister's daughter, Helen, is the salvation of the family, however, from her father's point of view. She obtains a degree in sociology and vigorously crusades to destroy organized crime, especially the gambling that contributed to the ruin of her brothers. It is largely through her work, in fact, that the younger brother is sentenced to jail.

The Policy King indicates that intelligent young Negroes are likely to drift into a world of crime because of the environment they are a part of. The ghetto breeds illegitimacy of many kinds, and illegal gambling offers a quick route to financial success for a black youth who is denied access to some of the legitimate businesses. The daughter, though, illustrates that with dedication, race pride, and hard work, a Negro can accomplish remarkable feats within the system that is operated and controlled by white America.

Caldwell offers a puzzling situation, though. By succeeding according to white standards, Helen Marshall is destroying her own brother and also one of the few businesses that gives a

Negro an opportunity. Presented as an exceptional person in the mold of Brown's Clotel or DuBois' "dark princess," Helen is, in effect, selling out to the white bigots who have kept the majority of her race in bondage. Caldwell is rather unsure of his allegiances and his novel deteriorates into a series of vignettes calling for race pride on the one hand and for submission to white society on the other.

The road to success for a black family, if it comes at all, is usually difficult in the novels of Afro-Americans. However, Odella Wood's *High Ground* (1945) is unique. The novel presents a black man who supports his wife and children in a more than adequate fashion with few problems. The protagonist moves from the South to Pennsylvania in search of a wife and an economic opportunity. Surprisingly, he finds both. Only when he takes his family on a trip back to Virginia are there any incidents of racial discrimination. Accustomed to being treated as an equal in Pennsylvania, the protagonist's wife is infuriated by the Jim Crow system of the South. Back in the North, though, everything goes smoothly and the family prospers.

Wood's sentimental story is weak, however, from a critical viewpoint. The melodramatic incidents of racism in the South, as contrasted with the almost complete lack of them in Pennsylvania, tend to distort the reality of black experience. The regional prejudice of the author is never justified in the book, for the success of the family in the North is not explained. The implication is that life in the North guarantees social and financial opportunities for Negroes. Wood paints a pretty picture of the promised land in *High Ground*, but the reader is limited in his view by the narrowness of the frame.

George Wylie Henderson, who in his first novel, *Ollie Miss* (1935), dealt with an isolated segment of black life in the rural South, changes his locale in *Jule* (1946). The sequel traces the career of Ollie's son as he moves from Alabama to Harlem. The novel emphasizes the promise of the North in comparison to the bleakness of the South, much in the manner of Wood's *High Ground*. However, there is an indication that Harlem is lacking in some of the wholesome qualities of rural life. The protagonist finds it necessary to marry a Southern girl in order to feel completely comfortable in the city. The implication is that the South is a paradise that has been ruined by the prejudice of the white man. The North, on the other hand, is a potential paradise which does not fulfill its promise because of the significance put on decorum and social status.

The novel begins with the typical flight motif, as Jule is forced to escape from Alabama after a fight with a white man. In the North, though, he discovers that there are opportunities that did not exist in Alabama. Jule finds a job in New York and, with the help of a white friend, even joins a labor union. In his efforts to improve himself he has affairs with several girls from the Harlem elite. When Ollie dies Jule goes back to the South for the funeral. When he returns he brings with him an Alabama girl. The South, he learns, possesses some values that are of significance. The girl is representative of the charm and honesty of life close to the soil in the rural South. Much of the exotic glamour of Harlem is artificial, a fact that Jule has time to reflect on during his trip home. Although he returns to Harlem he has a real part of the South with him as a reminder of the pastoral existence he had once shared with Ollie Miss. This idyllic situation, however, has been ruined by the intrusion of white bigotry.

Jule is a much weaker novel than its predecessor. Henderson is much more at home in depicting the customs and attitudes of a locale he is familiar with. The phenomenal success of Jule is presented in a manner that is unconvincing, as his rise is precipitated by coincidence and fantastically good luck. The protagonist is reminiscent of the heroes of the apologetic fiction of the first part of the century. The novel also exploits some of the primitivistic themes of the Van Vechten vogue by concentrating on the night life of Harlem in scenes that have no relevance to the development of the plot, and that are, in fact, contradictory to the major thesis that the Harlem elite is an artificial society. It is only when Jule returns to the South that Henderson regains control of the novel, but by then it is too late.

Attacks on the South and its racial practices are not unusual in the accommodationist fiction of the period. Will Thomas also unleashes some of his animosity on Jim Crow in *God Is for White Folks* (1947), which deals with the old theme of passing. Beau, the son of a white plantation owner, attempts to make his fortune as a white man in a Louisiana city where the secret of his Negro ancestry is presumably unknown. He injures a man in a fight over a woman, though, and his racial identity is revealed by someone from his father's plantation. The lynching party is called off when the injured man recovers. Beau's luck continues as he is able to win the favors of Elisse, the white woman who caused the altercation. Finally, the owner of the plantation acknowledges that the hero is his son by bequeathing his property to him.

The farcical treatment of race is essentially a satire on both the apologetic protest novel and the plantation tradition. The customary events of the early protest fiction occur, but the results are reversed. The benevolent white master of the plantation school is also presented, but he transgresses Southern decorum by recognizing his Negro son. Thomas further discredits the white concept of life on the old plantation in his bitter comments on miscegenation.

> White men had made the law and broken it, and the thing the law was supposed to prevent happened anyhow. Their own lusty sex urge, contemptuously ascribed to the animal blacks, had betrayed them, and it continued to do so. They bred mulatto children by sleeping with black women, and they bred quadroon offspring by those mulattoes, and after that nobody could be sure who was white or who was not, until finally the land was full of mixed breeds as white as their fathers.[1]

As this passage indicates, though, Thomas does not remain objective so that the absurd action can speak for itself. The tendency to condemn white racism through the use of such authorial comments is too strong and the novel suffers as a result.

Even such relatively unsuccessful novels as *High Ground* or *God Is for White Folks* indicate a concern for social equality and justice as applied to blacks. Lionel Trilling in "Manners, Morals, and the Novel" states that the greatness of the novel form is its ability to involve the reader in moral issues—to force him to examine his motives and concepts of reality. A serious book, according to Trilling, is one that presents some image of society for the reader to consider, to judge, and to question.[2] By reflecting the social situation of Negroes in the United States, novelists such as Thomas, Henderson, Wood, Caldwell, Swados, and the black proletarian writers, attempted to make a serious use of the novel. If many of these novels are rather insignificant as art, they do serve the purpose of calling attention to social ills. The failure to do justice to this purpose is due more to a lack of literary talent than to a lack of effort. The question of talent has been answered to a large degree in the following decades, but even in the forties there are black novelists of skill other than Wright, Himes, Smith, and Attaway.

One of them is Dorothy West. In *The Living Is Easy* (1948), an accommodationist novel, she satirizes the "counterfeit Brahmins" of Boston who are more interested in social status than in their own humanity. She reveals the insanity of imitating the false values of white society, while at the same time showing the pervasiveness of this practice. The Negroes who deny their blackness in accepting the standards of the white aristocrats are severely attacked by the author. Indirectly, West also condemns the white world which establishes the values, and worships them with a blind devotion.

The special target of this attack is Cleo Judson, the wife of "the black Banana King" of Boston, who is tremendously proud of her position among the social elite of the black population. Born in the South, she has known poverty and it makes her hungrier for the advantages of wealth. As a young girl Cleo had been sent to relatives in Massachusetts where her light complexion was expected to be an advantage for her. She realizes her goal by marrying Bart Judson, an enterprising young businessman. Once her security is assured, Cleo concentrates on advancing socially and on rescuing her sisters from their inferior positions; the fact that they are relatively happy does not enter her mind. In attempting to make proper Bostonians out of them, Cleo draws them out of their homes and eventually manages to ruin their lives by imposing her own specious values upon them from the sanctuary of her Boston mansion. Her extravagance in trying to support, and control, her entire family also contributes to the financial downfall of her husband.

The price of becoming socially respectable is high not only for the Judson family but for many of their friends too. The typical maneuver of the black social climbers is to trade the remnants of their humanity for a place among the elite. The author's contempt for the snobbishness of Cleo and her associates is epitomized in a scene at one of many social events. One of the prominent guests takes advantage of the opportunity to present the case of a black man in the South who has been unjustly accused of murder. The plea for financial assistance is met with indifference by the Boston ladies, however. The problems of the unfortunate Negro tend only to substantiate the opinion of the Bostonians that lower class blacks should be ignored.

Identifying with the poor and uneducated black masses is regarded as a breach of decorum.

Throughout the novel West points out the disgust displayed by the Judsons for anything associated with their black ancestry. Cleo is so upset by the darkness of Judy, her only child, that she resolves not to have any more children. It is ironic, then, that the family finally goes broke and Bart and Cleo are forced to struggle for a living like "common darkies." As a further comment on the justifiable fate of the Judsons, the author reveals that the accused black murderer is the husband of one of Cleo's sisters. This melodramatic insertion is hardly necessary, however, since from the opening pages Cleo has been thoroughly exposed as an opportunist and a selfish conniver. The flashback episode of Cleo's childhood in the South helps to explain her actions but it does not excuse them.

The major weakness of *The Living Is Easy* is West's failure to maintain an objectivity towards Cleo and her crowd of status seekers. These characters disengage themselves from their black ancestry and from their essential humanity with such ease that they lack conviction. The verbal irony, humorous in the first part of the novel, tends to dissolve into an open attack on Cleo in the later stages.

The portrait of Cleo Judson as an ambitious parvenu trying to compensate for the deprivations of her childhood makes *The Living Is Easy* interesting, however. The novel presents an antithesis to the stereotype of the black woman as an enduring and sympathetic matriarch—the black mammy of the plantation tradition. Cleo fulfills the opposite role, as through her own selfishness and perverted sense of values, she guides her family to destruction. Neither is Cleo the victim of white oppression in the usual sense; she has both wealth and position and it is her own greed that destroys the family. Cleo, though, is a victim of the dominant white culture in the sense that her dreams of emulating it tend to distort her personality. Like other counterfeit Brahmins, she has bought the concept of white superiority at the cost of her soul. The pressure is applied primarily by the black bourgeoisie which wants to dissociate itself from the poor lower class blacks. While *The Living Is Easy* does not depict racial conflict, the influence of the white world pervades the novel to the extent that Cleo Judson becomes a grotesque figure—a mad woman who concedes to the idea that white is right by living in a dream world in which she plays the role of a white aristocrat.

West's book is one of the better Negro novels of the decade. As in the case of most of the accommodationist fiction of the period, *The Living Is Easy* condemns white society, or a certain phase of it, without concentrating exclusively on depicting the Negro as a victim of white oppression. There are no metaphysical rebels in accommodationist novels, only individual characters with unique problems revolving around the inconveniences and hazards of adapting oneself to the racial practices of the whites. Racism, in one form or another, is a fact of life for most of them, but it is not necessarily the determining factor.

A small group of black novelists, however, chose to avoid, to a large degree, the special problems of black people by writing about white characters. The assimilationist novels are in a sense a rejection of the limitations of the Wrightian protest novel. By concentrating on whites, the writers are ostensibly free of the tendency to propagandize, and the white world with its multitudinous possibilities is open to them. If they cannot participate in it as citizens, they can as novelists. Yet there are few outstanding productions in the assimilationist field, as most of the energy of Negro novelists is expended on the fictional presentation of social and psychological problems related to being black.

An exception is the second novel of Ann Petry. In *The Street* (1946) she followed the protest tradition of Wright. But in *Country Place* (1947) she turns to assimilationism and incorporates into the book some of the protest elements that appear in the earlier work. It is an anatomy of the mores of a small New England town. The village tends to resist change and to cling to its old prejudices, including hatred of Catholics, Jews, and Negroes. Petry exposes the moral deadness of the environment with a vengeance. By concentrating primarily on white characters, the author maintains an objectivity that is lacking in her propagandistic novel, *The Street*.

The story is narrated by a pharmacist, who is something of a village historian and gossip. Basically, it concerns Johnnie Roane, a veteran returning to Lennox, Connecticut after World War II. The joyful anticipation of his arrival is marred by the warning of the Weasel, a taxi driver, who suggests that Roane's wife, Glory, has been unfaithful. This proves to be true, and Roane, ashamed and hurt by Glory's adultery, and tired of the confining atmosphere of the small town, decides to leave. He deserts both his wife and his father's business to become an artist in New York.

While Roane finds it necessary to flee from Lennox to assert himself, there are other inhabitants of the community who remain to fight on alien ground. The outsiders—Neola, a Negro maid; the Portuguese, a gardener; and Rosenburg, a Jewish lawyer—are free of most of the biases and opinions of the majority of the townspeople. Partly because of their social status, they have not been corrupted by the greed and hatred of the people around them. Much of the energy of these outcasts is directed at retaining their self-respect in the face of prejudice and ignorance. Like Lutie Johnson, in *The Street*, they struggle against a hostile environment. The marriage of Neola and the Portuguese gardener, which is approved by their white employer, is an act of defiance against the town. Mrs. Gramby, a representative of the old order of New England puritanism, not only supports the interracial marriage, but further declares her moral position by disinheriting her greedy daughter-in-law. Although at the conclusion the old lady is killed in an accident, she illustrates that the moral deterioration that has immobilized the village can be challenged. With Mrs. Gramby's death and the departure of Johnnie Roane, however, the task is shifted completely to the shoulders of the outcasts. Constructive change, it appears, will not come easily to Lennox.

Country Place illustrates that the pettiness of humans not only keeps them from realizing their full potential as individuals but produces atrophy in a community. Only the actions of those people with enough fortitude to fight the conventions and moral laxity of the majority are of significance. Marred by a melodramatic conclusion and a tendency towards polarizing the concepts of right and wrong, the novel is nevertheless one of the impressive artistic endeavors of the decade. The author enters the realm of protest by implicitly advocating a moral system of values and contrasting it with the inferior standards of most of the white people of Lennox. She demonstrates that protest elements can be an integral part of a novel that does not deal exclusively with racial themes. *Country Place* is concerned basically with the white response to prejudice and environmental handicaps. Johnnie Roane has an advantage over the protagonist of *The Street*, though, and he exercises his prerogative by simply fleeing to more fruitful grounds, an act not possible for Lutie.

In contrast to *Country Place*, which has broad social implications, Zora Neale Hurston's *Seraph on the Suwanee* (1948) is
more concerned with the psychological development of an
individual. It concentrates on the life of a neurotic white woman
from a poor family in Florida. This is in contrast to Hurston's
novels of the thirties in which she depicted isolated Negro life
in the South. In her third novel, though, blacks play only minor
roles, as the author deals primarily with the sexual complexes
of a woman who cannot face reality.

Arvay Henson is the product of a religious family in a rural
area. The fundamentalist approach to life tends to produce inner
tensions in the girl. She tries to repress her erotic feelings for
the local minister, who eventually marries her older sister. Arvay,
living a vicarious sex life, avoids other men. When they do
approach her, she discourages their advances by pretending
to faint, and for six years Arvay lives in mental adultery with
her sister's husband. However, the brash young Jim Meserve,
seeing through her behavior, wins her confidence, and then
seduces her. Arvay marries Jim, but although they prosper, the
relationship is never stable. Arvay still feels guilty about sex
and considers their demented son to be the embodiment of her
sins. The shock of discovering the degraded life her sister and
the minister live, however, helps to rid Arvay of her complex.
She is finally able to accept her husband for what he is, instead
of living with a romantic concept of a perfect lover, and the
novel ends in a happy reunion of man and wife.

The Freudian aspects of *Seraph on the Suwanee* are handled
effectively through much of the novel, but Hurston tries to reveal
the change in her protagonist through the use of melodrama
and contrived situations. The transformation of Arvay is nearly
miraculous. Unconvincing also is the treatment of racial matters.
The general tranquility between blacks and whites is comparable
to that displayed in the plantation tradition. Joe Kelsey, a Negro
employed by the Meserves, is the prototype of the faithful
retainer, and his son strives to fulfill the same role. When Joe
finally decides it is time to leave Jim's farm, he becomes the
wretched freedman who hastens back to the master's protection.
Despite her dislike of anyone black, Arvay prefers the Kelsey
family to the Portuguese family that her husband employs for
a time. Because of their strange customs, she does not consider

the foreigners as "real white people." The Kelseys, on the other hand, are predictable in their role as inferiors.

While an ideal relationship, from a white viewpoint, is shown to exist in regard to the white farmer and his colored help, a different kind of racial balance is applied to the shrimp boats. The author makes it clear that in commercial fishing all men are treated according to their ability by the employers. This form of equality produces no friction between the white workers and their black counterparts. However, the communal tranquility of the shrimp boats is presented through authorial comment rather than as part of the action of the novel. The author, in her attempt to portray racial harmony, strays from her major theme to present a rather distorted and contradictory view of the relationship between the races. This is a fault that Hurston avoided in her two earlier novels.

A more dynamic version of the communication between the races is revealed in A.Q. Jarrette's *Beneath the Sky* (1949). Also dealing primarily with white characters, it is a melodrama set on a plantation in South Carolina. The major conflict involves the plantation owner, a former Yankee, and his overseer, who hates every aspect of the North. The Yankee, himself a married man, falls in love with the overseer's daughter, producing a series of problems that result in the murders of the Yankee's wife and the overseer.

A subplot concerns a black family which resides on the plantation. Willie and David Johnson work in the fields under the direction of the white overseer. The latter hates the Johnson brothers because they are Negroes and fears them because he is sure that they will rape his daughters. When Willie is seen swimming with one of them, the overseer lynches him despite the intervention of the plantation owner.

Jarrette draws on the racial mythology of whites to depict a typical Southern tragedy. There is no attempt made, though, to explore the meanings behind the action in the novel itself. Lynching is merely an accepted form of Southern justice that is applied to Negroes. The demise of Willie is simply glossed over as if it were a common occurrence of no significance. While *Beneath the Sky*, on the whole, is the type of pulp fiction that does not often warrant criticism of any kind, the contrast with *Seraph on the Suwanee* is interesting. Hurston's apologetic portrait of racial harmony in the South is discredited by Jarrette as a matter of course in the least melodramatic section of the novel. Hurston stresses the point that blacks and whites can live, or at least work, together peacefully. Jarrette accepts racial tension as a fact of life. Both authors, however, fail to retain the objectivity promised in the early portions of their novels. Racial themes are not an integral part of either book, but both Hurston and Jarrette take the opportunity to editorialize on racial matters. One of the professed advantages of the assimilationist novel is the objectivity it allows the writers. Ann Petry in *Country Place*, for instance, comments on racial prejudice only through the actions of her characters, while at the same time avoiding the more sensational aspects of racial conflict. The tendencies to protest and to assert one's opinions have always been inherent to the writing of fiction. Petry merely succeeds artistically to a much greater degree than Hurston or Jarrette.

The forties also saw the arrival of a unique assimilationist Negro novelist. Frank Yerby, who began his career as a writer of short stories in a protest vein, became one of the most commercially successful black authors with his historical romances, perhaps rivaled only by the detective stories of Chester Himes in the sixties. Influenced by Alexander Dumas, the famous nineteenth century French novelist, who as a Negro was nevertheless assimilated into the culture of his country, Yerby departed for Europe, where he has turned out a number of best-selling romantic potboilers. *The Foxes of Harrow* appeared in 1946 and since then he has applied his formula to over twenty novels. The major characters are white and the favorite recipe of this "prince of the pulpsters," according to Robert A. Bone,

> contains a bold, handsome, rakish, but withal somewhat honorable hero; a frigid, respectable wife; a torrid anything but respectable mistress; and a crafty, fiendish villain. Structurally . . . the Yerby novel carries its hero from a sandbar in the Mississippi (symbol of the outcast, the pariah, the base-born, the bastard) to his Harrow (wealth, fame, and the founding of a dynasty). It is likewise customary for transient love to evaporate, as all obstacles which have separated the hero from his true love are removed. A dash of sadomasochism and a generous sprinkling of derring-do, and the formula is virtually complete.[3]

On the whole, however, the Negro novelists of the forties indicate a concern for the condition of black people in American society. This is especially evident in the protest novels, but it is also illustrated in the fiction that falls outside the Wrightian protest tradition. In turning away from this tradition, novelists such as William Attaway, Ann Petry, and Dorothy West were merely taking a different approach to the fictional representation of Negro life. While there is no organized movement that constitutes a revolt against protest, there is an indication of a dissatisfaction with the Wright school and its emphasis on metaphysical rebellion. This trend continues into the next decade as James Baldwin, Ralph Ellison, and others, attempt to broaden the fictional image of the Negro. The protest novel, though, makes a comeback in a different form.

CHAPTER V

Accommodationism in the Fifties

The revolt against the Wright school of protest that began to take shape in the late forties came into dominance in the following decade. The protest novel patterned after *Native Son* virtually disappeared, as a different form of protest fiction came into existence. The majority of the black novelists, though, pursued themes that were not limited to a depiction of racism. While several assimilationist novels were produced, the dominant trend was the accommodationist novel. This type of fiction explored various aspects of black life in America, without stressing the traditional role of the Negro as a victim of white society to the exclusion of other themes. Accommodationist fiction constitutes a literary movement in the sense that it basically opposes the Wrightian protest tradition and deals with the common theme of adjusting to life in a country dominated by whites. This aspect of the revolt against Wright, then, is an objection to protest as an end in itself.

In essence, every Negro novel of the fifties that deals with black experience includes some form of protest against the racial policies of whites. But while the traditional protest fiction stresses racism essentially for the sake of propaganda, the accommodationist novelists are more concerned with incorporating protest elements into larger themes. The aesthetic aspects of the production generally play a more important role, as the author strives for an objectivity that is often surrendered in a protest novel. The black characters of accommodationist fiction are not merely victims of bigotry—they are individuals with multiple problems and aspirations that may be only indirectly related to the fact of being black. The protest novels of the fifties, in contrast, depict the Negro as a victim of a society that uses physical violence and a corrupt legal system to keep him from attaining his human rights.

The Wrightian protest novel came under the attack of several Negroes after World War II in the form of critical essays, as well as in fiction. In 1949 James Baldwin's "Everybody's Protest Novel," an article appearing in *Partisan Review*, discredited protest fiction because of its tendency to exploit the romantic illusion that a society based on universal equality is possible in the United States, an idea that Baldwin discredits in the light of the experience of the Negro in America. Protest novels such as *Uncle Tom's Cabin*, according to Baldwin, are merely fantasies that foster false hopes of racial harmony. The case of *Native Son* is different, according to Baldwin, in the sense that Bigger Thomas reverses the role of Uncle Tom and accepts a theology that denies him life. He admits his bestiality and searches for his individuality on those terms. But the main point is that both Bigger and Uncle Tom are denied the right to live as humans. To Baldwin,

> The failure of the protest novel lies in its rejection of life, the human being, the denial of his beauty, dread, power, in its insistence that it is his categorization alone which is real and which cannot be transcended.[1]

Baldwin continued his attack on *Native Son* in "Many Thousands Gone," an essay published two years later in the same periodical. He was not alone in his criticism. In 1950 William Gardner Smith suggested that the monotonous repetition of offenses against blacks in protest fiction tends to defeat the purpose of the writer. Although these offenses constitute truth, they do not constitute art.[2] Smith abandoned his own advice, as did Baldwin, after an unsuccessful venture with an assimilationist novel, but the views expressed by these writers are typical of the literary atmosphere around 1950. Saunders Redding echoed the opinions of Baldwin and Smith in an autobiography (1951) by stating that

> I hope this piece will stand as the epilogue to whatever contribution I have made to the 'literature of race.' I want to get on to other things. . . . The obligations imposed by race on the average educated or talented Negro . . . are vast and become at least onerous. I am tired of giving up my creative initiative to these demands.[3]

Redding was among the first of this new breed of black writers to publish a novel that illustrated his literary philosophy. *Stranger and Alone* (1950) is a study of Negro education in the South and its effect on a passive and unexceptional individual. As in the case of O'Wendell Shaw's *Greater Need Below* (1936), Redding's novel exposes the inadequacies of the Negro colleges, which are basically training grounds for servants and laborers. These schools are established by white Southerners to maintain a racial status quo. The emphasis is on the teaching of black inferiority and the necessity of becoming trained in menial capacities that will aid the white economic system. Rather than concentrating on the overt effect of discrimination, Redding emphasizes the efforts of the protagonist to find a place within the existing racial system.

Shelton Howden, a shy young man of only average intelligence, becomes a part of this atmosphere as a result of his desire to become a doctor. During his tenure at New Hope College, however, he is encouraged to forget his ambitions and to plan on a career more in line with his abilities. All of his life Shelton has been aware that the white people had the authority and the power to do what they wished. Thus, he accepts what they tell him. In Dr. Posey's class, for instance, Shelton can find nothing to contradict the books which declare that blacks are innately inferior to whites. The Negro student thus longs to be white, and attempts to emulate his designated superiors.

Upon his graduation Shelton takes a job as a pullman porter. Although he had higher hopes, it is not a bad position for a Negro with a college degree, by Jim Crow standards. Through the help of a black professor, though, Shelton wins a scholarship to a graduate school in New York. After obtaining his master's degree he accepts a position at Arcadia State College, back in the South. Here he comes under the influence of P. T. Wimbush, a Booker T. Washington type of administrator, who favors Shelton because of his inferiority complex. The accommodationist college president, who works within the system of white supremacy, promotes Shelton to the role of his assistant. Together they work to keep the system working smoothly at Arcadia, dismissing any teacher who shows signs of teaching racial equality. Shelton assumes the personality of Wimbush and begins to dislike "common darkies" almost as much as he hates radical Negroes. At the conclusion of the novel he informs Judge Reed,

71

an influential white racist, of a secret plan by which the black citizens of the county hope to win some of their voting rights. Shelton prefers to maintain his position within the Southern system rather than to cast his lot with the rebellious blacks. Thus he turns to Judge Reed who has the power to stop the Negro plot, and therefore save Shelton's career.

Redding's portrait of Shelton Howden, a mulatto who accepts his inferior status in society as a justifiable designation, is a comprehensive analysis of the subtle effects of racism. Howden is brainwashed to the point that he dissociates himself from black people. Like Cleo Judson in *The Living Is Easy* he thinks of himself as a white person whose interest is served by keeping the black masses in subordination. Through Wimbush, Howden's mentor, the author attacks the philosophy of Booker T. Washington, the black educator who advocated the kind of vocational education that is ridiculed in *Stranger and Alone*. Wimbush, the prototype of the black Southern educator who is later incorporated into Ellison's *Invisible Man*, summarizes the patronizing attitude of Washington by telling his assistant that

> 'Darkies who go around saying they don't give a roaring hoot what white people think, and who think they're independent of every and any white man born, just show their ignorance. . . . White folks don't have to give a damn. But we do. We have to give more than a damn about them because no matter whether you love or hate 'em, the country's theirs by a kind of right of eminent domain, and, in a way, people like you and me are theirs too.'[4]

According to Wimbush, as long as the whites own the country and the black people that live in it, the best that a Negro can do is to play along with the game. Personal advancement, under the direction of whites, is the goal of Wimbush and his prime student. Opposition to the system is a refuge of fools who are doomed to defeat. The thing to do is to accept the fact that you are a Negro in a white man's world, and then do everything you can to erase the handicap.

While Redding's novel attacks white racism, it does so only by implication. The real villains are Howden and Wimbush, who recognize the corruption of the educational system, and choose to support it anyway. Indeed, Alain Locke accuses Redding of not projecting the characters sympathetically enough to throw the blame on the society where it belongs.[5] But that is part of the strength of *Stranger and Alone*. Redding presents just enough evidence to demonstrate the reasons for the actions and opinions of the protagonist. There is no need for further comments on the environmental deficiencies that shaped Howden. His actions are more than self-condemnatory. If the novel lacks vitality it is significant for what it has to say about racism and about an individual response to environmental and moral pressures.

The problem of adjusting to an environment which is unfavorable to blacks is a recurring theme in the Negro novel. Philip B. Kaye explores the difficulties faced by a family from Harlem that moves to a predominantly white neighborhood. *Taffy* (1950) is the story of a black youth of seventeen who is so attached to the ghetto that he fails to adjust to life in Brooklyn. The problem of accommodation is intensified, of course, by the white neighbors who torment the Johnson family, but there is more involved than the boy's response to bigots. In Harlem, Taffy Johnson was a member of a gang that gloried in its defiance of the white world. Harlem was his turf, the place where he felt at home, and it took more than a nice house with a room of his own to replace it.

For a time, Taffy is enthralled with the new environment and his new acquaintances. But the feeling soon disappears as he discovers that the whites hate him, and that the few Negroes in the neighborhood are snobs. Depressed, he hangs around Harlem, looking for the excitement of the old days. The atmosphere is not the same as it once was, though, and Taffy takes out his frustration by killing a white man. A short time later Taffy and an innocent companion are killed by two policemen who are primarily concerned with shooting "niggers" rather than with making an arrest. Martha, Taffy's mother and a candidate for the state assembly, is greatly grieved by the death knowing that she has been negligent in her responsibilities toward her son as a result of her personal ambitions. She refuses, however, to use her position to incite the Negroes of the area into a retaliatory action against the policemen. The fate of Taffy shocks her back to reality and she vows to put her personal life into a proper perspective in lieu of her search for political power.

The protest elements of *Taffy* are fused into a complex plot that develops several themes. Racism plays a major role in the novel but it is only one aspect of the complicated problems of the Johnson family. Taffy's troubles stem partly from the conflict between his father, a docile man who spends most of his time at his job as a pullman porter, and his mother, who demands more love and respect from the members of her family than they have to offer. At the same time, she offers nothing in return. As a result Taffy takes to the streets where violence is a way of life. By the time he moves from Harlem, Taffy has the stamp of the ghetto on him, and when he finds difficulty in adjusting to his new world he tries to return to the old. He is no longer accepted as a peer by his Harlem acquaintances, though, and he attempts to compensate by an act of violence. The action is not a form of rebellion, as in the case of Bigger Thomas, but a sign of resignation to the fact that he no longer has a home—a place where he is regarded as an equal. The ideal time of boyhood is gone, even if it did take place in a ghetto, and the protagonist cannot adjust to the complexities of life in a white neighborhood. Rejected by both Harlem and Brooklyn, Taffy turns to violence as a desperate means of recovering the past.

Taffy is a remarkable novel in the sense that it attempts to analyze the problems of a black family on both a personal and a racial level. It almost succeeds, but Kaye is not quite capable of controlling his thematic line. The novel breaks down into several separate stories loosely held together by the figure of Taffy Johnson, who is too narrow a character, though, to bridge the gaps. One is left with the feeling that Kaye wanted to write a protest novel in the tradition of *Native Son*, but yielded to the temper of the time.

William Demby's first novel also deals with a Negro youth who has difficulty in adjusting to a new environment. *Beetlecreek* (1950) revolves around a fourteen-year-old boy who leaves Pittsburgh, where his widowed mother is hospitalized, to stay with his aunt and uncle in Beetlecreek, West Virginia. Life in the small town is depressing for a boy from the city, though, and Johnny Johnson becomes as disenchanted as most of the people who live there. He is trapped by the provincial attitudes of both whites and blacks, and in attempting to accommodate himself to the mores of the community he commits an unpardonable act of inhumanity.

The characters who have the closest contacts with Johnny are his relatives, Mary and David Diggs; Bill Trapp, an old white man who lives alone at the edge of the black section of the community; and several black youths who are part of a gang that Johnny eventually joins. All of these people are trapped in the village, which tends to stifle the lives of its inhabitants. Bill Trapp, for fifteen years a recluse, attempts to communicate with some of the town youngsters and is ostracized by both the white and black citizens. David Diggs, a frustrated artist who can find only menial jobs, seeks relief from the stifling atmosphere by drinking with Bill Trapp and having an affair with Edith, an old flame. Mary, his wife, compensates for a loveless marriage by her activities in the Woman's Missionary Guild, an organization that is guilty of spreading malicious gossip about Trapp among the black community. The Nightriders, Johnny's gang, reflect the prejudices of Beetlecreek by applying pressure on Johnny to sever his relationship with the old white man.

It is the figure of Bill Trapp that evokes the pettiness of most of the residents of the town. He draws suspicion by befriending Johnny and his uncle. Enthralled by the sharing of his life for the first time in years, he invites a number of children of both races out to his home in rural Beetlecreek. This rather pathetic attempt at communication turns the village against Trapp. His brief period of happiness comes to an end, as even his Negro friends desert him, and he climbs back into his lonely shell. Johnny does not believe the rumors about the immorality of Trapp, but he succumbs to the influence of the Nightriders and sets fire to the recluse's house as a part of the initiation rites that are necessary for acceptance by the gang.

Johnny's act is representative of the hatred and the moral depravity of a community dominated by people who are primarily concerned with conforming to a perverted sense of decency. The efforts of a man to express his love for people are misinterpreted because any positive action in the morally dead town is suspect. An outsider to begin with, Trapp is tolerated as long as he exists in his personal vacuum, but the minute he transgresses the border of the citizen's morbid version of respectability by inviting a mixed group of girls to a party, he is in for trouble. Rumors spread that he is a child molester, and not even Johnny, who had at one time mentally equated Trapp with Jesus Christ, can withstand the pressures exerted by the bigots. His fiery feat is a symbolical crucifixion performed by all of Beetlecreek, which is itself a miniature replica of the modern world. In attempting

75

to adjust to the conventions of the village, Johnny commits himself to immorality.

Robert A. Bone suggests that the novel presents an existentialist definition of evil in which man attempts to express himself in negative and destructive ways if no other confirmation of his existence is available.[6] Demby leaves little doubt that the inhabitants of Beetlecreek, both black and white, embrace evil without considering an alternative. Racism, although it exists in abundance, is only an aspect of the general sickness of the community. In Ann Petry's *Country Place* there are several brave individuals who speak out against injustice, but in Beetlecreek no one commits himself to the side of virtue. Even Bill Trapp spends the greatest part of his life in denying his own humanity. His friends, Johnny Johnson and David Diggs, surrender to the mediocrity of their surroundings.

Demby attempts to convey his vision of the world through the use of recurring images and symbolic actions. However, he stresses too much the idea that Beetlecreek is a village of death. The descriptions of the thoughts and feelings of the characters are designed to reveal that Beetlecreek is responsible for the plight of its inhabitants. They are unable to escape from the trap that society creates. In displaying the despair of the more sensitive individuals of the town, the author suggests that those who possess the capacity for constructive action are doomed to failure. Demby proclaims the guilt of mankind, but his deterministic manipulation of the characters detracts from the total effect of *Beetlecreek*.

The problems of a black youth in adjusting to an unfriendly environment, a popular theme in the fifties, are again depicted in Owen Dodson's *Boy at the Window* (1951). Originally published under this title and later released as *When Trees Were Green*, the novel is more objective than *Beetlecreek* in dealing with the difficulties of a young Negro boy in facing an atmosphere of hostility. Dodson's characters possess an element of freedom that is absent in Demby's novel. While the protagonist's situation is basically the same as that of Johnny Johnson, his life is not entirely predetermined by his environment. It is limited, however, by the deprivations usually associated with a ghetto.

Coin Foreman spends his early years in New York, but when his mother, Naomi, dies he is sent to Washington, D.C. to live with Uncle Troy, a blind man who has more than enough troubles of his own. Without the protection of Naomi, Coin discovers many of the unpleasant aspects of life, including what it is to be a "nigger." The boy decides that he will not live with his uncle after observing that the blind man is more concerned with drinking and sex than in being a replacement for his mother. Fortified by memories of Naomi and visions of biblical heroes, Coin prepares to leave his new home as the short novel concludes. He is determined to find love in a world that has suddenly deteriorated.

Dodson uses a stream-of-consciousness technique to reveal the thoughts of the young protagonist. It is largely through the recording of the mental responses of the boy to the things around him that the author is able to convey his impressions of life in a ghetto. One of the revelations that makes an impact on the protagonist is the indignity innately related to being black. The impressions of Coin are revealed after he has traveled by train to Washington.

> Coin knew something was wrong with the way everyone had acted but he didn't know where to place the blame. One thing he had learned: what nobody would tell him. He knew now what a nigger was. His mother really had been right. A bad person. What confused him was that it meant much more than that. Maybe you weren't a bad person but you were colored and they called you nigger.[7]

Coin's severest problems are more personal, though, than those stemming from the color of his skin. He is primarily concerned with establishing a companionship that can take the place of his mother's love and understanding. In his search for fulfillment, the boy discovers some of the handicaps of being among the disadvantaged, but he refuses to become discouraged. The scope of the novel is extremely limited, however, as Dodson tries to channel his material through the consciousness of a ten-year-old boy. The book is almost too short to explore fully some of the problems it presents, but within these limitations it is an interesting portrait of the various aspects of the maturation of a youth from a ghetto.

The novels produced by blacks in the first year or two of the fifties, before the publication of Ellison's *Invisible Man* or Baldwin's *Go Tell It on the Mountain*, indicate the concern for fiction that transcends the protest novel in its depiction of Negro experience. The reaction to the Wright School of Protest is revealed in the tendency of authors to employ themes that are basically universal. The characters are human beings before they are Negroes. Yet, the necessity to protest against the treatment of blacks by the white majority persists. Integrity demands that the truth about the racial situation be known. The problem is to convert an individual version of truth into an artistic form that is not a racial tract. Writers such as Kaye, Redding, Demby, and Dodson were able to produce novels that relegated protest to a secondary role and that were at the same time moderately successful on an artistic level. Ellison and Baldwin exceeded the artistic success of their predecessors, though, and popularized the accommodationist novel.

The publication of *Invisible Man* (1952) is the climax of the revolt against the Wrightian protest novel. Ellison, in continuing the trend of his predecessors, carried the accommodationist novel to its logical conclusion by producing a book that effectively fuses protest elements into art. In triumphing over this fictional problem, the author demonstrates his concept of the basic unity of human experience. Racial elements are merely a part of the more universal questions associated with a chaotic world, such as moral responsibility, identity, and reality. Ellison does not indulge in overt propaganda except in the sense that the total effect of the novel indicates a concern for sanity and understanding in regard to racial matters. But the major emphasis is on the blind faith exhibited by the protagonist in his efforts to accommodate himself to the society around him—and his subsequent realization that the world is not at all similar to the inculcated version that he had believed in.

Ellison, in an effort to repudiate the limitations of the Wrightian protest novel, presents a protagonist who endures a variety of experiences that tend to summarize the history of the Negro in the United States. The nameless narrator remains invisible throughout the novel as he assumes the various roles that the whites create for him. In his innocence, though, the invisible man believes in what he is doing despite the fact that he is victimized by the people he meets. Only after observing life for a number of years does he realize that he has been a pawn in the hands of the power system—that he has been invisible not only to others, in their failure to recognize him as an individual, but to himself also, as the result of his unawareness of the racist world around him. He asserts his humanity only when he recognizes his various roles for what they are.

The novel is composed of four major episodes which reveal

much of the black experience in America. Their more immediate consequence, though, is to serve as a framework in the protagonist's journey from innocence to a form of knowledge that accepts moral responsibility. In the Prologue, the narrator-protagonist speaks from his home in the coal cellar of a building rented strictly to whites in an area that borders Harlem. He reflects on the past events that have led to his present situation in which he resides in his rent-free hole in the ground in a section of a basement that was abandoned and forgotten in the nineteenth century, with the added comfort of the electricity that is tapped from Monopolated Light and Power. The 1369 lights help to confirm the reality of the protagonist, who has learned that he is invisible to whites. The fact that he is recognized only as a stereotype, as a Negro in a particular role, induces him to be socially irresponsible as a means of revenge on the world that has wronged him. His present mood is indicated in a dream in which an old slave poisons her master for refusing to set her free despite his promises to do so.

The trouble all started, the protagonist relates in the first chapter, when his grandfather shocked the entire family with his death-bed speech. He advises his heirs to

> '... keep up the good fight. I never told you, but our life is a war and I have been a traitor all my born days, a spy in the enemy's country ever since I give up my gun back in the Reconstruction. Live with your head in the lion's mouth. I want you to overcome 'em with yeses, undermine 'em with grins, agree 'em to death and destruction, let 'em swaller you till they vomit or bust wide open.'[8]

The words of the ex-slave are a constant puzzle to the hero, who is advised to forget them by his parents. Although the youth is a model of decorum and is praised by the most lily-white men of the Southern community, he is haunted by the idea that he is being treacherous. His grandfather's words become a curse to him as he cannot understand the need for warfare against whites when everything is right with the world. He envisions himself as a potential Booker T. Washington, and, in this state of innocence, the old man's advice is incongruous but disturbing.

The first major episode occurs on the protagonist's graduation day. He is invited to speak, as an outstanding member of his high school class, at a meeting of the town's leading white citizens. Before the oration is to be delivered, though, the whites have a battle royal planned, in which ten black youths, including the hero, are blindfolded and instructed to fight until only one remains on his feet. After being entertained by a naked blond dancer, the men call for the battle royal. The protagonist survives with only a cut mouth. Then all of the boys are "rewarded" with money that is thrown on an electrified rug. Worried about whether the entertainment will detract from the dignity of the occasion, and with his mouth full of blood, the young scholar finally delivers his speech on the importance of humility in attaining racial progress. He gets a briefcase and a scholarship to a Negro college for his performance.

The battle royal scene establishes the comic tone of the novel. More importantly, it exposes the role of the Negro as a ritualistic scapegoat. The white men force the youths to perform for them in a manner that satisfies their own perverted tastes. The reward for the labor of the Negroes, in a historical parody, is a few coins that they have to scramble for on their knees. The irony of the situation is stressed when the hero makes a mistake in his speech on humility by mentioning social equality. He continues only after apologizing for his error. Another spurious reward is presented in the form of a scholarship to a college for Negroes that is controlled and supported by whites, and that teaches blacks to take their proper, or inferior, roles in society as a laboring class for white industry. The climax of the episode is an event that foreshadows the future action. The protagonist dreams that he finds in his new briefcase a document which reads: "To Whom It May Concern, Keep This Nigger-Boy Running."[9]

With his innocence still basically intact, the young student goes to college where, in the person of Dr. Bledsoe, he encounters the doctrine of accommodationism. Bledsoe, a black college president in the mold of Redding's P. T. Wimbush, or Booker T. Washington, supports the Southern system of keeping the Negro in an inferior position. At the same time he occupies a powerful position himself, and one way of maintaining it is by demanding proper behavior from the students. The protagonist transcends the code of ethics by driving Mr. Norton, one of the rich benefactors of the school and a "bearer of the white man's burden," into the back country where the poorest blacks reside. Norton questions one of the farmers, an uneducated man named Trueblood, who has become a local celebrity among whites because of his incestuous relationship with his daughter. The tale of incest horrifies and entertains the Bostonian to the extent that he rewards the sharecropper with a large sum of money. Norton becomes ill after his experience and requests a stimulant. The hero makes another mistake by attempting to accommodate the old white man at the Golden Day, a notorious road house that caters to the black inmates of a neighboring mental institution. The chaos at the Golden Day shocks Norton back to normal and he reports the incident to Bledsoe on his return to the campus. The protagonist is expelled from school and sent North with a letter of recommendation from Bledsoe.

The second major episode exposes the fallacies of the Southern system of education in the manner of Shaw's *Greater Need Below* and Redding's *Stranger and Alone*. But the college career of the invisible man does more than that: it reveals how Northern liberals support racism. Norton, haunted by the need to fulfill the expectations of his abolitionist ancestors, acts the role of a philanthropist while he is actually contributing to the concept of white superiority. The visit with Trueblood confirms Norton's own sense of superiority while at the same time it assuages his guilt in connection with his erotic feelings for his own daughter. Again the Negro is rewarded for acting as a scapegoat, although the white liberal is willing to pay much more for the expiation of his guilt than the Southerners, who merely hold Trueblood up as an example of Negro depravity. Trueblood, an exception among Negroes, is nevertheless the kind of black man whites are glad to know, as he demonstrates the validity of repressing the entire race.

Another of the important figures of this section of the novel is the mad vet, a former doctor who visits the Golden Day with the rest of the Negro mental patients. The vet, describing himself as a brain surgeon who is unable to practice in the United States because of racial prejudice, attempts to analyze both the protagonist and Norton. He tells the student that the philanthropist is a great believer in the wisdom of the maxim "white is right." But his blindness to the underlying nature of Negro psychology makes him a potential vehicle for the personal advancement of an enterprising black. However, the hero is not perceptive enough to take advantage of the situation. Indeed, the mad vet summarizes him as a walking zombie, an invisible personification of the Negative who has learned to repress his humanity. He is a mechanical man who registers the facts of life with his senses but not with his brain.[10]

Still not convinced of the truth of the advice offered by his grandfather, the mad vet, and even Bledsoe, who tells him how the whites respect a Negro who plays the proper role, the protagonist heads for the industrial center of the North with hope in his heart for a bright future. In New York, however, he discovers that Bledsoe's letter is treacherous. Instead of recommending him to a prospective employer, it implies, in essence, that this black boy should be kept running. He eventually finds employment with Liberty Paint, a company that manufactures the famous Optic White paint. His career as a laborer is far from pleasant, though, as he becomes involved in a labor dispute. The factory has been hiring blacks as scabs in its battle with the union. The hero finds himself in the precarious position of being distrusted by both sides. Assigned to work with Lucius Brockway, the indispensable Uncle Tom who regulates the equipment in the basement of the plant, he gets into a violent argument about labor problems. In the heat of his diatribe against the union, Lucius neglects his gauges and an explosion occurs in which the protagonist is injured. Subjected to shock therapy in a hospital, he is eventually released to the streets of Harlem.

The Liberty Paint adventure illustrates the historic exploitation of the Negro by American industry. Ellison, in a symbolical fashion, echoes the proletarian aspects of his literary predecessors in his portrait of the migration of black laborers to the North, where they are hired mainly to offset the pressures of the white labor unions. Brockway represents the skilled black laborer who is taken advantage of by the white capitalists, who, in his quest for security, considers other blacks as threats to his position. Thus, he opposes any change in the company policy, even if he is exploited. The hospital scene stresses the identity theme. The protagonist, treated in a strange electrical machine that ostensibly cures him from the damages suffered in the explosion, is nevertheless left with a partial loss of memory. He cannot remember his name, although flashes of his past life occur to him. With his identity uncertain, he is released from his job and told to find something for which he is better prepared. Symbolically, his treatment implies the attempt of the white society to make the Negro impotent and to destroy his individual identity. To the hospital staff he is just another black face that represents a threat to Aryan culture. The electrical machine, indicative of the industrial age, gives the invisible man a new life at the same time that it limits this life to the boundaries designed by the people who refuse to recognize the humanity of blacks.

The fourth major division of the invisible man's life, before his descent to the underground, deals with his experiences in Harlem, especially with the Brotherhood. Overcome by feelings of alienation and hostility in the ghetto, the protagonist exists for a while on his compensation money. He is still obsessed with the question of his identity and the direction his life is taking. Mary Rambo, a black woman from the South, gives him a room and encourages him to be a credit to his race, but he is still confused by the implication of his grandfather's curse as tempered by his experiences. In an incident involving the eviction of an old Negro couple from their decrepit apartment, the hero discovers he still possesses his oratorical powers. The cruelty of the eviction awakens his sense of solidarity with the black race, and he delivers a speech protesting the injustice of dispossessing the aged Negroes from their home. He is subsequently recruited by the Brotherhood, a radical political organization, and a thinly disguised version of the Communist party, as a speaker and rabble rouser. He turns out to be too militant, however, and Brother Jack orders him to study pacifistic methods of organizing and educating the people of Harlem in terms of Marxist ideology.

As a spokesman for the Brotherhood the hero infuriates Ras the Exhorter, militant leader of the Black Nationalist Party. Ras embraces his black separatist philosophy with all the gusto of a Marcus Garvey. He has a special hatred for the Brotherhood, which he feels is merely using Negroes for ideological purposes. The invisible man himself begins to suspect the motives of the organization when Tod Clifton, an intelligent black member of the Brotherhood, is so offended by the policies of the organization that he abdicates his high position and turns illegally to hawking Sambo dolls among the white people of the city. Clifton is senselessly killed by a white policeman and the hero ignores party discipline to speak at the funeral of the popular figure. He still does not entirely abandon his belief in the Brotherhood as the savior of all mankind, though, until a curious incident occurs. In leaving a committee meeting he finds it necessary to disguise himself to escape from Ras. He is immediately mistaken for an ambiguous person called Rinehart, who apparently fulfills several roles in the fluid world of Harlem where invisibility is recognized and taken advantage of. When the emphasis of the Brotherhood shifts from Harlem to international issues, then, the protagonist is on the verge of discovery.

In considering the Brotherhood's decision to abandon the Harlem phase of their activities, the narrator is forced to compare the treachery of the organization to the deceitfulness of Rinehart in his multiple impersonations. He realizes that if the Harlemites can accept Rinehart as a preacher, a charlatan, and a numbers runner, invisibility exists. He concludes that he, too, is invisible, especially to the white people who have been using him. But the multiplicity of Rinehart offers new possibilities. As an invisible man he can turn the tables on the blind white world that sees only a commodity in the Negro. His life had been an absurd joke, but with the recognition and acceptance of his invisibility he will no longer be an innocent victim. At last he understands his grandfather's curse. Behind the mask of his black face the invisible man decides "to do a Rinehart," and overcome the blind white people with yeses and undermine them with grins.

> They wanted a machine? Very well, I'd become a super-sensitive confirmer of their misconceptions, . . . Oh, I'd serve them well and I'd make invisibility felt if not seen, and they'd learn that it could be as polluting as a decaying body, or a piece of bad meat in a stew. And if I got hurt? Very well again. Besides didn't they believe in sacrifice? They were the subtle thinkers—would this be treachery? Did the word apply to an invisible man? Could they recognize choice in that which wasn't seen?[11]

Before the invisible man has time to put his grandfather's advice into action, however, Harlem explodes into a battlefield directed by Ras, who is now the Destroyer. Everything that is owned by whites is the target of Ras and his ghetto troops. Despite his argument to the contrary the protagonist is unable to convince Ras that he is no longer a dupe of the Brotherhood. He escapes from Ras but is pursued by a gang of whites. In his flight he falls through a manhole into a coal cellar. Invisible in the coal, he eludes the pursuer, and then falls asleep to dream that his enemies have castrated him—an imaginary act that emphasizes his thwarted existence.

In the Epilogue, the narrator, from his hole in the ground, attempts to analyze his experiences and decide on a future course of action. He feels inclined at first to stay underground to avoid the tendency of the modern world to make a man conform to a pattern. Only in division, he realizes, is society healthy. Life is full of infinite possibilities, as illustrated by Rinehart. With these thoughts running through his mind, the invisible man begins to lean toward the acceptance of his version of a socially responsible role. Finally he decides to end his hibernation and emerge into the world with his black skin, in all its invisibility, proudly displayed. The fact that few will see beneath it enhances his possibilities to play the roles he prefers.

The Harlem section of the novel, which is over half of the book, concentrates primarily on the historical Negro role in the Communist party. Ellison lucidly summarizes the response of the black intellectual to communism by indicating the promise it offers. The chance to be important socially and politically, however, is complicated by the decision to abandon the masses of the ghetto for the sake of international politics. Thus racial loyalty is tested against party ideology. The decision made by the invisible man is aided by Tod Clifton and Rinehart. Clifton leaves the Brotherhood to sell Sambo dolls as an indication of the role the Negro plays for the organization. Rinehart, despite his tendency to exploit his fellow blacks, represents the possibilities inherent in invisibility if applied to the white society that manipulates the lives of Negroes. Ras the Destroyer offers a more contentious alternative to white racism. The first of the militant revolutionaries to appear in a novel since Wright changed the course of black fiction in 1940, Ras and his violent philosophy are rejected by the narrator. He prefers to consider the significance of his grandfather's advice to "agree them to death and destruction." The question is how to put this concept to a socially responsible use.

The criticism generally directed at *Invisible Man* is that it is too episodic. The passive hero is involved in a series of adventures that illustrate his invisibility. The author strives to make each scene more intense than the preceding one, but is doomed to failure after the brilliance of the battle royal and the college episodes. The last section of the novel dealing with the Brotherhood is dull in comparison. The resurrection of the hero after the explosion in the paint factory promises more than it fulfills, and the Epilogue provides an optimistic conclusion that is not supported by the major portion of the novel. These flaws do not seriously detract from the significance of *Invisible Man*, however. Ellison explores the nature of race prejudice and the history of the Negro in the United States in a manner that displays his rhetorical skill to the utmost. The comic tone of the novel is maintained by the author's mimicry of the tall tale, the political address, and the Negro sermon; his exposure of stock racial attitudes in bizarre scenes; his portrayal of the hero's innocence in the face of discrimination; and in his use of symbolism and surrealism in depicting events of serious import. The absurdity of the world, especially in regard to racial matters, is epitomized by Rinehart, the shadowy figure who exploits his invisibility by his multiple existence.

The tendency of Ellison to emphasize Negro history is illustrated by his use of the briefcase the hero is given upon his graduation from high school. The objects that he carries in it at different phases of his career reveal the story of the black man in America. His diploma is symbolic of the unsatisfactory educational system of the South. Bledsoe's letter indicates how blacks are used against each other within this system. The minstrel bank he steals from Mary Rambo represents economic exploitation. The leg shackle given him by a member of the Brotherhood is a symbol of slavery, which, in a sense, still exists. Tod Clifton's Sambo doll represents the servile role played by blacks in most phases of American life. Brother Jack's letter identifying the hero as a party member illustrates the willingness of the Communists to use the Negro as a political pawn. Finally, his dark Rinehart glasses are indicative of the invisibility of blacks in a society in which their humanity is denied.

In illustrating the black experience in America in this manner, Ellison is able to show the effects of racism without concentrating on it to the exclusion of themes that are more universal in nature. The major emphasis is on the response of the protagonist as he gradually becomes aware of his position in relation to the reality of the world. His experiences, in this sense, are basically the same as those of any person who moves from innocence to knowledge. He is invisible not simply because he is a Negro, but because people of both races fail to recognize his individual characteristics. In their attempt to assert themselves or their ideas they see only a face that offers no resistance to exploitation. Only by an awareness of this situation can the hero begin to establish a personality of his own. Only by a knowledge of mankind in general, and himself in particular, can he have any control over the stereotypes which automatically form in the eyes of most of his beholders. This is the state that the invisible man advances to. Ellison does not reveal what he does with the knowledge gleaned from his experiences, but the important thing is that he has arrived as a human being.

Ellison's novel, then, indicates that protest can be an integral part of a supreme artistic creation. Unlike the author of *Native Son*, Ellison does not limit himself to a didactic presentation of human depravity. In its overall quality, its ironic exposure of the faults of American life, its symbolic use of history, its linguistic skill, and its concern for the privacy of the individual, *Invisible Man* claims a place with *Absalom, Absalom!* and *The Sound and the Fury* among the great novels of twentieth century America. But it is only one of the novels of the period that illustrates an interest in describing an aspect of the black experience without using the framework of the protest novel. Several of Ellison's predecessors began the trend and James Baldwin continued it with his first novel, *Go Tell It on the Mountain* (1953).

One of the most vocal of the critics of *Native Son*, Baldwin, in his own novel, concentrates on the internal problems of a black youth who is primarily concerned with escaping from the trauma of racial discrimination rather than in challenging the white world in the manner of Bigger Thomas. The protagonist attempts to adjust to the barren world around him by devoting his energy to the attainment of a religious conversion. In order to ease the hardships of his life he withdraws into the protective custody of the ghetto church. Instead of striking back at the white world he attempts to reconcile himself to it by sublimating his hostilities.

The action of the main plot takes place on the fourteenth birthday of John Grimes, but in a series of flashbacks Baldwin reveals the backgrounds of the boy's mother, aunt, and stepfather. The lives of these people illuminate the situation of John in the Harlem of 1935. Gabriel, his stepfather, and Gabriel's sister Florence were reared in the South. They both rejected the entreaties of their pious mother to live in a religious manner. Florence, jealous of the attention given to her brother, left home to seek a better life in the North. Her husband finally deserted her because of her stress on social status.

Gabriel became a preacher after his mother's death. He married a woman who bore him no children, and also carried on an affair with another woman. The infidelity resulted in an illegitimate son. Gabriel, after the death of his wife, eventually migrated to Harlem where, through his sister, he met Elizabeth. Anxious to atone for his treatment of his first wife, Gabriel married Elizabeth despite the fact that she was the mother of an illegitimate infant son, John.

In the present action of the novel, John and Gabriel regard each other with suspicion. Gabriel, a religious zealot who is filled with a sense of his own importance, ignores both Elizabeth and John. His love has been focused on Roy, his son from the union with Elizabeth. Roy, however, rejects both his father and religion. On the day of John's birthday he is wounded in a knife fight with white youths. John, meanwhile, who clings to his mother and the church as protection against a hostile environment, feels sorry for himself because he has to work on this special Saturday as if it were any ordinary day. He compares his household chores to the ordeal of Sisyphus, who is doomed to push his boulder up a hill for eternity. However, Elizabeth gives him some money and allows him to buy himself a present.

As John wanders through the streets of New York City he reflects on the way white people live. His father says that all whites are wicked, that they hate all "niggers." John is not so sure about the inherent evilness of whites, but he does admire their world. He is also aware of some of the subtleties of racial discrimination. Standing on a hill in Central Park, he feels like a giant who might destroy the city in his anger, for the glory of the Lord. The author takes advantage of the reflective state of the protagonist to reveal some of his thoughts on the status of a Negro in New York.

> He remembered the people he had seen in that city, whose eyes held no love for him. And he thought of their feet as swift and brutal, and the dark gray clothes they wore, and how when they passed they did not see him, or if they saw him, they smirked. And how their lights, unceasing, crashed on and off above him, and how he was a stranger there.[12]

Unlike Ellison's invisible man, John Grimes rids himself of most of his illusions at an early age. He accepts his role as an outsider, but to compensate he turns to his mother, his religion, and to Elisha, a Young Minister in the Temple of the Fire Baptized, in an effort to find love and protection. On Saturday evening, then, John experiences his conversion and becomes one of the elect. The ordeal on the threshing-floor of the church awakens in him a sense of freedom. For the first time he is able to face Gabriel without fear. But in his moment of glory it is to Elisha that the youth turns. The young man offers him the encouragement and love that Gabriel is incapable of expressing. With an identity established within the church, John feels that he is on his way, that he is capable of combating the world on whatever terms are necessary.

The religious conversion of the boy is in a sense a sexual experience. The problem of masculine identity is essential to a black youth who grows up in a society that tends to emasculate Negroes, especially if the father is absent or is inadequate. Edward Margolies suggests that the church partially fulfills the psychic needs of this type of individual by providing an Old Testament God of authority and masculinity. In order to be accepted by this God he must reject his worldly and sensual impulses and passively await the insemination of divine grace, thus momentarily assuming female characteristics in the quest for masculine identity.[13] The hint of a homosexual relationship between John and Elisha is, from Baldwin's point of view, therefore justified.

Perhaps just as important to the development of the novel as John's conversion are the flashbacks involving the early lives of Gabriel, Florence, and Elizabeth. This method of delving into the past, according to Marcus Klein,

> allows Baldwin to hold within a single vision the experience of a long history of the Negro in America. He can incorporate into it slavery and abrupt emancipation, the frustrations and the extremes of the life of the peasantry of the Old Country, the battle within the peasantry, and intimately within the family, for order, continuity, and moral stability. At the same time he contains within the vision the development of a religion that is an instrument at once of ethical prohibition, of promise, hatred, and of emotional deliverance. In the same moment he can contain the Negro experience of the trek to the North, with its sharper frustrations and its greater desperations.[14]

The conversion of John Grimes is part of a predictable historical process. The emotional pressure caused by the white power structure turns John to religion as a means of survival, repeating the experiences of his relatives in the past. The conversion is not only a religious act, it is part of a sexual awakening that is also related to white oppression, which emasculates black males and concomitantly increases the significance of the female's role in family life. Further, the economic conditions of the family contribute to the religious fervor. Years of struggling for a living under adverse conditions, in both the rural South and in the ghetto, increases the attractiveness of a religion that offers a definite sign of salvation. The ascendency of John Grimes to the elect is thus an important event in his life, but of more immediate importance to him is that it provides an alternative to living with fear in an inimical environment. It means that he is less likely to end up full of hate, trying to fight the world with violence, as in the case of his brother, Roy.

The life of Baldwin's protagonist is different from that of the invisible man in the sense that the former is congenitally affected by the psychological pressures of white oppression. Life in a ghetto is a struggle for survival that is somewhat softened by religion. The hero of Ellison's novel, on the other hand, indulges himself in the American dream of success. He becomes disillusioned only after years of experience. His response to the fact of being invisible is intellectual rather than emotional, but he has been exposed basically to physical aspects of discrimination, partly because in his innocence he does not allow the psychological elements to penetrate. To John Grimes racism is primarily a psychological force from which he withdraws through the promise of a passionate deliverance.

The main difference, in the novels, though, are in tone and scope. The detached, ironic humor of *Invisible Man* is geared to explore the gamut of black life. Baldwin's historical vision is much narrower as he concentrates on the psychological problems of individuals. The emotional intensity of the characters is reflected in the prose. Much of the book is written in the feverish pace of a Calvinist sermon. Baldwin, who attempts less, makes fewer mistakes, but his novel is marred by the failure to make the flashbacks of more immediate relevance to the plight of the protagonist. *Go Tell It on the Mountain* stands well on its own, although it is small in comparison to *Invisible Man*.

With the publication of these two novels, however, the form of protest inaugurated by *Native Son* was effectively pushed into the background. While a different form of protest began to take shape in the fifties, Ellison and Baldwin stole the attention of the critics, and to a large extent, the public. This is not because of a lack of emphasis on racial matters, which are prevalent in both novels, but because of the artistic skill displayed and the tendency to deal with universal human problems. The protagonists are representative of the twentieth century man who searches for meaning and identity in a world that tends to alienate sensitive individuals.

Wright himself acknowledged the fact that the day of the formula protest novel was over, by producing *The Outsider* (1953). Influenced, as so many novelists have been, by Camus and Sartre, Wright presents his own version of the existential man in Cross Damon. A Negro post office employee in Chicago, Damon stresses the fact that being black is of no importance to him. What is significant is that he is an outsider, a man who purposely rejects the laws and norms of society. His life is spent searching for meaning in a godless world in which man is only what he makes himself. To adapt himself to this situation, the protagonist creates his own standards.

Tired of his job and his family, Damon takes advantage of a subway accident to assume the identity of another person. Taking the name of the dead man, Damon watches what is supposedly his own funeral, and later is forced to kill a man who recognizes him. He flees to New York where he becomes involved with Communists. He discerns that they merely intend to use him for their own purposes, though, and he retaliates by killing two of them, plus his racist landlord. Ely Houston, the district attorney, discovers the true identity of Damon in their long philosophical discussions, but cannot obtain proof of the murders. However, Damon is shot by Communists and on his deathbed he intimates that he was mistaken in living by an individual value system.

As an outsider, Damon is impervious to the political maneuvering of the Marxists. He sees behind their ideological webs and recognizes that their social crusade for Negroes is merely a facade to undermine the American government. Cross Damon realizes that he needs other people to fulfill his own potentials, but he is not ready to accept any ideology until he is sure that it will not reduce him to "a creature of nervous dread." Thus he attempts to create his own future with nothing to guide him but his own will. He rejects his past life and, as much as society will let him, dissociates himself from his black skin. Free of obligations, Damon's struggle is now for the realization of himself. He is obsessed with his nonidentity. What he needs is the type of responsibility that will test him so that he is able to feel his worth. However, in ridding himself of the claims of others, he finds that he foolishly drifts in an opaque world that he cannot become related to. Wright states that

> It was this static dream world that had elicited those acts of compulsion, those futile attempts to coerce reality to his emotional demands. There was in him a need to stabilize his surroundings. The world of most men is given to them by their culture, and, in choosing to make his own world, Cross had chosen to do something more dangerous than he had thought.[15]

Adrift in this world, Cross Damon succumbs to his own weaknesses. He kills when it is not absolutely necessary and once his bloody deeds are done he talks himself into the necessity for another murder. Damon's personal feelings conquer his intellect and his fate gets out of his control. On his deathbed, then, he recognizes his mistakes, but at the same time he tells the district attorney that he is "innocent." Judged by his own standards he is innocent in the sense that he was merely trying to go his own way in a world burdened by absurd inhibitions. His mistake is that he let his emotions interfere with his philosophy. This is the danger of searching alone, Damon realizes, and he implies that what is needed is men who are responsible for others as well as for themselves.

Russell Carl Brignano suggests that *The Outsider* is actually a rejection of the nihilistic-existential premises of the protagonist. In pointing out the fallibilities of Damon and his philosophy, Wright is advocating a humanistic type of reform based on a concern for the common good. The destruction left in the wake of a man who walks outside of history and society tends to illustrate the risk of accepting a philosophy that recognizes no laws. The life of Cross Damon implies the need for a moral discipline in a world dominated by industry and science.[16]

Wright, however, does not control his novel well enough to make his position clear. The theme of the protagonist's search for identity in a chaotic world is the author's primary concern —and he overworks it, to say the least. The book is composed mostly of long philosophical discussions and the reflections of the protagonist on his fate. Scenes of violence are interspersed to relieve the monotony. While Wright makes some interesting comments on the ideological inclinations of man, the power of *Native Son*, and of his autobiography, *Black Boy* (1945), is not present in *The Outsider*.

Although Wright avoids race to a large degree in the novel, Cross Damon does take advantage of the stereotyped racial attitudes of whites to help him in the assumption of a new, if random, identity. He uses his invisibility only when it is necessary, though. Most of his time is spent in searching for a role that accommodates his philosophy. In concentrating on existentialism from what is essentially a nonracial standpoint, Wright divorces himself from the emotional atmosphere of *Native Son* only to find himself in a frigid intellectual mausoleum that is largely devoid of artistic significance.

Gwendolyn Brooks, a Pulitzer Prize winning poet, also published a novel that has accommodationist characteristics. *Maud Martha* (1953) is thematically in the popular tradition of the fifties which deals with the coming of age of a young Negro in a society which necessitates a personal adjustment to the effects of racism. The heroine, in the manner of Dorothy West's Cleo Judson, is concerned with obtaining a favorable economic and social position. She is not a fanatic like Cleo, but she is worried about the darkness of her complexion and about being accepted in the neighborhood. Maud Martha also has a husband who is basically oblivious to her needs and desires. It all adds up to a lot of trouble for the young lady.

Maud Martha is first presented as a girl of seven who is fat and unloved. As an adolescent she suffers through dates, living in a romantic dream world. It is as a young bride, though, that the protagonist learns the real pains of life. Living in a drab apartment with a husband who spends his energy trying to advance in a business that discriminates against him, Maud Martha soon becomes disillusioned. Bearing children and working for white bigots does not improve her view of life, but she learns to endure the hard times and to enjoy the good ones when she can, in the meantime retaining her self-respect. After suffering a series of indignities from her employer, she decides to quit for the simple reason that

> one was a human being. One wore clean nightgowns. One loved one's baby. One drank cocoa by the fire—or the gas range—come the evening, in the wintertime.[17]

Maud Martha is the type of enduring black woman that has become a stereotype. The impressive aspect of the novel, though, is the stylistic presentation of the protagonist. The book is composed of thirty-four poetic fragments, or chapters, each of which is a slice-of-life episode. The impressionistic vignettes reveal the various attitudes of the heroine towards life with a minimum of words. In comparison with the protest novels of the forties, *Maud Martha* resembles a series of sonnets. If the material is rather scanty for a novel, and a plot is lacking, the elegance and economy of the language partially compensate for it.

Much of the mental anguish of Maud Martha stems from the fact that she is black, but the book actually stresses the triumph of the human will over all difficulties. Chester Himes' *The Third Generation* takes the opposite course in depicting an entire black family that is destroyed by the psychological pressures of racism and by individual weaknesses. Himes, too, stresses the development of a Negro youth, but in this case the progression is towards the negative as the protagonist is warped by an unhealthy environment and is unable to reconcile himself to the chaotic society around him.

The Third Generation (1954) presents, in Lillian Taylor, a shrew who matches Cleo Judson in her insatiable passion to be white. Lillian tries to dominate her husband and is responsible for driving him from one job to another. She hates the pronounced Negroid features of the man, and the marital difficulties that result from this hate not only cause Professor Taylor embarrassment in his position as a college teacher but make their home life extremely unpleasant at times. Charles and his brother, then, grow up in an atmosphere that is far from ideal. Lillian teaches them that her ancestors were rich white people and that her light skin is a sign of superiority. Professor Taylor, gradually becoming neurotic under his wife's harping, loses teaching positions at Negro colleges in both Missouri and Mississippi and is finally reduced to a janitor in Cleveland, Ohio.

In the meantime the once happy boyhood of Charles has disappeared to be replaced by the continual frustrations of insecurity and loneliness. Charles never lives up to the promise he had shown as a youngster, when he was insensitive to the tensions between his parents. As the conflict increases over the years it eventually adversely affects him. He finally goes to college but the idea of learning no longer appeals to him. Himes explains that he is more interested in an artificial sense of freedom.

> Temporarily he had escaped from the constraining authority of his parents, his mother's constant nagging and fear of his father's defeat. It was as if he'd shed a great burden he'd borne for many years, or got rid of an irritating sore. He could do as he chose, go where he pleased. He felt that he'd grown wings.[18]

But he is never free from the psychological burdens that have

94

accumulated over the years and he misuses the physical freedom that he is granted by indulging himself in debauchery. In gaining a measure of revenge on his domineering mother, Charles tends to ruin himself. The old problem of female dominance in the Negro family haunts the Taylors. Without the strong masculine hand to counteract Lillian, Charles disintegrates under the combined pressure of society and his own sense of inferiority. Like other of Himes' male characters he tries to compensate for his mental emasculation through drinking and sexual encounters, but he only increases his problems.

As in the case of Baldwin's *Go Tell It on the Mountain*, Himes depicts the internal strife of a black family. The pressures on John Grimes, however, are mollified by the love of his mother and the emotional catharsis provided by the church. Charles Taylor finds no constructive outlet for his problems. His mother, in the manner of Cleo Judson in *The Living Is Easy*, accepts a value system based on white superiority and the ensuing psychological problems are self-destructive. The major fault of *The Third Generation*, though, is the tracing of the self-destructive processes in a naturalistic style that becomes tedious in its compilation of evidence to justify the protagonist's behavior. The vitality of the first half of the novel dissipates in proportion to the worsening condition of Charles Taylor and his family.

The psychological implications of racism that are prevalent in the protest novels of the forties also play a major role in the accommodationist fiction of the fifties, as indicated in works such as *The Third Generation*. However, in the Wrightian protest novels psychological oppression leads to violence. There is no standard response to racism in much of the later fiction, as individual artists struggle with the problem on their own terms. Julian Mayfield in *The Hit* (1957) illustrates how gambling plays an important part in the lives of the inhabitants of a ghetto, many of whom hope to escape from it by making a "hit." Gambling provides an outlet for the frustrations of the urban Negroes who feel that they are trapped in a web patrolled by the white power structure.

The novel shows how the numbers game affects a Harlem family. Hubert Cooley, a building superintendent, plans to abscond with Sister Clarisse when his number pays off in the illegal policy racket. Gertrude, his wife, who does most of the work while Hubert dreams about escaping the ghetto, tries to save enough money to pay the bills. When Hubert steals the money that was put aside for the gas and electric bill, his wife takes to the streets to try and get it back before he places his bet. In the meantime, their son, James Lee, has to prove his manhood by fighting an Irish mechanic at his place of employment. As he comes triumphantly home from work he finds his father sitting patiently in front of his apartment. Hubert made his hit for over four thousand dollars. However, Sister Clarisse refuses to leave with him, and to make things worse, the pay-off man has left town without delivering the money. As the novel ends, Hubert, refusing to believe his dream is shattered, continues to wait for the man to appear with the cash that will take him out of Harlem.

The pervasiveness of the numbers game and the dream it represents is revealed in the prayer of a minister.

> Lord, I'm needing a new church so I can help set these people back on the path of righteousness. I saw a nice big store at One hundred and thirty-sixth and Lenox, . . . It's the perfect site for the Blessed Lamb Holiness Church. . . . The number is 471, Lord, and I have played it in a six-way combination. Now if in your loving kindness you could see fit to make things go that way, O Lord, we would be eternally in your debt as we are already. All these things we ask in Jesus' name. Amen.[19]

The policy racket thrives among the poor people of the ghetto, who dream of making that one big hit that will send them on their way to success. The fact that the odds are thousands to one does not detract from the dream. In concentrating on this aspect of ghetto life, Mayfield reveals the despair of being trapped within the boundaries designated by white society. The episode involving James Lee Cooley and his battle to prove himself to the white people who antagonize him underlines the theme of oppression that dominates the novel. The author is adept at selecting the material which pinpoints the aspirations and personality of his characters. Within the narrow framework of the novel he does a more than adequate job of disclosing the comic, as well as the tragic, aspects of daily life in Harlem.

The same is true on a lesser level in Mayfield's second novel, *The Long Night* (1958). It deals with the adventure of a Harlem youth who is sent to collect a small hit made by his mother, who jokingly advises him not to come home without the money. When the older members of Steely's gang take the money from him, the boy embarks on a night long expedition to beg, earn, or steal the amount of the hit. In the process he discovers his father, who had deserted the family years ago. The author uses flashbacks to reveal the story of the father's desertion, which was due largely to the pressures of trying to succeed in a society dominated by whites. Mayfield, however, is not very convincing in *The Long Night*, which is contrived and melodramatic in comparison with *The Hit*.

Another novel that deals with the numbers game is Langston Hughes' *Tambourines to Glory* (1958). Appearing twenty-eight years after his first novel, *Not Without Laughter*, it exposes the way in which religion is exploited by a couple of Harlem opportunists. The tone of the book is comic, though, as Hughes reveals how Essie and Laura, middleaged women from the ghetto, discover that religion is something they can collect on. They start their own church, and, with an emphasis on music, it soon attracts a lot of sinners who are willing to contribute a little money for the privilege of being a part of the audience. Business picks up even more when Buddy wins the confidence of Laura and begins to use the church as a front for his gambling operations. Buddy becomes too independent in his use of both the church and Laura, though, and she kills the numbers man for revenge. Essie, innocent of much of the illegal and selfish activities of her partner, continues to operate the church, thinking with some justification, that she is providing a service for the community.

Hughes' novel is a delightful portrait of the Harlem crowd that will believe in anything that promises an escape from the realities of existence. While it is shown that poverty and oppression motivate the religious activity, Hughes competently depicts the humorous aspects of this zeal. With the introduction of Buddy and the numbers game, though, the comedy tends to be replaced by a serious note that dissipates into melodrama. *Tambourines to Glory* illustrates some of the techniques that have made Hughes a popular poet, short story writer, and folklorist, but it does not enhance his literary reputation.

Even Hughes, however, is indicative of the trend away from the Wrightian protest novel that emerges in the fifties. The concern with art, and with the attempts of the majority of blacks to adjust, in some way, to the racism that is prevalent in American society, as epitomized in *Invisible Man* and *Go Tell It on the Mountain*, is as strong as the necessity to protest. The best novels of the period are those that strike a balance between the depicting of the significant aspects of Negro life and an objective manner of presentation. The most popular theme is the awakening of a young Negro to the facts of oppression, and the discovery of a method of accommodating himself to life under this handicap.

Other black novelists of the period, though, took different approaches to their fiction. The assimilationist novel, which deals primarily with white characters, briefly attracted such authors as Himes, Baldwin, and Wright. But the main challenge to the Ellison-Baldwin domination was the protest novel which depicted the Negro as a victim of physical and legal violence—a movement that was headed by Ann Petry and William Gardner Smith, but that also saw the return of Himes and Wright to the protest field.

CHAPTER VI

Assimilationism and Protest in the Fifties

The urge to protest has been basic to the Negro novel since its inception. The revolt against protest, headed by such writers as West, Redding, Ellison, and Baldwin, was directed only at those novels patterned after *Native Son*. Protest elements, in most cases, were incorporated into the work in some form. However, novels designed specifically to reveal the Negro as a victim of racism continued to be produced in the fifties. The metaphysical rebel disappeared, but the militant revolutionary showed signs of developing. At the other extreme, though, was the assimilationist novel which avoided racial themes by presenting white characters.

The theory behind the assimilationist novel is that the elimination of racial material will give the black writer a literary freedom that will allow him to concentrate on art rather than on protest. The tendency to write propaganda is very strong when one attempts to depict Negro life. In writing about whites, on the other hand, a novelist is free to explore any aspect of life that appeals to him. The fallacy of this argument, though, is in the mediocrity of the fiction itself. The black novelists were merely avoiding the issue that they were primarily concerned about, as evidenced by the fact that most of these writers produced racial protest novels of a superior quality. Of the assimilationist novels produced in the fifties only Baldwin's *Giovanni's Room* is of any significance, and it is essentially a propagandistic book.

William Gardner Smith, whose *Last of the Conquerers* (1948) was the first racial protest novel to break away from the Wrightian

99

formula, abandons racial themes in *Anger at Innocence* (1950). Smith's second novel deals with a timid white man who falls in love with a woman young enough to be his daughter. Theodore Hall, separated from his wife, falls in love with Rodina, a sultry young pickpocket. Hall is haunted by feelings of guilt as a result of his adulterous affair, however, and he finds little satisfaction in it. Yet, he cannot resist the sexual charms of Rodina. Complications arise when the girl tries to change Hall into her idea of what a man should be. The man refuses to relinquish completely his version of decency, though, and Rodina retaliates by killing both Hall and herself.

Smith's melodrama is concerned basically with sexual frustration. Besides the problems caused by the puritanical view of Hall and the possessive traits of Rodina, the author presents two other afflicted characters. Juarez, a moody Mexican, is jealous of Hall's success with Rodina, and he helps to create the friction that leads to the catastrophe. Hucks, a truck driver, attempts to rape Rodina. The story, centered on these four misfits, is replete with thwarted passions and perverted values. Most of the typical defects of sensationalism, which Smith managed to eliminate from his earlier protest novel, occur in *Anger at Innocence*. The characterization of Theodore Hall is interesting, but on the whole the novel's obscurity is deserved.

Willard Motley followed his popular *Knock on Any Door*, (1947) with a novel of political corruption in Chicago in the years after the second World War. *We Fished All Night* (1951) traces the career of Don Lockwood as he ascends from a Polish ghetto to the political leadership of the city. In the process the author exposes the machinations of the local government in the hands of opportunists. Lockwood, who as a young man is a champion of civil rights and an amateur actor, becomes corrupted as he advances politically. He realizes what is happening to him but he cannot stop while power beckons.

Motley attempts to reveal disillusionment on a large scale as he ties together the lives of several families that come to know the protagonist. Much of the book is devoted to problems in the labor unions and discrimination against Jews. As in *Knock on Any Door*, the author substitutes other minority groups for blacks to illustrate the effects of prejudice and oppression. Despite his ability to analyze many influential aspects of society that are exerted on an individual, Motley is a crude stylist who exploits the sordid side of life for the sake of sensationalism.

Motley, encouraged by its popularity, produced a sequel to *Knock on Any Door*, his first novel. Concerned with the illegitimate son of Nick Romano, *Let No Man Write My Epitaph* (1958) follows the same pattern of its predecessor except that the son is saved from the fate of his father through the help of sympathetic friends. The novel attacks the narcotics business by revealing the nefarious effects of dope. The inner core of the city of Chicago is shown to be a natural breeding ground for crime. While Nick Romano, Jr. is rescued from the corrupting influences of the city, the inherent danger of the place is stressed, especially from the standpoint of those who are born in poverty. Motley also indicates the power of race prejudice in a subplot involving an uncle of the protagonist and a Negro girl. Although they are in love, the pressures of society will not allow them to marry.

Although Motley tried to spice up the sequel with the addition of the interracial love affair and the introduction of several colorful characters, it is basically a regurgitation of *Knock on Any Door*. The stylistic improvements are negated by the repetition of themes and melodramatic incidents. Motley's novels are essentially protest novels in the sense that they try to prove that environmental factors victimize individuals. He advocates constructive change in reform schools, local government, and drug legislation, but while exposing the evils of life in the city, Motley tends to satisfy the public taste for violence and melodrama.

Chester Himes' assimilationist novel, *Cast the First Stone* (1952), also deals with the need for reform. The book depicts the inadequacies of a prison, specifically on the life of Jim Monroe. A young white man, Monroe learns the intricacies of the prison's system of keeping the inmates in check, as well as the ways in which one can accommodate the ruthless guards. The barbarity is underlined by the killing of a Negro prisoner, but it is not until a fire kills a number of inmates that a prison reform bill is passed. With that propagandistic aspect of the novel taken care of, Himes concentrates on the mental condition of the protagonist. Monroe considers suicide as a result of his imprisonment, but he finds relief in the friendship of Duke Dido. Although the men are not homosexuals they are branded as such. The fallacious charge induces Duke to commit suicide. Monroe, however, tries to rationalize the situation and he looks forward to his imminent freedom with some optimism.

Cast the First Stone is concerned primarily with the inhumanity of penal institutions. From this viewpoint the novel is relatively effective, but when the author focuses on the inner turmoil of the protagonist there is a sharp decline. The ambiguous relationship between Monroe and Duke verges on the sentimental, although Himes attempts to make it a valid part of the plot by introducing the homosexual aspects. This theme illustrates further the cruel treatment of the prisoners, as the conditions of the prison are shown to be conducive to homosexual activities. The second half of the novel, however, resembles an afterthought on the part of the author in which he injects an existential theme to emphasize what he had already stated in the first part of the book.

Richard Wright joined the assimilationist trend with the publication of *Savage Holiday* (1954), a book that was rejected by Wright's regular publishers. Basically it is an exercise in psychological hack writing. Erskine Fowler, the white middle-aged protagonist, is a study in repressed sexuality, resembling Theodore Hall of Smith's *Anger at Innocence*. His problems are intensified by the attractive young woman who lives in the next apartment. In a series of melodramatic coincidences the lives of the two people become intertwined. The predictable result is violence.

Wright, in an effort to abstain from the racial themes that he had popularized in *Native Son*, presents only white characters in this small potboiler. The protagonist works out his Freudian complexes under the spell of Mabel Blake. Victimized by his Protestant training that emphasized negation, Fowler goes berserk when he is confronted with temptation. Wright not only establishes a Freudian atmosphere, he explains much of his own symbolism, which is relatively obvious to begin with. Although the book poses several serious questions about the nature of guilt in an oppressive environment, there is no deep exploration of them. In attempting to show that race does not dominate his thoughts, Wright merely displays an inability to deal with something he is not particularly interested in—a situation that is partially remedied in a later protest novel.

Another famous black author abandoned racial themes entirely in a novel of the period. James Baldwin, in *Giovanni's Room* (1956), deals with a homosexual relationship between white males in France. David, an American, finds that he is in love with both Hella, his fiancée, and Giovanni, an Italian bartender. The love he experiences with the transplanted Italian youth is terminated when Hella arrives in Paris. Giovanni responds by degenerating into a beggar who eventually murders a man. David, upset by the knowledge of his homosexuality and the news of Giovanni's arrest, withdraws from Hella into a world in which only his guilt exists. After the Italian is executed, David engages in a wild homosexual escapade. Hella finally calls off their engagement and David faces the future with pessimism.

In his second novel, Baldwin attacks American culture from a different angle. Rather than stressing the oppressive forces of white society on the black subculture, he exposes the puritanical corruptness of America that makes the expression of love impossible. The American protagonist is unable to give himself completely to others, due largely to the Christian background that taught him self-denial. Margolies suggests that

> Christian love has here been transfigured into masculine love, the one redeeming grace in Baldwin's neo-Calvinist vision of a corrupt and depraved world. David's failure is that he has failed to 'bear witness' to Giovanni's suffering—that he has failed to give him the love Giovanni demanded in order that he might survive.[1]

Failing as a Christian, and consequently as a lover, David embraces his homosexuality as a part of the cross he has to bear. He can no longer accept Hella, a symbol of the American Christianity that has led him to the hell that yawns before him. He recognizes too late the purity of Giovanni's love, but he vows to worship the spirit of his departed savior even if it leads to self-destruction in a world that brands him as a pervert.

Although Baldwin has a command of the language that allows him to communicate with power, *Giovanni's Room* is probably his least successful work. His argument for homosexuality as a source of pure love in comparison to the spiritual bankruptcy of American puritanism is his primary concern. Despite the presentation of scenes that rival those of Poe or Hawthorne in their evocation of the atmosphere necessary to convey the full significance of the author's material, the characters are relatively shallow. They are often mere mouthpieces for Baldwin's point of view, which he tries desperately to establish, knowing that it will be hard to accept. The novel is therefore more propagandistic than *Go Tell It on the Mountain*, which deals with racial themes.

In taking into account the assimilationist novels of the fifties, it is obvious that the freedom ascribed to the absence of racial themes did not produce great literature. In fact it did not produce much freedom. Motley and Himes campaigned for social reform. Smith, Wright, and Baldwin condemned puritanical attitudes toward sex. None of these novels celebrated life as Ellison did in *Invisible Man*. None of them illustrated a zest for combating life as Dodson did in *Boy at the Window* or Brooks in *Maud Martha*. The novels of white life published in the fifties reveal a morbid concern for social problems. Significantly, Himes, Smith, Wright, and Baldwin all wrote much better novels when they concentrated on the problems of black people. Also, except for the historical romances of Frank Yerby, the assimilationist novel virtually disappeared in the following decade.

The great Negro novels of the fifties, of course, are the ones that deal freely with aspects of black life. A protest trend is discernible, though, which, while it did not reach great heights in the decade, eventually developed into a dominant literary force. These are the novels which depict the Negro not only as a psychological victim of white society, but as a target for eradication. The racial protest novels of the fifties illustrate that whenever a black steps out of the boundaries assigned to him, or whenever the whites are looking for a scapegoat, he pays with his life. The difference between these protest novels and the books designated as accommodationist is that the protest fiction concentrates exclusively on revealing that Negroes are refused full participation in American life by the threat of physical violence, or by legal manipulations. In contrast, the nonprotest literature reflects the various individual responses to the condition of being alive, and also being black, in a country where whites make the rules.

There is no dominant pattern of protest as in the previous decade, however. The influence of *Native Son* is present only in a general sense. Only one novel presents a metaphysical rebel that bears a resemblance to Bigger Thomas. Chester Himes in *The Primitive* (1955) delineates the career of a black novelist who cannot escape the Bigger in his mind. Jesse has an affair with Kriss, a white woman from North Dakota who has trouble adjusting to the Bohemian life she seeks. Jesse's third novel has just been rejected because the publisher thinks that the public is tired of protest fiction. Jesse, though, feels that he can only write about life as he sees it.

The angry black writer and the confused white woman, then, are drawn together by their frustrations. Kriss is attracted to the Negro because of the primitivistic sexual image he represents to her. Jesse turns to Kriss as a form of revenge on the white world in general. The hopelessness of their affair is stressed through the inanity of a television program Kriss periodically watches, and by their pseudo-liberal friends who have to force themselves to accept the interracial romance. After a drinking bout Jesse exacts his full measure of revenge by killing the woman.

Although the protagonist is an educated man who has had some success in the literary world, he finds an identity only in violence. Because society defines him as a "nigger" he responds by acting in the expected way. In fulfilling the role of the brute Negro by the murder of the girl in, presumably, a state of insanity, Jesse is subconsciously accepting the inferior position assigned to him at the same time he is striking back at white society. The murder is an act of self-assertion that is also a denial of his own humanity. As in the case of Bigger Thomas, Jesse becomes visible to whites only through a violent act, but even in this state of visibility he exists merely as a specific stereotype. In a moment of madness, though, he decides that being recognized as a brute is preferable to not being seen at all. When he realizes what he has done, Jesse consoles himself by reflecting on the fact that in fulfilling his role he has descended to the level of the people that created it—he has become a member of the human race.

In a chaotic and unjust world the protagonist strikes back by asserting his own extreme form of injustice. Himes is careful to draw the parallel with *Native Son* even though his protagonist is completely different from Bigger Thomas. To American society he is a Negro, however, and that categorization is very limited indeed. *The Primitive* stresses the effects of racism on a black man, suggesting that a potential Bigger Thomas is omnipresent in a person who is not recognized as an individual. In concentrating on this theme, though, Himes' novel is limited in scope and weak in artistic merits. The last overt protest novel of the author, who has turned to farces and detective stories, it is also the last novel to be patterned after *Native Son*. Himes merely substitutes an artist for the depraved proletarian of the earlier novels, but the result is, unfortunately, essentially the same as in the other imitations of Wright's book.

More typical of the protest fiction of the period is Lloyd Brown's *Iron City* (1951) which continues the apologetic trend of presenting a promising Negro who is physically destroyed or severely punished by racists. A novel of prison life, it illustrates the process of legal lynching that is employed by the law enforcers. Lonnie James, a Negro on death row, tells the story of his arrest and conviction to a couple of black men who are involved with communism. James has been framed and forced into a confession of a murder that he knows nothing about. A Defense Committee is formed in behalf of the convicted youth, but every effort to free him is defeated by the testimony of the same policemen who were paid to frame him to begin with. Despite the discovery of a witness that can free James, the Supreme Court upholds the death sentence.

Brown's novel is a typical product of the period with its portrayal of communism as a potential savior of the black race. This concept is retained throughout the book and, although the protagonist is not rescued, his cause is valiantly presented to the bar of justice, such as it is. But Brown makes it obvious that James does not have a chance against the elements of racism. Despite his innocence, the white policemen, in need of a black scapegoat, hold him for sixteen days without a charge until they are able to beat a confession out of him. They then fix the trials to protect themselves and to assure the conviction of the victim. This is Brown's comment on American society. *Iron City* is designed to expose the inhumanity of legal racism and, if the novel is weak stylistically and generally unimpressive, it does emphasize a significant weakness of the legal system and of the country in general.

A similar miscarriage of justice occurs in Herbert Simmons' *Corner Boy* (1957). The novel reveals the malicious effects of an unsavory environment on Jake Adams, a black youth who leads a gang in a St. Louis ghetto. Jake becomes a dope pusher, one of the jobs that commands respect from his peers. Because of his connections with the major hoodlums of the city, the youth manages to stay clear of the law. However, when he becomes romantically involved with a white girl, he is pushing his luck too far. When the girl is killed in an automobile accident involving Jake's car, the legal authorities try to convict him of rape. Jake, who was not responsible for the accident, is guilty of being in the company of a white girl, and it is essentially for this that he is sentenced to prison, although he does escape the death penalty. Jake knows that when he gets out of jail he will go back to "the corner" where he got his education in the hard facts of life. The ghetto is the only place he can go, and the chances are good that he will end up back in prison.

The environment is stressed in the first part of the novel. Simmons shows how the limitations of the ghetto affect the lives of the corner boys. Reared in an atmosphere in which crime is a respectable occupation, the youths from the ghetto develop attitudes that are much different from those of their white counterparts. The protagonist is a typical product of this environment. He knows how to make his way in the jungle that imprisons him. However, when he begins to date a white girl, the situation is out of his control. A case is built against him by the white policemen before the accident occurs. He has violated the most serious taboo known to white racists, and it is only a matter of time before the police "defend white womanhood" by eliminating Jake Adams. The fact that the girl loves him makes preventive action all the more necessary, from the perverted viewpoint of the law enforcers.

Simmons is adept at presenting the intricate aspects of life in the ghetto. Part of the novel is an objective portrait of Jake and his gang. Much of this material, however, is irrelevant to the catastrophic events of the second half of the novel. Simmons resorts to the inevitable melodrama as the plot progresses. The protagonist is the victim of a conspiracy to frame him on a charge of rape, although there is no evidence. The point is, of course, that no black is protected by law when the legal system is controlled by racists. *Corner Boy* is weak in the sense that while it shows the forces that shape the protagonist, it does not illustrate how the attitudes of whites are formed. White racism does not directly affect the youth until he violates an unwritten code of decorum. Racism then takes over as the theme of the novel, but it is expressed only through sensationalism.

The legal manipulations used to keep Negroes from attaining justice, as stressed in the fiction of Lloyd Brown and Herbert

Simmons, represent one form of racism. More common in the protest novels of the fifties, though, is the use of violence by whites. The primary excuse for resorting to violence is miscegenation, which may be interpreted as the mere presence of a black male with a white female. The threat of physical force is often sufficient to prevent blacks from expressing themselves freely. In case of transgression, murder is almost inevitable.

Ann Petry's *The Narrows* (1953) is basically concerned with the love affair between a black bartender and a white woman from high society. More significantly, it marks the flowering of the apologetic protest novel which had been revived by Savoy and Smith in the late forties and continued by novelists such as Brown and Simmons. Petry's third novel traces the life of Link Williams, the adopted son of Abbie Crunch, a respectable widow who lives in the Narrows, a black ghetto in the city of Monmouth. Link receives his education in surviving in a white world from Bill Hod, a Negro who owns the bar across the street from the Crunch residence. In a series of flashbacks, Link's struggles to attain self-respect in the face of discrimination at school are revealed. Hod, with the help of a teacher, gives the boy lessons in black history and develops a sense of pride in him. Link eventually graduates from college. He takes a job as bartender for Hod while he works on a history of slavery in America.

Link's plans are interrupted by an affair with Camilo Treadwell Sheffield, a blond fashion expert, who does not announce that she is married. Ignorant of the ghetto and its inhabitants, the white girl becomes involved with the Negro to an extent that she had not imagined possible. Their affair is tumultuous, though, as the pressures caused by racist attitudes begin to mount. Link worries about whether he is just a vehicle for Camilo's lust. He cannot believe that she loves him once he finds out that she belongs to one of the most prosperous families in the city. He accuses her of being a "rich bitch" looking for extramarital thrills. Camilo retaliates by charging him with rape. The woman's mother and husband attempt to help her by bribing the local newspaper owner to attack verbally Link and the people of the Narrows. When their efforts to convict the Negro fail, the two conspirators, Mrs. Treadwell and her son-in-law, without the knowledge of Camilo, murder him.

The novel is much richer than a brief synopsis can indicate. The minor characters add a lot to it. Mrs. Treadwell and her son-in-law, rich to the point of arrogance, are nevertheless forced to dirty their hands with violence in order to protect their good name—which they fail to do anyway. Bullock, the editor of the *Monmouth Chronicle*, considers himself independent until he is pressured by Mrs. Treadwell. Jubine, the hippie photographer, tries to convince Bullock of the power of society to make people conform—a fact that the editor later learns from Mrs. Treadwell. Powther, the black butler at the Treadwell estate, is fastidious in his professional role. But he cannot control his voluptuous wife, Mamie, whose amorous adventures interfere with her housekeeping chores. Her small son, J. C., is left to fend for himself most of the time and the results are often disastrous, except when Abbie, Powthers' landlady, rescues him. Abbie's best friend, Frances Jackson, is a mortician who has made her peace with white society. Bill Hod cannot make peace with racists, though, and the white society to him is an object of scorn and hate. Al, the Treadwells' white chauffeur, hates "niggers," but he likes Powther.

The Narrows, the finest of Petry's three novels, attempts to broaden the perspective of protest fiction. The variety of characters that the author supplies, all representing different views towards life and race, tends to diffuse the impact of the protest elements. It is not just Link Williams and his tormentors that are involved, but an entire community. The emphasis, though, is on racism as it applies to the protagonist. All that Link has learned about black pride is meaningless in comparison to the ignorance and hatred that are responsible for his death. Link realizes that he has broken a taboo and, according to the tribal laws of the society, that he must pay with his life. That is the only reality.

The concept of white superiority negates the teaching of Bill Hod. Under the direction of the tavern owner and his employee, Weak Knees, an old Negro who has experienced the facts of racism, Link is introduced to the philosophy that black is something besides a symbol for evil or inferiority. In a flashback episode the author states that

> They proved to him, Weak Knees and Bill Hod, that black could be other things, too. They did it casually. Ebony was the best wood, the hardest wood; it was black. . . . The best caviar was black. The rarest jewels were black; black opals, black pearls.
>
> After a month of living with Bill and Weak Knees he felt fine. He felt safe. He was no longer ashamed of the color of his skin.[2]

But he is not safe from a physical standpoint, especially where a white girl is concerned. That is just the mistake the omnipresent white vigilante committee is looking for.

Ironically, however, it is this education in black pride that precipitates Link's death. He reacts to Camilo's position in society in a stereotyped fashion by classifying her as an exploiter of blacks on a sexual basis. Link is so aware of the historical tradition of sexual racism that he fails to judge Camilo on her individual merits. The implication is that racial consciousness does not necessarily negate the psychological dangers of racism. Link's knowledge increases his hatred of the collective white world, and, with the discovery of Camilo's background, Link can no longer identify her as a distinct human being. His physical demise, then, is merely the climax of a life of spiritual deprivation.

Petry is often brilliant in her attempt to soften the horror of her novel. The characterization, the humor, and the exploration of various aspects of life, are reminiscent of *Invisible Man*. The major problem with *The Narrows* is that these ingredients are not completely integrated into the novel. The author is telling two stories. One is a comedy on domestic life and the other is a grim tale of blood and lust. If Petry does not quite succeed in weaving these elements together, her attempt is valiant. *The Street* (1946) is a Wrightian protest novel of some merit, and her *Country Place* (1947) is one of the few good assimilationist novels. *The Narrows* is, in a sense, a combination of these two earlier efforts, and it surpasses both of them not only in reflecting the effects of racism but in analysing the human condition.

A flair for melodrama is perhaps Ann Petry's greatest weakness. In this respect she is at least matched by Richard Wright. From his French refuge the author of *Native Son* preferred to abandon overt racial themes in *The Outsider* and *Savage Holiday*. Violence and sensationalism remained part of his work, though, and in his return to protest fiction Wright continued the trend in an apologetic novel. But he was somewhat out of touch with America and *The Long Dream* (1958) looks backward rather than forward in its stylistic and thematic aspects. The novel makes no concession to the work of Ellison or Baldwin in its harsh portrait of racism in the South which denies the youthful protagonist the opportunity to develop his potentialities.

Wright was never completely irrelevant to the racial temper of his time, however, and *The Long Dream* catches the violent mood of the South in a vivid fashion. The story of a black youth who comes to maturity in a small Mississippi town, it concentrates on the friction between the races. Fishbelly Tucker is nursed on a hatred for whites, who are a constant physical threat, and he disapproves of his father, Tyree, a mortician who cooperates with the white power structure. Fishbelly is faced at an early age with the choice of trying to fight the system or of stepping into the dual roles occupied by Tyree, who is a leader in the black community but a pawn of the influential whites. The experiences of the protagonist make him realize that neither alternative is plausible.

In his educative process Fishbelly witnesses a variety of discriminatory practices. The white population runs the town with complete authority. The young protagonist is constantly haunted by the fear of white women after an experience in which one of his acquaintances is murdered for being caught in a room with a white prostitute. When Fishbelly is picked up by the police for swimming on private property, he is so afraid that the picture of the white girl that he keeps in his pocket will be discovered, that he faints. Because he is the son of Tyree, though, he is released. The police make a good profit from protecting the illegal businesses of Tyree, who decides that it is time for Fishbelly to learn something about the extracurricular operations.

When Tyree is killed for pushing his luck too far with the police chief, his partner in crime, Fishbelly takes his father's place. When he refuses to cooperate with the police department he is framed, although he fails to take the bait in the form of a white woman. Fishbelly is thrown in jail anyway, but he is released when the Chief decides that he is necessary to the operation of the illegitimate concerns. Fishbelly takes the opportunity that is offered him and escapes from the Mississippi town—all the way to France as a matter of fact. He refuses to play his father's role and he knows there is no way to change the social order.

The abdication of Fishbelly takes a long time. The financial profit to be gained by playing along with the white people almost closes his eyes to the reality that he is merely being used by them to the detriment of his own race. Early in his life he had been aware that the real reality of the lives of his people were negated; the *real* world lay over *there* somewhere—in a place where white people lived, people who had the power to say who could or could not live and on what terms; and the world in which he and his family lived was a kind of shadow world.[3]

Fishbelly finally escapes from the world that has emotionally crucified him. His refuge is a foreign land where, he hopes, racism is not an unalterable fact of life.

A sense of outrage pervades *The Long Dream* as the protagonist's existence is continually threatened by violence. Rather than fighting the injustice of the world in the manner of Bigger Thomas, Fishbelly decides to regard it as a hopeless case and to search for a new world in which he is not defined by the color of his skin. He admits defeat as far as living as a human being in the South is concerned. The novel attempts to illustrate the reasons for the protagonist's actions through the extended use of melodrama and by authorial comment. Wright's narrative, on nearly every page, reflects the hatred that exists between races. *The Long Dream* adds little to the literary reputation of the author, however, and even less to his views on the racial situation, which had been presented more poignantly in *Native Son* and *Uncle Tom's Children*.

Before Fishbelly Tucker eventually decides to run, he indicates a mild interest in challenging the white power structure. Perhaps the most significant development in the protest fiction of the decade is the introduction of the militant Negro. Ras the Destroyer made his appearance in *Invisible Man* and, although the protagonist of the novel rejects Ras' philosophy of violence, the militant Negro is a memorable figure. Just two years later similar rebels appear in the novels of John Oliver Killens and William Gardner Smith. The publication of the two books marks the birth of the militant protest novel which flourishes in the following decade.

Killens' *Youngblood* (1954) is a lengthy propagandistic tract that presents one episode after another of racial confrontations and injustices. The black Youngblood family of Georgia struggles to maintain a semblance of dignity in the face of white oppression. The life of Joe Youngblood is one of hard work for little reward. The whites take advantage of him economically and he can object only at the risk of his life. His son, Rob, suffers through the same indignities, but on a slightly different level. The racial atmosphere changes under the influence of young militants who work to improve the situation of the Negro in employment, and who instill black pride through the South. Rob Youngblood becomes involved in this movement through his high school teacher.

The personification of the racial problems that confront Rob is the challenge of a white girl. The author elaborates on the danger of white womanhood throughout the novel and includes a long flashback episode built around this theme. On the other hand, black women are shown to be the victims of sexual indignities which they can do nothing about. Rob manages to avoid being lynched, however, and after his high school graduation he takes a job in a hotel. It is at this point that his father is seriously wounded by a white man as a result of his demanding his correct wages, after being cheated for years. Violence erupts in the small Southern town, which becomes a battlefield as the blacks protect themselves from the whites, who want to make sure Joe Youngblood is dead. His crime of standing up to a white man is unpardonable. Killens adds a further touch of melodrama by producing a white man, once having been saved by a Negro, who volunteers to donate his blood to Joe. The wounded man dies, though, and Reverend Ledbetter announces his challenge to the white population at the funeral. In attempting to console Mrs. Youngblood, he tells her to

'... look all around you at your brothers and sisters, thousands of them, and Great God Almighty, fighting mad, and we're going to make them pay one day soon, the ones that're responsible. There's going to be a reckoning day right here in Georgia and we're going to help God hurry it up.'[4]

This speech, coming from a minister, emphasizes the militant tone of the novel.

Youngblood is perhaps unique only in its militancy. Killens reflects the mood of some of the young blacks in their impatience with the American way of life. Appearing in the same year as the Supreme Court's famous decision on the segregation of public schools, the novel is prophetic in its portrait of increased activity in the field of civil rights. A year later Rosa Parks refused to sit in the back of a bus in Montgomery, Alabama and Martin Luther King, Jr. took advantage of the situation to begin a peaceful revolution that shook the South. But a significant number of blacks preferred more forceful means of demanding their rights. In *Youngblood* the initiative is provided not by the young rebels but by old Joe Youngblood, who finally decided that he would no longer passively accept being exploited and cheated. In an act resembling those of Bigger Thomas, he strikes back at a white man. Once he has performed his act of rebellion, Joe is shot, but he inspires others to take a militant stance. The load is shifted from the individual metaphysical rebel to the young people who are prepared to emerge as revolutionaries—who are ready to organize into groups that are dedicated to changing a discriminatory way of life.

Killens is far from a polished writer. His style is essentially an imitation of Richard Wright at his worst, and his concern for violence and sensationalism is also reminiscent of his predecessor. But *Youngblood*, for all its crudeness, is a prophetic novel: it indicates the shape of much of the fiction of the sixties as well as the historical events that have affected the country since 1954.

William Gardner Smith, after an experiment in assimilationism, also produced a militant novel. *South Street* (1954) carries the implications of *Youngblood* farther along the way towards revolution. The book deals with a black bourgeois family in Philadelphia. The three Bowers brothers wear white carnations in their lapels as a reminder that their father was lynched by a white mob. Michael is a militant who declares his hate for whites and becomes disenchanted with his brothers for not doing the same. Claude, a noted writer who has just returned from Africa, has grown relatively content with his position in society. Philip, the third brother, withdraws into a world of his own. Michael organizes the Action Society in an attempt to neutralize police brutality, but his brothers refuse to join.

A main focus of the novel is on Claude and a white girl, Kristin. Although they are forced to endure many indignities they decide to get married. White bigots continue to put the pressure on the mixed couple, though, and in desperation they prepare to depart for Canada, where they expect to live without the prejudice that they encounter in Philadelphia. In the meantime, Michael continues to stress the need for militancy and black nationalism. In one of his speeches for the Action Society he maintains that the whites

' . . . have told us, in their books, and in their schools, and in their newspapers, that the black man has made great and continual gains in a steady upward rise since the days of slavery; and they lie; for, all the years since Reconstruction, through depression, social revolution and two earthquaking wars, have been but a desperate striving, continually, and in pain, to reach again the human heights we occupied in the triumphal years immediately after the Civil War. So have we fought, and still we fight.'[5]

His way of fighting includes instant retaliation for any act of violence committed against a Negro.

The pivotal point of the plot is the death of Philip, the pacifistic brother. He is killed by an angry white youth who had earlier been beaten by blacks in one of Michael's retaliatory measures that got out of control. Shortly before his death, Philip had denounced the Negro Action Society for its use of violence. The murder of his brother changes Claude's plans: he decides not to go to Canada but to stay and fight for the rights of blacks, even if it means giving up his wife. He realizes that his place is on South Street with his brother Michael.

Smith is a better craftsman than Killens. He depicts the lives of various people of the Philadelphia ghetto, much in the manner of Ann Petry in *The Narrows*, who are not directly related to the major plot but who add a great deal to the understanding of the main characters and the incidents in which they are involved. Smith, in fact, integrates these minor characters and events into his novel more effectively than does Petry, but *South Street* depends too much on melodrama and coincidence. The Bowers brothers are over-idealized and the novel itself is much like the apologist fiction of an earlier day.

As in the case of *Youngblood*, though, the militant tone tends to be the dominating aspect. The rebels who appear are not in the class of those that populate such novels of the sixties as *Sons of Darkness, Sons of Light*, or *The Spook Who Sat by the Door*, but they illustrate the awakening sense of pride and race consciousness that leads to the confrontations with the white power structure. Violence is matched with violence despite the danger of a full scale race war. Michael Bowers is an early version of Malcolm X, who rallies his people against white tyranny. Smith does not take him to the point of advocating an overthrow of the local authorities, though, or of initiating violent action. The Action Society is basically a vehicle for defense, although some of the younger extremists go beyond that. It is unwarranted violence on the part of blacks that

115

indirectly causes the death of Philip. Smith's warning, then, is to use violence only when it can be justified by the brutality of whites. In the meantime the fight for equality must go on as swiftly as possible on legal grounds.

The militant novels of Smith and Killens did not immediately induce other novels of the same type, and it was not until the sixties that this kind of protest fiction became popular. But several novels of the late fifties show the influence of the militant trend although they adhere more closely to the apologetic tradition that was popular before the publication of *Native Son*, and that was revived in the fifties. The writers make use of historical events to add authenticity to their comments on the racial temper of the time. Frank London Brown's *Trumbull Park* (1959) is the story of the migration of black families from the slums of Chicago to the public housing project on the perimeter of the city, a move that Brown actually made. Edmund Austin's *Black Challenge* (1958) is a fictional account of Marcus Garvey's "Back to Africa" movement. W. E. B. DuBois' *Black Flame Trilogy* is essentially the history of the Negro in America as fictionalized by a man who participated in many of the important events.

Brown's novel describes the ordeal of Buggy Martin and his family in Trumbull Park. Buggy, a black proletarian, decides to make the move to the new housing project after years of living in the South Side ghetto. Although white mobs are harassing the other Negro families who have been brave enough to try to live there, Buggy thinks that anything will be better than the dilapidated buildings of the ghetto. When the white people of the vicinity begin to throw rocks and bombs into their house, the Martins wish they were back where they came from. Living with the constant threat of violence is almost more than they can stand. Police protection is required at all times and Buggy has to be escorted to work in a patrol car. Although some of their black neighbors crack under the pressure and leave Trumbull Park, there is a hard core that refuses to move. Buggy emerges as the leader of this group as a result of having nerve enough to walk through the mob, and he and his wife decide it is time to take the initiative instead of depending on the police for constant protection. The novel ends as Buggy and a friend make it home from their jobs safely on their own, despite the omnipresent white mob that threatens them at every step.

Trumbull Park is a very narrow novel which is stylistically immature, but within these limitations it is effective propaganda. Brown concentrates on the psychological strength of the protagonist in his existence under the constant pressure of mob violence. Buggy wavers many times, but survives when he decides that not even death can stop the triumph of justice. The strength supplied by associating himself with a cause allows him to challenge the mob. Buggy's victory over the mob is a small one. He knows the same people will be there to torment him the next day, but he has won a victory over his own fears. He realizes that he can endure as long as they can. Not even death can stop him now, for he has given impetus to a fervor that envelops his compatriots. From a mental standpoint, Buggy is as militant as Michael Bowers.

Edmund Austin's *Black Challenge* presents a different sort of hero. Marcus Cox symbolizes the Negro hope for equality and is a challenge to the social and economic structure of white America. Like Ellison's Ras the Destroyer, Cox is a West Indian who rallies the people of Harlem into a sense of race pride. The threat of violence represented by the protagonist and his cohorts keeps the white community at a respectful distance. However, the black characters are idealized to the point of ludicrousness. The parallels to the career of Marcus Garvey are obvious as Austin attempts to make a mythological figure out of his protagonist. Garvey was a magnetic individual who surrounded himself with Dukes of the Nile and the Niger in his efforts to promote blackness, but Austin's novel depicts only the heroic side of the man. It is in the apologetic tradition except that Marcus Cox emerges as a militant superman.

The trilogy of W. E. B. DuBois is basically a record of his own career thinly disguised as fiction. The first novel, *The Ordeal of Mansart* (1957), deals with the major events involving blacks in America from the period of the Reconstruction to 1916. The famous sociologist, who had first tried his hand at fiction with *The Quest of the Silver Fleece* (1911), describes the problems of Manuel Mansart as he tries to fight white prejudice and the Uncle Tom Negro leadership represented by Booker T. Washington, who, according to DuBois, sacrificed racial integrity for economic expediency. Probably the most important event depicted is the organization of the Niagara Movement, which the author himself was mainly responsible for. In *Mansart Builds*

117

a School (1959), DuBois concentrates on Negro education in Georgia from early in the century to the beginning of World War II. He echoes many of the ideas expressed in Redding's *Stranger and Alone* about the fallacies of Southern education, as he calls on his own experiences at Atlanta University. As a means of combating the propagation of white superiority, Mansart introduces black study programs.

In *Worlds of Color* (1961), DuBois, again posing as Manuel Mansart, Negro educator, reflects on the international response to the problems of racism. He concentrates mostly on discriminations against black people in the United States, though. Mansart discovers that almost every move made by the government is an act of aggression against colored people, including the Korean War. He hears of a conspiracy against Franklin Roosevelt because of the President's lenient racial policies. The white power structure of Mansart's own school tries to get rid of him because of his liberal views. The combination of events leads to his rejection of the American capitalistic system. Shortly before his death Mansart calls for black pride and socialism as answers to the problems of the Negro. As the old man is dying his younger relatives vow to do anything necessary to establish their rights. Their patience has disappeared with the dawning of a new age of militancy.

DuBois, over ninety years old at the publication of his last work of fiction, nevertheless sounded the note that was to dominate the decade of the sixties. The progression of the militancy in the trilogy indicates that the sociologist, who moved to Ghana in his last years, was himself running out of patience with the racial policies of his native country. The increased interest in protest displayed by the author in *Worlds of Color*, though, detracts proportionately from his minimal skills as a novelist. The portrait of Mansart as a part of the historical processes of the country seen in the first two novels dissolves into mere gibberish, so that even the recounting of history is suspect in the concluding book. However, if DuBois was not a good novelist, even in his senility he could predict the direction that American society was going to take.

In the sixties protest fiction arrives not simply as the dominant trend, as in the forties, but as the dominant form of art. Despite the greatness of *Invisible Man* and the promise of some of the later novels in the accommodationist vein, the best novels in the sixties are mostly in the protest realm. The militant protest novel, given impetus by Killens and Smith, is the most significant innovation. The interest in aesthetics, and the variety and universality of the black experience, as promulgated by Ellison, does not disappear, but with the major exceptions of the books by Kristin Hunter and Paule Marshall, it is absorbed in the fiction that emphasizes unresolvable racial problems. The capitulation of James Baldwin to this field, after he had been the major critic of protest fiction and one of the chief exponents of the autonomous Negro novel, is indicative of the shape of the sixties.

CHAPTER VII

Accommodationism in the Sixties

The best novels of the sixties, with a few exceptions, are in the protest field and the emergence of the militant protest novel is the major development. This type of fiction stresses an organized retaliation on the part of blacks against white oppression. Apologetic protest in the decade continues to depict the Negro as a victim of racist practices and attitudes; however, a number of novels of the period do not deal specifically with these themes. This nonprotest or accommodationist fiction concentrates basically on the adjustment an individual makes to function in accordance with the standards of white society. This adjustment includes a resignation to the existence of racism and the search for a meaningful identity that will serve as a compensatory stratagem. The individual accommodates himself to the conventions of the dominant culture in order to survive, or because there seems to be no plausible alternative, but at the same time he hopes for a positive change in his life.

The accommodationist fiction of the sixties does not, then, exclusively emphasize the exploitation of blacks. This is an aspect of life that is taken for granted, and the characters respond to it as merely another part of their existence. While an accommodation to this kind of a society is an acknowledgement of the white power structure, militancy is rejected as a panacea. Racial confrontations and scenes of violence are rare in these novels, as the conflicts take place essentially on a psychological level. The characters accept their fate, or wrestle with their conscience in an effort to find mental peace in a ridiculous world. A third alternative is to work for change in an individual and intellectual manner within the system. A major aspect of the fiction is the quest for a racial identity. An individual, if he is not to be defeated by his environment, must identify with his black heritage. An accommodation to white society cannot include a denial of one's blackness. Racial pride, in perspective with one's essential humanity, is the savior of the individual.

Prevalent in some of the accommodationist fiction is the existential theme of man as an outsider in an absurd world, in which only death is a certainty. The influence of such French writers as Sartre and Camus is apparent, as heroes are portrayed who merely drift along in a world that seems devoid of meaning. A person accepts the standards of his society because he does not know what else to do. Concurrently he feels alienated from this society and its inhibiting laws and customs. Freedom is attainable only through scorning the absurd world. With this attitude, one is able to assert his independence; but most people are not capable of attaining their freedom, according to the novels of the period. They continue to exist within the confines of absurdity. Unlike Sisyphus they are unable to scorn their fate.

Charles Wright's *The Messenger* (1963) presents a black protagonist who listlessly exists in the chaotic world of New York. In the existential pattern, the novel is composed of a series of scenes designed to reveal the absurd aspects of life in the crowded city. The protagonist is lost and confused in this strange world and he reflects nostalgically on his boyhood experiences in Missouri. He learns how to adjust himself to the pace of his new life to some extent, but his dominant feeling is that of being an alien who is full of despair. A solitary traveler in the city, he realizes that he has to leave. The problem is that he does not know where a black boy can run.

The narrator is a young black man named Charlie who works for a messenger service. A variety of misfits parade in and out of Charlie's life, most of them as lost and lonely as he. Moving like an uncertain ghost through the white world, in which he is constantly reminded that he is a Negro, the messenger survives mainly on the memories of his boyhood. Life had been a joy then, but during the war in Korea he learned, from a soldier's viewpoint, that most people suffer unbearably. This is verified by his life in the city. He decides that he must leave, but he makes no attempt to do so until he is evicted from his midtown

apartment because of his hippie way of life and his odd assortment of friends. The novel ends as these friends give Charlie
a party, which is itself a comment on the protagonist's view
of existence. Horrified by the knowledge that he is facing the
reality of his own empty life, he concludes that the party has
turned into a microcosm of the world. His drunken friends are
searching for the crazy kick that will "still the fears, confusion,
and the pain of being alive on this early August morning."[1]

The messenger is a man alone in an alien world. Like Ellison's
invisible man, he ponders his future with uncertainty.

> Now, at twenty-nine, I am not expecting much from this world. Fitz-
> gerald and his green light! I remember his rich, mad dream:
> 'Tomorrow we will run faster, stretch out our arms farther.' But
> where will this black boy run? To whom shall he stretch out his
> arms?[2]

The question remains unanswered, but the messenger eventually
leaves the sanctuary of his New York home and ventures forth
into an unknown world. There is no hint of optimism, though,
as the messenger's move is precipitated by his eviction. The
road ahead also looks bleak.

Charles Wright's book is dedicated to Richard Wright, but
his writing bears more resemblance to that of Ellison and Gwendolyn Brooks. *The Messenger* is much like *Maud Martha* in the
sense that it is a series of vignettes depicting various aspects
of the life of the protagonist as he progresses from youthful
exuberance, to disillusionment, to a condition of resignation
to one's fate, tempered by a faint aura of hope. Charles Wright
draws principally from Ellison, though, as he presents a black
boy who is kept running by the white establishment. The
emphasis is on the chaotic world in which the protagonist is
merely an observer of the absurdities around him, or an object
to be used by other people. The novel itself, in its episodic structure and its lack of plot, is a reflection of the messenger's state
of mind. The book solves no problems or makes no special pleas;
it simply describes a world which is a private version of hell.
The Messenger is a short but poignant work that tends to summarize the existential point of view that is repeated in many
of the novels of the decade, none of which match Charles
Wright's book in quality.

Bill Gunn's *All the Rest Have Died* (1964) echoes the theme
of *The Messenger*, but the book is encumbered by a melodramatic plot. It depicts the career of a Negro actor who finds peace

only when he realizes that life is of little significance. The discovery allows him to rid himself of his complexes and to take his fate into his own hands. The ridiculous aspects of life are minimized by the acceptance of this responsibility. Racial themes are of less significance than the stress on this theory, but Gunn, in the manner of Charles Wright, indicates that racism is merely another aspect of the absurd condition of the world.

Barney Gifford is a man who lives in the memories of the past. His life is built around the influence of his cousin, Taylor, who was killed in a senseless accident, and who had earlier passed for white and joined the army during the Korean War. However, the pressures of living with men who stated their hatred for Negroes finally affected Taylor and he was granted a medical discharge. At the time of his death he had hoped to become an actor. Barney, tormented by the absurdity of the accident that killed his older cousin, nevertheless tries to fulfill the career of Taylor by becoming an actor himself. His life is only a series of bizarre incidents, though, that is climaxed when a friend commits suicide in his presence. The act convinces him that freedom can be found only in scorning the world. Gunn stresses the significance of the death by exploring the protagonist's mind.

> The idea of Bernard dying came to me last night; . . . The terrible picture of his face as he succeeded in falling from that boat, the expression of victory and strength. It was not a fall but a breaking loose, tearing away from the earth, a flypaper existence. I tried to feel remorse, but the visitation of that expression gave me peace.[3]

Fortified by this concept of freedom, Barney accepts the fact that he has to live his own life, rather than Taylor's. He asserts his liberty by marrying a white girl who has been in love with him for years. They are no longer held back by the conventions of society that tend to limit the choices of a Negro. At the end of the novel Barney is a man who is willing to take the responsibility for his actions.

All the Rest Have Died carries its version of existential philosophy to a logical conclusion. The protagonist discovers the meaning of freedom and acts on that basis. The novel is carefully designed to reveal this intellectual growth, and Gunn is successful in presenting his philosophical argument. An actor himself, as well as playwright, the author depends heavily on a stream of consciousness technique to depict the action as it is seen through the eyes of Barney Gifford. This method tends to lessen the melodrama of the incidents and give them instead an intellectual significance, since the stress is on the protagonist's response to them. But the novel is very limited in scope; Gunn is content to explicate his philosophy, and the racial materials that he presents are mere comments on a social situation rather than an integral part of the book.

The absurdity of man's condition in a chaotic universe is stressed to perhaps a greater degree in Robert Boles' *Curling* (1967) than in any other novel of the period. The book presents a black protagonist with the unlikely name of Chelsea Meredith Burlingame who is adopted by a rich white couple. The action of the novel takes place on a winter weekend in Massachusetts. Chelsea joins his white friends on a trip to Cape Cod, participates in a wild drinking party, goes to a zoo as part of a drunken excursion, and eventually is robbed in a bar in New Bedford. Chelsea kills the man who stole his wallet, is freed from any guilt in the incident, and, as the novel closes, prepares to return to his job in Boston.

Most of the novel takes place in the mind of the protagonist. Chelsea is haunted by the memories of the past which curl into one another until there seems to be no escape from madness as he recalls the past that has been designed and directed by the rich white man. The major problem of Chelsea is his lack of racial identity. His black skin makes him feel like an outsider in the white society in which he exists. There is no answer to his dilemma, though, since the action of the novel serves to point out the absurdity of the world that he cannot escape. Although he temporarily deserts his white friends, the irony of his plight is illustrated when he becomes dependent upon a white lawyer after his arrest. Resigned to the fact that he is inextricably bound to the society he resents, he decides to return to Boston.

Boles' novel is a private view of hell that does not escape the limitations of its stylistic weaknesses, but it is indicative of the concern with identity in much of the fiction of the period. In a world that is presented as chaotic, the necessity of being associated with a semblance of order is dominant in the characters, who, unlike Barney Gifford in *All the Rest Have Died*, are not strong or perceptive enough to accept the responsibility of shaping their own lives. The tendency is toward resignation, as in the case of Chelsea Burlingame in *Curling*, or toward blindly groping for a resolution to the universal confusion, as in *The Messenger*.

125

In Melvin Van Peebles' *A Bear for the FBI* (1968), the emphasis is on resignation. In revealing the life of a Negro youth in episodes that conclude with his graduation from college, the novel illustrates the emptiness of life in a society that values conformity. The protagonist is concerned primarily with living in a typical middle class manner. The pressures of being a Negro are subjugated to those connected with being an average American boy. Thus the hero describes his adventures in the Boy Scouts with gusto, but by the time he becomes a college student much of the enthusiasm for life is gone. With an increased awareness of some of the facts about American society, especially its lack of tolerance for Negroes, the protagonist becomes disillusioned. His graduation is a sad affair summarizing his attitude and predicting a rather grim future. Van Peebles is a humorous writer of some capabilities, but his novel, much like *The Messenger*, is basically a series of vignettes that is admirable in spots but, on the whole, presents only a few interesting observations on modern America.

A novel in a similar vein is Al Young's *Snakes* (1970), The protagonist is a black youth who attends a high school in Detroit and who finds solace only in his music. Reared by his grandmother in a ghetto which is rife with dope and gambling, MC manages to survive by becoming engrossed in the playing and composing of jazz. When he graduates from school, he realizes that he has to leave for New York just to escape from the stifling atmosphere that he associates with his home. As he boards the bus that will take him away MC feels, for the first time, that he is not trapped. Although he does not feel as if he understands what freedom is, or what he expects to find in New York, the important thing is that he is at least temporarily leaving an environment that he considers oppressive. It is a blind attempt at finding a meaningful identity. Young is not particularly skillful at presenting a cohesive narrative and the novel is significant only in its portrait of the activities and language of the ghetto inhabitants.

The search for identity in an absurd world also emerges as the major theme of LeRoi Jones' *The System of Dante's Hell* (1965). This esoteric novel deals with a young Negro soldier who deserts the army for two days while he is entertained by a fat prostitute. He realizes that the escapade must come to an end and he attempts to make his way back to the base. He is intercepted by a gang of blacks who resent his light complexion and his city mannerisms. Soundly beaten, the protagonist wakes up two days later surrounded by white men. Figuratively he is in hell, his search for security and order frustrated by an insane society.

Jones, a famous militant poet and dramatist, departs from his vitriolic attacks on whites in his novel. The book is almost impossible to understand, though, since Jones defies most of the accepted rules of language and of the novel form. The thin stream of narrative that is discernible among the fragmented prose and erotic recollections illustrates the alienation of the protagonist from both the black and the white worlds. He is a man who refuses to accept his role as an outsider but who is beaten by the hostility of his environment. His experiences lead only to chaos.

A primary aspect of existentialist fiction is a search for order or meaning. A requisite for attaining success is the acceptance of one's racial status. The condition of being black is neither denied nor asserted militantly. The facts of discrimination are acknowledged as a part of life. The object is to accommodate oneself to the system as comfortably as possible, or to pronounce one's independence by ignoring the existing conventions. A direct challenge to the white society is avoided. In the existential fiction of the period racial themes are sometimes of secondary importance to the broader aspects of existence in an indifferent world. However, a number of novels in the sixties concentrate primarily on racial identity. The emphasis in this accommodationist fiction is on conciliation with the white world as tempered by individual views of race pride and of morality. The individual adjusts to society in his own way.

Herbert Simmons' *Man Walking on Eggshells* (1962) is a portrait of a man who is forced to make a choice between a militant organization and a personal belief in nonviolence. The novel indicates how discrimination by a society can produce a retaliatory hatred that leads to violence, though black militancy is itself exposed as an ineffective method of dealing with racial problems. Moderation, according to Simmons, is a difficult and individual route that is necessary for survival.

Ray Douglas, a jazz musician, turns to drugs after his wife dies. His work suffers as a result, but under the influence of old friends he makes a comeback in the musical world. His friends, who have experienced years of oppression, emerge as militants. They use the popularity of Ray to support their cause and he becomes known as a spokesman for extremist Negro groups. Ray is disenchanted with his role, though, and decides to take the advice of his grandfather and go his own way. The militants try to force him to remain in their camp, but he adamantly refuses. He persists in acting only as an individual of intelligence and integrity in all phases of his life.

Simmons, the author of *Corner Boy* (1957), offers no solution to race problems in his second novel. He merely illustrates one man's response to the pressures of society. The book is weakened by the author's use of coincidence and melodrama in tracing the stormy career of the protagonist. Simmons himself wavers between the moderate views of his protagonist and the militant views of some of the other characters. The most profound and enlightening statements on racial matters are made by the militants, who are later discredited by rather crude manipulations of the plot. This is perhaps Simmons' way of revealing the difficulty of the problem, but it is not an artistic resolution.

William Demby's second novel, published fifteen years after *Beetlecreek*, is a story of the development of race pride in an American expatriate. *The Catacombs* (1965) takes place in Rome against a background of newspaper reports telling of racial violence and hatred in the United States. The narrator, in relating the details of a romance between a black actress and an Italian count, is actually exposing his own needs for personal fulfillment. He associates the racial incidents in America with the activities he observes in Europe, and decides that he prefers to be a part of his native country. He favors an active participation in life to a sterile existence in a foreign country.

The narrator is a friend of the young black actress, Doris, who relates her adventures with the Count to him. Doris realizes that the narrator is in love with her. She carries on two affairs at once, then, and eventually becomes pregnant, presumably by the Italian. The baby is born dead and shortly afterward the disenchanted nobleman informs the girl that he is leaving the country. Doris somehow becomes lost in the Catacombs and the narrator, given impetus by the disappearance of the girl, returns to the United States to assume his racial identity.

Doris, who engages in a personal struggle with the Count, matching her animation against his stagnancy, represents the vital aspects of life to the narrator. She possesses the vitality of Africa and the tempestuous nature of America. The Italian, on the other hand, signifies death and the moral decay of Europe. The triumph of the Italian over the American girl illustrates the necessity for the narrator to return to the United States before he, too, is destroyed by Rome. On his decision to return, the death images associated with the city are replaced by hints of resurrection, as a new Pope is elected and Easter approaches. Even the racial bigotry of the narrator's native land is preferable to Rome once his religious convictions have given him the courage to face again the prospect of being an American Negro.

Demby's stylistic improvisations are impressive as he attempts to convey a sense of illusory motion reflecting the thoughts of the narrator. His symbolism and imagery revolving around death and the promise of resurrection comprise the most effective aspect of the novel. On the whole, the author's talent is wasted on a flimsy plot and a vapid thematic line that appears to be almost an afterthought. A modern version of Hawthorne's *The Marble Faun*, the book is nevertheless more of a literary exercise than a significant artistic contribution or social commentary.

A major aspect of adjusting to white society is the psychological problem of maintaining race pride in the face of the national belief that white is right—that white people in their superiority are to be emulated. Carlene Hatcher Polite concentrates on the pressure this concept creates in regard to young black intellectuals in *The Flagellants* (1966). The novel illustrates that Negroes must maintain their self-respect and make a special effort to adjust themselves to a society in which the males tend to be emasculated and the females tend to emerge as the dominant force.

Ideal and Jimson engage in a tempestuous romance which is complicated by the latter's inability to find suitable employment. An intelligent young man, Jimson retaliates to Ideal's harrangues by explaining the situation of the black man in America. The paradoxical tragedy of the Negro, according to Jimson, is that his intelligence has been thwarted by the white-is-right doctrine to the extent that emulation of the white man is his primary goal. Racial progress is stymied by the Uncle Toms who still cling to this philosophy. Ideal learns to respect the opinions of her lover, and their affair runs relatively smoothly until Jimson takes a position in a library under the direction of a white woman. Ideal becomes jealous, provoking an argument on sexual mythology which develops into a treatise by Jimson on the continued existence of the enduring black matriarch. A remnant from the days of slavery, the modern version of this figure, represented by Ideal, according to Jimson, persists in assuming the dominant role in the household, at the same time robbing her mate of his masculinity.

Ideal, however, defends the black matriarch concept as a vehicle for survival on an economic basis, as the woman still receives the majority of the job offers while a high percentage of black men are unemployed. The tendency of whites to entrust black women with domestic responsibility is not often applied to males in the labor market. She is able to sympathize with Jimson's position, as she relates to him her idea of the typical Negro marital status.

> 'Naturally, the man resents his lack of self-esteem when his woman assumes the role normally assumed by him. Living within a frustrated, suppressed, anxiety-hatched cocoon flagellates the hell out of both of them. Regarding him as a ne'er-do-well, she resents him, thinks of him as a weakling, a pimp. He in turn, sees her as a shrew, authoritative, overbearing, a frustrated woman wanting to be a man. . . .'[4]

What Ideal herself would prefer is for Jimson to assume his proper role, but neither of them can transcend the stereotyped positions assigned to them by society. Ideal, the matriarch, and Jimson, the slave, continue to flagellate each other as the novel closes.

The failure of the characters to assume an identity other than the traditionally designated roles is basically the result of their own mental blocks. Society, of course, contributes to the problem, but it is essentially a matter of resigning oneself to a personal concept of martyrdom. The flagellation is to a large degree self-inflicted. At the same time, their arguments, a defense mechanism against a cruel environment, tend to reveal much of the black experience in America. The novel consists mostly of poetic dialogue that often develops into a tirade or exposition on a racial subject. The lack of a complicated plot does not detract from the author's attempt to present a panoramic view of the American scene from the black standpoint. The intense concentration on the thoughts of the two characters is unalleviated, though, and the novel eventually dissolves into an endless mental debate that gradually loses its poignancy.

While the Negroes in *The Flagellants* are unable to accommodate themselves to their society, Margaret Walker's *Jubilee* (1966) presents a heroine who forces herself to adjust to slavery and the almost equally unpleasant existence in the Reconstruction era. The novel depicts the life of an enduring black matriarch, the prototype of the figure that is discussed in Polite's book. Walker, in the tradition of the apologetic writers of an earlier period, emphasizes the ability of Negroes to survive in the face of great tribulations.

Jubilee spans the Civil War as it follows the career of Vyry, a black woman who is born into slavery on a plantation in Georgia. Vyry grows up as a slave in the years preceding the war, when the talk of freedom fills the air. She becomes romantically involved with Randall Ware, a free Negro who owns his own blacksmith shop, before the whites rob him of his property. Vyry, who experiences the horrors of the auction block and the whipping post, is left to fend for herself when the war breaks out. With no other prospects she stays on at the plantation, nursing the declining white Dutton family. When Ware fails to come back from the war, she eventually attempts to make a home with Innis Brown, a former slave. They are driven from one farm to another by whites, who will not allow them to live in peace. They never give up, however, and when Randall Ware finally appears he is forced to the realization that Vyry, with her quiet resolution to live in peace with her white tormentors, is not the woman for him. A prosperous man, Ware is nevertheless too race conscious to try to win back the passive and forgiving Vyry.

Throughout the novel Vyry maintains her Christian humility and her respect for the decadent white aristocrats who treated her like an animal. Although Ware berates her for being a "white man's nigger," she refuses to change her attitude. She insists that she will not beat the white man at his own game of killing and hating and she bears him no ill will for enslaving her. In presenting this black matriarch, Walker creates a female version of Uncle Tom. Vyry is the ideal Christian who suffers immeasurably while retaining her faith. Randall Ware, on the other hand, is a black hero patterned after the protagonists of Sutton Grigg's *Imperium in Imperio* (1899) or Walter White's *The Fire in the Flint* (1924). He is an exemplary figure who rises to a prominent position despite the handicap of being black. It is this tendency to create stereotypes, including a Faulknerian portrait of a decaying Southern family, that detracts from *Jubilee*. It is nevertheless a relatively competent historical study of the Civil War period.

In fulfilling a role that is assigned by white society, a Negro is in danger of losing his individuality. This is Randall Ware's contention in *Jubilee*, and is also the theme of Cecil Brown's *The Life and Loves of Mr. Jiveass Nigger* (1969). The latter novel makes the point that in acting the part of a black stud, a role that the white bigot fearfully designates for the Negro, the protagonist is actually "jiving" himself. Instead of gaining a measure of revenge on the white man, he is merely pandering to the white world. He is entertaining the white women by fulfilling their erotic desires and dreams associated with the mythical black potency, while, at the same time, he is serving as a scapegoat for the envy and hate of white men.

Brown's novel traces the adventures of George Washington, a pragmatic black man who hopes to launch a successful career as a gigolo in Denmark. His life is based on the theory that one must constantly try to outsmart whites in a battle that is continually waged between the races. The idea is to "jive," or take advantage of, the white man in the way that will hurt him the most. Knowing the sexual fears of the racists, George decides to become a professional stud. In the pursuit of his career, though, he eventually discovers that he is being used by white people in this capacity also. He rejects his role and resolves to return to the United States. He realizes that he has been thinking from a white point of view and has therefore been another pawn in their hands. George learns that he must live his own life rather than to act in a manner prescribed by whites.

The farcical tone of the book, and its emphasis on sex, does not disguise its serious nature. In dealing with the theme of racial identity, Brown illustrates the necessity of coming to terms with the role one plays in his relationship to the white world. When the protagonist realizes that he is a mere puppet and becomes instilled with race pride, instead of a juvenile desire for revenge, he matures as an individual. Before this can happen he must reconcile his blackness with his humanity—he must discover that he is a human being who happens to be socially defined as a Negro, rather than to consider himself as a black person who is innately alienated from his fellow humans. His racial identity consists of an acknowledgement of his heritage, in which he takes pride, while concurrently he places his pride in perspective with the condition of being human, so that he becomes a proud man who recognizes the solidarity of all people. In treating this difficult problem, Brown manages to explicate it with a degree of competence. This is a relatively notable achievement, since the novel is sensationalized to meet the public taste.

The discovery of what it means to be black is often a traumatic experience, and in Gordon Parks' *The Learning Tree* (1963) it is a part of the process of growing up in an environment in which racial violence is always a threat. The novel reveals the difficulty a black youth faces in choosing between racial loyalty and the concept of justice. It is only at this point, when a moral decision may result in violence, that the boy realizes the terrible responsibility involved in being a Negro in a community dominated by whites.

Newt Winger, a teenager on a Kansas farm in the 1920's, experiences an eventful boyhood. His favorite girl is impregnated by the son of a respected white judge. His major enemy, Marcus Savage, the son of a Negro alcoholic, attempts to kill him. The most dramatic incident, though, is a murder that Newt witnesses, and the subsequent trial. Booker Savage, Marcus' father, kills a white man during an attempted robbery. Another white man is the major suspect. Newt, however, eventually informs the authorities of the real killer rather than see an innocent man convicted, knowing that the truth may incite the white residents of Cherokee Flats to violence. The guilty man commits suicide and the peace of the community is kept intact by the calmer heads among both the whites and the blacks.

The environment of the small Kansas town is much the same as that anywhere in the country in regard to racial discrimination. The Negroes merely adjust to it. On the Winger farm, though, Newt has a chance to develop his potentialities to a greater degree than the inhabitants of a ghetto. His parents, though poor, are able to make a living from the land. The rural atmosphere, pervaded by the moral teachings of his elders, produces a sense of duty in the youth that makes his final decision in the murder case a matter of necessity.

Parks, a famous photographer who wrote, directed, and produced the motion picture version of his novel, illustrates that blacks and whites can live peacefully in juxtaposition if the blacks are willing to be subjugated. This does not prevent, though, a striving for equality through patience, faith, and education. The hope for the future is embodied in such young people as Newt Winger, who may be able to impress the bigots with their exemplary behavior. However, the melodrama and the obvious didacticism of the novel, presented in a crude naturalistic manner, keep it from being a significant work.

Hog Butcher (1966) explores the same problems. Written by Ronald L. Fair, it depicts a young Negro boy who witnesses a murder. The novel concentrates on the integrity of the boy in the face of the pressure that is extended by corrupt elements of the police department. This integrity is maintained as a result of an identification with the victim, a Negro basketball star. The athlete is one of the few black persons that the protagonist can admire, and he is not going to allow him to die in disgrace.

Cornbread, a hero to the young people of the ghetto because of his success in basketball, is mistaken for a criminal as he lopes down the street. The two policemen, one black and one white, shoot him when he refuses to stop. Wilfred Robinson witnesses the incident and vows to defend his fallen hero, but he is warned by a policeman not to testify in behalf of Cornbread. Although he is severely frightened, Wilfred refuses to cooperate and tells the truth in such a convincing manner that the men who did the shooting are forced to admit that Cornbread may not have been the person they were looking for.

The courage displayed by the protagonist is primarily a result of his sense of identity with the victim. Aware of some of the discriminatory practices of the law in dealing with blacks, and the scarcity of Negroes who are given an opportunity to be heroes, the boy resolves to speak out at any cost. It is a matter of race pride, as well as justice, that motivates him. Fair's book is not particularly outstanding in any respect, but it does indicate the general trend towards the establishment of a racial identity in the fiction of the period.

Hog Butcher illustrates the need for a young black person to identify with a prominent Negro. The adjustment to the standards of white society is much easier for an individual to make when he possesses a degree of race pride. The absence of this factor contributes to the bleakness of life in a ghetto. Louise Meriwether, in *Daddy Was a Number Runner* (1970), shows how disillusionment becomes dominant in the existence of a young girl from Harlem, primarily because the people she admires turn out to be just ordinary humans. The novel points out the various facets of Harlem, during the 1930's, which make life miserable for its inhabitants.

Francie, a girl of eleven, helps her father in his job in the illegal policy racket. Adam Coffin informs his daughter that making a hit in the numbers game is the only chance a person in Harlem has. The girl worships the numbers runner, the one ray of light in her barren environment. The Coffin family does not prosper, though, as the police crack down on gambling and a son is arrested for allegedly killing a white man. In the meantime marital difficulties arise and Adam spends little time with his family. Against this tumultuous background Francie tries to live a normal childhood, an impossibility in her environment, and by the time she is thirteen Francie realizes that the ghetto is a trap from which she may never escape. Dissatisfied with her father and most of her acquaintances, the girl seeks in vain for an element of race pride that will enlighten her life. She settles instead for a resignation to her fate.

Meriwether's novel is concerned specifically with exposing the hopelessness of a ghetto existence. The effective scenes are those which are not directly related to the plot, which is merely a device from which to explore the lurid elements of Harlem. The book is basically a series of vignettes, revolving around Francie, to which several melodramatic incidents are attached. While it is weak technically, it presents some vivid scenes of the ghetto which tend to document the author's contention that a child of Harlem is doomed.

Harlem is merely an epitome of the hundreds of other ghettos of the country. In *Howard Street* (1968) Nathan C. Heard explores the sordid side of black life in Newark in an attempt to show that the ghetto inherently produces corruption. The author presents a number of characters who have surrendered to the depravity of their environment. Rather than struggling against the oppression that tends to reduce them to animals, they resign themselves to the idea that the world is a cruel and meaningless place in which values exist only on a personal level. Anything that produces a kick, or that is necessary for survival, is indulged in without a thought of the law or mortality. The rules and conventions of white society do not exist in the ghetto except as applied from the outside.

The major characters of *Howard Street* are a prostitute, her pimp, and a man who tries to live according to the standards of white morality. Although the latter holds his own in the psychological battle with his iniquitous acquaintances, he is shown to be an exception. The typical response to the environment is to turn to alcohol or dope. Heard concentrates almost exclusively on orgiastic scenes in which depravity is revealed to be the ordinary way of life in the ghetto. This is the inevitable result of white oppression, according to the author. The characters do not concern themselves with race pride or the maintaining of self-respect. They accommodate themselves not to the white world but to a black version of hell that is intended to be an escape from the oppressive atmosphere created by whites, but that is self-destructive to an extent equal to the banefulness of racism. In this sense *Howard Street* is unusual since there is little effort made to adjust to the outside society, and no attempt to challenge the dominant white world. Heard, in stressing this resignation to oblivion, necessarily limits himself to the portrayal of lurid scenes that become repetitious. Art is sacrificed for sensationalism and the result is not flattering to the author.

The quest for a racial identity is a major theme of most of the accommodationist fiction of the decade. The theme extends also into fiction dealing with colonialism. In *Where the Hummingbird Flies* (1961), Frank Hercules deals with the process of decolonization in Trinidad. This involves the surrendering of traditional values on the part of whites. The natives, in their effort to gain freedom and power, challenge the colonizers not only on political and economic grounds but in racial matters. At stake is the colonial belief in racial superiority, a concept the black people must struggle against in their attempt to establish race pride. Hercules' novel examines the effects of the resulting societal turmoil on both blacks and whites.

Francis Herbert, an educated black, focuses on the problem of winning racial equality for the natives of Trinidad. The country is undergoing change in its system of government due to the pressure applied by the sense of nationalism of black people around the world. With the support of two important whites, Griffths and Herrick, the young Negro attacks the racist governing practices of the white power structure of the island. The British colonists, reluctant to allow change, are aided in their conservative approach by some of the Negro elite, who are given prominent positions in exchange for loyalty. Herbert is eventually arrested for his revolutionary activities and, despite the defense of Herrick, an influential white lawyer, he is exiled. However, Herrick and Griffths, with the aid of most of the black population, devote their time to the task of winning political freedom for all of the people of the island.

While the author attacks colonialism, with its inherent racist policies, he also censures the black bourgeoisie. The status seekers of the island society are satirized in the tradition of Dorothy West's *The Living Is Easy*. Both the colonizers and the black elite are forced to yield somewhat to the pressure of the masses, although it is a painful process. The exile of Herbert is a desperate act of a dying system. The novel illustrates the awakening of the oppressed, a significant twentieth century phenomenon. Hercules, though, does not explore the problems involved in de-colonizing to any depths. The dynamic process of a shift of power from a few whites to the black masses is handled with a conspicuous lack of drama by the author. He only scratches the surface of the turbulent world that he presents.

A more penetrating study of an island civilization in turmoil is Paule Marshall's *The Chosen Place, the Timeless People* (1969). The novel analyzes the people of Bournehills, an island in the West Indies, as they search for their own version of independence. Rather than accepting the aid of the American or British government, the natives attempt to help themselves and to define freedom from their own viewpoint, which includes the concept of pride in their racial heritage. The book also explores the response of individual whites to a people they do not understand. This failure to comprehend the customs and psychology of the Negro inhabitants of the island is where the trouble between the races begins. The action of the novel is given impetus by a group of Americans who are sent to Bournehills to make a preliminary study for a government project intended to improve the economic status of the area. Saul Amron, plagued by a sense of failure due to his past performances as both an anthropologist and a husband, is in charge of the expedition. Harriet, his wife, is from a rich family and it is largely through her influence that Saul gets the job. They are both frustrated, though, by their lack of progress with the native people. The islanders refuse to cooperate with Amron on a professional basis, and Harriet, with her aloofness towards black people, is unable to make friends.

137

The island itself, for years controlled by British colonial forces, is dependent on sugar cane for its income. The major factory is owned by whites, a fact which the natives resent. Inspired by the legend of Cuffee Ned, a slave who led a revolt in the past, the natives set fire to some of the property owned by whites as a culmination of the spirit of rebellion that is sweeping the island. Amron, as he becomes involved with the people of Bournehills, realizes the fallacies of the government project and sympathizes with the revolutionary tactics. He believes that only a violent act on the scale of Cuffee Ned's rebellion will redeem the island for the black masses.

The embodiment of the spirit of Cuffee Ned is Merle Kinbona, a middleaged black woman who is primarily responsible for the conversion of Amron to the side of the people. Although she does not lead a revolt, she is the epitome of the type of Negro who will no longer be a pawn in the hands of whites. She takes pride in the deeds of the legendary slave and inspires Amron to think in the same way. Although the small revolution fails, basically because the natives are not yet psychologically prepared for it, and his project is also on the verge of disaster, the anthropologist feels that he has become a real human for the first time in his life. The price is high, though, as his wife, angered by the fact that he loves Merle, uses her power to get him recalled from the government assignment. Harriet, haunted by the shame of losing her husband to a black woman, finally commits suicide. Amron, disenchanted with the world in general but richer as an individual, returns to the United States. Merle, meanwhile, after giving Amron the courage he needs to begin life anew, goes to Africa to delve further into her racial heritage.

The novel is much more complex than Hercules' book, for Marshall not only examines her major characters at great depth, and explores the political and racial atmosphere of the island, but presents subplots which reveal the local color aspects of Bournehills, and that contribute to an understanding of the major actions. The economic exploitation of the native population is a primary factor in keeping them under control, and the author shows how the desire of the blacks to control their own resources strikes fear into the hearts of the British landowners. The latter respect only power, and do not recognize the natives as individual humans. Cuffee Ned, a hero to the blacks, is merely the prototype of a "bad nigger" to the whites. It is this lack of understanding, as Saul Amron discovers, that makes the emergence of a new Cuffee Ned a necessity.

While violence is not a major aspect of the novel, the author implies that it may be the only answer to the problems of blacks. In this sense *The Chosen Place, the Timeless People* is in accordance with the dominant trend of the period, the militant protest novel. However, Marshall stresses the point that the natives themselves are not aroused enough to stage a revolution. The damaged property is the result of the enthusiasm generated by the annual carnival in which the revolt of Cuffee Ned is celebrated, but it is obvious that the discontent of the blacks is steadily increasing and the threat of an explosion is imminent. Marshall is objective in her treatment of the turbulent country, though, and propagandistic elements are kept to a minimum. The characters work out their own destiny against a background of political upheaval in a manner reminiscent of Joseph Conrad's *Nostromo*. The book is one of the fine accomplishments of the era.

The Chosen Place, the Timeless People aptly illustrates the tendency of an oppressed people to establish a racial identity in which they can take pride. Fortified by the assurance that they possess a noble ancestry, the natives are better able to accommodate themselves to their current situation. The danger, of course, from the white viewpoint, is that this pride will develop into a desire to challenge the white society instead of adjusting to it. Frantz Fanon, the famous black psychiatrist, wrote in 1961 that colonized people make use of particular incidents in this history of the country to give them a feeling of unity and to keep alive the revolutionary zeal. The instigator of the remembered action, although he may be an outlaw to the established power, is a hero to the oppressed people and is capable of inspiring another insurgence.[5] This is the situation that exists in Marshall's novel, a work which tends to bridge the gap between the accommodationist novel and the militant protest novel.

Another of the great novels of the period which tends to stand alone in terms of categorization and literary quality is Kristin Hunter's *God Bless the Child* (1964). The book depicts the efforts of Rosie Fleming, a black girl from the ghetto, to escape from the poverty she has known all her life. In her desire to acquire wealth and a home of her own, the girl ignores all ethical codes. Consumed by her passion, Rosie does not face reality, and, when it is forced upon her, the disillusionment is fatal.

Living with her mother, Queenie, in a small apartment infested with cockroaches, the young girl makes plans for the day she can move into a decent neighborhood. Rosie, imbued with the philosophy that money is the only answer to her problems, works at a variety of jobs, not all of them legal. Her constant battle with poverty, her alcoholic mother, and the roaches, take a heavy toll on the thin girl, but she eventually manages to purchase a house in a white part of town. Rosie is not concerned about the fact that she is integrating the neighborhood. She dismisses the blacks who rally in her support and ignores the insults of her white neighbors. With her mother, her grandmother, and her lover, she intends to enjoy her palace regardless of the cost. But her wild way of living eventually catches up with her. Weakened by tuberculosis and the effects of an abortion, Rosie's last bit of strength is drained from her when she discovers that her new house is also plagued with roaches.

The story of Rosie Fleming is a typically American one. In her pursuit of material goods she loses her own humanity. The fact that she is born in a ghetto, and deserted by her father, intensifies her passion to escape to a dream world. Rosie almost achieves her dream but she overlooks many important factors in her climb to material success. Finally aware of the fact that she has pushed her frail body too far, she pauses to wonder about the wisdom of what she has done. She realizes that she has been a fool. In her effort to emulate rich white people she has not taken into consideration the fact that whites also have houses with roaches in them—that they too have dandruff and falling hair. Dying, she reflects on her life and concludes that it

> had been like hurrying through a series of doors leading to a party, hearing the gay music and the tinkling laughter always receding, always one room away. But when you got to the next room, it was dark and empty, too.[6]

The disillusionment of Rosie begins in earnest when she moves into her new house, and is climaxed when she discovers roaches in it. Almost as difficult to withstand is the realization that Granny, her favorite person, is less than perfect. The old lady is proud of her granddaughter, but she rebels when Rosie allows Larnie, her lover, to sleep in the new house. In a revealing scene the kindly exterior of Granny is refuted and she is transformed into a Duessa. Discovering the couple in bed, she is shocked into

140

exclaiming that she can always find another home. To Rosie, Granny looks like an elfin child in her robe and with her long white hair let down. However, when Granny persists in her objection to the presence of Larnie, Rosie notices the change in the old lady. The author describes the scene as follows:

> With a sudden movement she turned on the light that mercilessly exposed shriveled skin and watery eyes, turning the child into a hag.
> Terror crossed Granny's face, the terror of stricken vanity at the thought of being discovered in that light. . . . Her hand darted out quickly, but it faltered before it managed to extinguish the lamp. Rosie saw it tremble, and knew that in that moment her grandmother had begun to die.[7]

Rosie's recognition of Granny's fallibility is an important step in her own downfall. She begins to realize that her destiny is out of her control. Her problems do not stem particularly from the fact that she is black but from her attempt to buy happiness. She takes her materialistic society too seriously and becomes a victim of her insatiable passion. Rosie is an heroic figure, though, as she struggles against her fate, not yielding even when she knows her chances are nonexistent.

God Bless the Child is an accommodationist novel in the sense that it presents a protagonist who attempts to embrace the values of the white world, not only to adjust to this society but to accept the values of whites whether they are valid or not. But Rosie's motives are more complex than a simple acceptance of white society. Her childhood gives her the impetus to emerge from the ghetto, and the only place for her to go is among the rich white people. Once she obtains her fine house, though, she concentrates on being her own exciting, pathetic self. One of the most vividly portrayed characters in black fiction, Rosie is a female version of Sammy Glick in Budd Schulberg's *What Makes Sammy Run?* Hunter maintains an objectivity in the novel as she presents a tragic situation in a humorous tone. Rosie takes her enjoyment when she can to compensate for her unhappy life in the ghetto. Her zest for life is reflected in the prose style of the author, who is perhaps second only to Ellison as a literary stylist among black novelists. Her major weakness is a tendency at times to be too explicit in her use of symbolism, to the point that it intrudes upon the narrative instead of functioning organically.

In *The Landlord* (1966) Hunter parallels the fine performance of her first novel, and the tragic nature of *God Bless the Child* is replaced by an emphasis on comedy. The major characters, a confused young white man who is alienated from his rich father and humanity in general, learns something about life by associating with an odd assortment of blacks, the tenants in his apartment house. The problems of the tenants tend to make those of the landlord seem insignificant in comparison. In an effort to solve the problems of his new acquaintances, the young man becomes involved in life for the first time.

Elgar Enders, the son of a rich manufacturer, decides to make an individual move of authority. He becomes a man of property and obtains the title of landlord, thus giving himself an identity and at the same time disassociating himself from dependency on his father. However, upon meeting his tenants he wonders if he has done the right thing. Marge Perkins, alias Madam Margarita, is a huge black soothsayer who has gone through fourteen husbands in as many years. Fanny Copee is a nymphomaniac and her husband, Charlie, is a demented black militant. Their three children are nothing but trouble. P. Eldridge DuBois is a con artist patterned after Ellison's Rinehart. Occupying the fourth apartment is an old Negro couple who never leave home because they think that the pension checks they receive are a mistake, and that government officials are looking for them.

In trying to collect the rent from his tenants, Elgar becomes involved in their lives. He finds a cause to fight for when his building is condemned, and he vows to save the homes of the residents. However, when he does not meet with instant success his feelings of insecurity continue to haunt him as the tenants turn against him. At one point he dons a suit of armor to visit Borden, his analyst. Clanking down the street, he feels temporarily safe from the hostility of the world. Hunter describes his sense of security by stating that

> Now he could cope with Copee's anger, with the poisoned darts of Marge's black arts, with the combined enmity of all the other residents of 709 Poplar Street. . . . It was a bit cumbersome, dragging all this protection around with him, but it was safe. When speed of transportation was required, he could always get himself a tank.[8]

The fortunes of Elgar change, though. He saves his building, acquires Fanny as a mistress, and establishes her in a business enterprise. He turns the knowledge of DuBois to productive ends by interesting him in an Urban Renewal program. He persuades Marge to return to her career as a blues singer. He wins the recognition of his father for the first time. Perhaps more important, he wins the love of Walter Gee Copee, one of Fanny's three sons, a Negro boy who simply admits that Elgar is his friend. The reaction of the young white man is described in the following manner:

> And all at once the burdens and the stiffness slipped from Elgar's shoulders, along with plaguing questions of identity and role. You knew me all along, Walter Gee. Not your Great White Father. No. Your small scared pink friend.[9]

Basically, what Elgar has been searching for is just that—a friend who can recognize him as an individual. At last he feels that he is more than an heir or a landlord. He has established a meaningful human relationship that is not based on heredity, economics, or sex. Walter Gee appreciates him for what he is. With the aid of Walter Gee, and his brothers, Willie Lee and Wesley Free, Elgar finds what success is about.

The Landlord presents a humorous version of the quest of identity, but Hunter is skillful enough to deal with serious problems at the same time. In the manner of Ralph Ellison she explores the American system of values through the use of a comic exterior. The implications go much deeper, though, as attitudes toward race and materialism are revealed in the zany antics of the protagonist and his unusual cohorts. Hunter discloses nothing new about society in her book. She indicates that a lack of communication between people, who are concerned only with their own interests, is the major fault of the modern world. However, she reverses the typical fictional patterns by presenting a white protagonist who discovers that he is invisible in a society that recognizes only wealth and significant accomplishments. It is only when he becomes a successful businessman and saves the building from being condemned that he is noticed. Even this victory is hollow until Walter Gee expresses his friendship. The humor of the novel, then, and its fresh approach to the old problems of identity and race, make it a memorable production.

The third of Kristin Hunter's novels is not of the same magnitude as her earlier works. In *The Soul Brothers and Sister Lou* (1968) she turns to a theme that was popular in the accommodationist fiction of the fifties by dealing with the effects of a ghetto environment on young blacks who are searching for a meaningful existence. Of major importance is the need to find an outlet from the pressures of a racist society. Without the means of channeling their energy into something productive, the youngsters are prone towards a violent retaliation against the police, who are the emblems of an oppressive white society.

Louretta Hawkins is a teenage girl from Southside, the part of the city in which recreation takes place in the streets. Lou longs for an opportunity to engage in constructive activities, but her friends are more interested in combating police brutality. Lou attempts to organize a musical group in an abandoned church that her brother rents, but the building is soon taken over by a number of young black militants who plan to turn it into a fortress for their battle with the police. Lou finally persuades them to put their talents to use in a more productive manner, though, and their tendency towards violence is converted into literary and musical endeavors. One of the results is the formation of a successful singing group, The Soul Brothers and Sister Lou.

The novel is an argument in favor of solving racial problems through the rehabilitation of the ghettos. While Hunter condemns militant action she illustrates why many blacks consider rebuilding necessary. The discriminatory practices of the police and the despair of life in the inner core of the city are presented vividly. Given the opportunities, though, the same youths who become militant rebels will turn into productive citizens. They will establish a racial identity and adjust to the white society by taking pride in their accomplishments. The book is so obviously contrived to make this point, however, that much of its effectiveness is lost. The realistic portrayal of the various aspects of life in Southside that is maintained through much of the novel is eventually abandoned for the sake of a conclusion in which the problems are neatly solved.

While *The Soul Brothers and Sister Lou* is much inferior to *God Bless the Child* and *The Landlord*, it illustrates the prevalency of accommodationist fiction of the period in which black characters show a concern for finding a racial identity that will allow them to function within the mainstream of American life. By establishing a racial pride they do not emulate whites blindly, but basically accept the standards of the society, despite the predominence of prejudice and oppression that denies them full participation. In most of these novels, the emphasis is on a character's desire to become a complete American citizen, regardless of the absurdity of the world, and the special handicap of being discriminated against, while concurrently retaining both an individual and a racial identity.

The accommodationist fiction of the sixties represents the moderate view of American society. It implies that there is a chance that it will survive—that blacks and whites can exist together in a country that has many problems to solve other than racism. But the decade is primarily a period of racial emphasis, as indicated even in many of the accommodationist novels. The commitment to militancy is illustrated in the work of such writers as Hari Rhodes, Ronald Fair, Sam Greenlee, John A. Williams, and, somewhat surprisingly, James Baldwin. During the same period apologetic protest reaches new heights of artistic respectability, especially in the hands of Williams, Baldwin and Ernest Gaines. The major trend of the decade, then, as reflected in fiction, is towards racial confrontations which question the validity of American values.

CHAPTER VIII

Apologetic Protest in the Sixties

The apologetic protest novel of the sixties concentrates on revealing the Negro as a victim of the brutality and prejudice of white society. It follows the pattern of the apologetic fiction of the early twentieth century in which an exemplary black character is physically destroyed by whites. In the sixties, though, violence is sometimes replaced by psychological pressure as a destructive vehicle, and the demise of the protagonist is not necessarily the inevitable conclusion. Blacks are depicted as being thwarted in their attempts to exercise their human rights, exploited by the white power structure, and alienated from their native country. Apologetic fiction of the era differs from the accommodationist novel in the sense that in the former the actions and the attitudes of whites prevent the blacks from joining the mainstream of American life. It differs from the militant protest novel from the standpoint that it does not depict an organized retaliation by blacks against their white oppressors.

The apologetic tone is epitomized in the work of John A. Williams, who later in the decade turns to the militant protest field. In his first novel, *The Angry Ones* (1960), Williams presents an enterprising young Negro who enters the publishing business only to discover that there is little opportunity for a black. The novel stresses the point that blacks are exploited by the business world that is controlled by whites. Negroes serve primarily as scapegoats for their white employers and friends, according to the author. The black response is one of anger and frustration, tempered by the knowledge that oppression can be overcome

147

by patience and a continual striving for excellence on an individual basis.

Because of discrimination, the protagonist, Steve Hill, must take a job with a vanity publishing firm which specializes in producing books financed by the authors themselves. He does most of the work but is unable to get a raise. He clings to the position simply because no other job is available to him; he realizes that a college diploma is worth nothing to a Negro. The agony of his situation is increased when a black friend commits suicide because of his inability to find employment, and, further, when a white friend accuses him of stealing the affection of his wife. Hill finally decides to quit his job and take a chance on facing the hostile world.

The Angry Ones is the weakest of Williams' five novels of the decade, but it presents some of the important themes of the period. The economic exploitation of blacks, and their sense of alienation from American society, are topics that are stressed throughout the novel, but of greater significance is the role of the Negro as a sexual scapegoat. The sexual mythology concerning black virility causes the protagonist's white friend, burdened by an unfaithful wife, to become insanely jealous of the Negro. To appease his own frustration, the white man physically attacks Steve Hill, although the guilty person is actually another white man. In another case, the manager of the publishing firm, a white homosexual, tries to take sexual liberties with Hill by promising him raises that he does not intend to pay. Although the protagonist resists his tormentors, he realizes that he is fighting another form of prejudice that is rooted deeply in the minds of white Americans. As Calvin C. Hernton has pointed out, the racism of sex in the United States exists not only on a psychological basis but is also maintained by a economic-political-social system that makes it both profitable and convenient to discriminate sexually against Negroes. The Negro male is kept in submission by the fact that any objection to the actions of whites is met with further injustices in the employment of the black.[1]

The Angry Ones is basically overt propaganda that is not objectified into art. This situation is corrected to a large degree in Williams' second novel, *Night Song* (1961), which is an examination of prejudice from a sexual viewpoint. A white man, David Hillary, is rescued from skid row by two blacks. One of them, Eagle, is a famous jazz musician. The other, Keel Robinson, is the proprietor of a coffee house in Greenwich Village. Hillary, a former college teacher who became an alcoholic after the death of his wife, is employed by Robinson. In the course of his rehabilitation, he becomes involved with Della, Robinson's white girl friend. The racial prejudice of the teacher, who thinks of himself as a liberal, is manifested in the competition over Della. He is unable to hide his jealousy of his black friend.

The depth of Hillary's bigotry is revealed when he watches Eagle being assaulted by a policeman and makes no move to help the man who had been primarily responsible for his recovery. The author describes the teacher's ambiguous reaction to the incident by stating that

> Eagle had stopped trying to defend himself, but the club continued to come down. Hillary could not turn his sight from the thundering club; he felt guilty but somehow joyous. The officer stopped. Watching the somber adagio, Hillary found himself waiting for another blow, just one more to finish out a subtle rhythm, he itched to have the officer strike once more. . . . David Hillary, somewhat surprised to find himself in the last row of the crowd, peering from behind other people's heads, walked away thinking grimly that he should have done something, he should have.[2]

His inability to act emphasizes his subconscious hatred and fear of blacks. He is able to recognize the affliction, though, and Hillary retaliates by accepting the fact that he is unable to win Della from Robinson simply because he is a lesser man.

Robinson, angered by the weakness of Hillary, responds by ridding himself of his fears of the white world that had made him sexually impotent. He discovers a confidence in himself in the same manner that Hillary recognizes his shortcomings. Both of them adjust to the new situation, as Robinson establishes his relationship with Della, and Hillary prepares to return to his profession. It is Eagle who suffers. Wounded by the white man's failure to assert his friendship for him, Eagle engages in one last bacchanal before succumbing to an overdose of drugs.

Night Song stresses the prejudice that even liberal whites sometimes possess, especially in sexual matters. The fear and jealousy that Hillary experiences because of the affair between Della and Robinson is illustrated in the pleasure he takes in Eagle's beating. A conciliation between the races, Williams implies, cannot be realized until such bigotry is recognized and combated by the individual. In the meantime, blacks will continue to be victimized by racists, which includes the majority of whites. The author allows the action of the novel to speak for itself, though, and by remaining out of the narrative he establishes an objectivity that is lacking in *The Angry Ones*. Perhaps the major fault of *Night Song* is its depiction of stock situations to reveal the inner nature of the characters, but Williams is able to overcome this to a large degree by presenting both the white and the black views with authenticity and sympathy.

In *Sissie* (1963) Williams concentrates on illustrating the malicious effects of a ghetto environment on a famous black entertainer. The novel stresses the point that a childhood spent in a ghetto leaves a lasting impression on an individual. In the case of Iris Joplin, the bitter memories of poverty, discrimination, and the constant battle between her parents, have affected her to the point that life in America is impossible. She is unable, in fact, to forgive her dying mother for the treatment she received as a child, although the old woman herself is primarily a victim of her environment.

Iris, and her brother Ralph, return to their home in California where Sissie, the mother, is on her deathbed. Iris, a famed European singer, and Ralph, an American playwright, discuss their early life during the process of their journey home. Iris is infuriated by the kind of life Sissie and her husband, Big Ralph, led. The problems associated with the unemployed male in combat with the black matriarch were intensified by Big Ralph's tendency to drink and carouse. The consequent hardship placed on the children alienated Iris from her parents, and her bitterness persists. Young Ralph also has suffered greatly from the depravity of his youth and the racial incidents that have occurred over the years, but he is able to forgive his parents to a large degree as he realizes that white oppression is the main reason for their failures. Sissie, meanwhile, reflects on her past life as she awaits the arrival of her children, and death. Her husband had at one time been a promising young man but he was unable to cope with a society that denied him his masculinity. His compensatory devices created tensions in the family that were never resolved. As Iris and her brother arrive at Sissie's side the drama centers on whether Iris will forgive her mother. Iris' mind has been corrupted by the years of hatred and self-pity, though, and Sissie dies with the wrath of her daughter still upon her.

While the anger of Iris is directed at her mother, it is the racism of American society that is basically responsible for Iris' perverted views. Sissie and her son, Ralph, are strong enough to withstand the environment and oppression, but Iris and Big Ralph succumb to the pressures in their own way. Iris sympathizes to some extent with her emasculated father. Sissie is the object of her hate largely because Iris blames her for Big Ralph's impotency, but Sissie was merely fulfilling the role that was passed on to her by the dictates of a society in which the black male tends to be denied his manhood. The obtuse Iris fails to realize the true situation, for racism, compounded by her own shortcomings, has destroyed her vision. *Sissie* lacks the poignancy of *Night Song*, though, as Williams places a heavy emphasis on the propagandistic elements of the novel without a concomitant artistic development. He belabors the theme of oppression to the extent that his style is not capable of supporting it without resorting to diatribe.

Williams, however, is primarily responsible for the establishment of the apologetic novel in the sixties. His first three novels deal with talented or educated blacks who are severely thwarted as individuals by racism. Williams also presents the theme of interracial sexual relationships in which racial prejudice is evoked. In *The Angry Ones* and in *Night Song* he illustrates the dynamic nature of sexual racism. This is the dominant theme in the apologetic fiction of the period. The racist attitudes of whites are revealed primarily through their responses to the sexuality of blacks, which is often the only aspect of Negroes they are willing to recognize. On the other hand, blacks either take out their hatred of the white world on their white lovers, or they are made aware of the barbarity of prejudice through a sexual relationship with a member of another race.

James Baldwin, in *Another Country* (1962), stresses the desire for revenge against the white world that blacks experience. The author uses two pairs of racially mixed couples to illustrate his thesis. The Negroes involved attempt to destroy their mates, consciously or unconsciously. The racist attitudes of whites makes it impossible for the blacks to live without gaining vengeance on the people who control their fate. However, the process of avenging oneself is a means of self-destruction unless it is qualified with the knowledge that one is dealing with individuals rather than a representative of a race. Baldwin points out this concept in his treatment of Rufus Scott, a black musician, and Ida, his sister.

Rufus, a successful musician at one time, deteriorates under

151

the pressures of living in a white world. He torments Leona, his white mistress, to the point that she is driven insane. Full of hatred for society and for himself, Rufus commits suicide, but his spirit lives on, in the person of Ida. Her thirst for revenge against the oppressive system that drove Rufus to his death leads her into a relationship with Vivaldo Moore, a friend of her brother. She tries to destroy him simply because of the color of his skin, but her plans are disrupted when she discovers that she loves the white man. She confesses her plight to Vivaldo who accepts her without fully understanding the hatred that the girl feels for his race in general.

Baldwin complicates the plot by introducing Eric Jones, a white homosexual from Alabama. Jones, an actor who has been employed in France, returns to America and becomes involved with the friends of Rufus. He has sexual affairs with Vivaldo and with Cass, the wife of one of Vivaldo's friends. Largely because of their experiences with Jones, Vivaldo and Cass return to their respective mates with a fuller understanding of themselves and the nature of love. Jones himself is reunited with his French lover, a youth named Yves.

From a racial theme, then, Baldwin moves to the redeeming power of love. Rufus, a victim of racism and his own hatred is destroyed by the indifference of the world, but Ida is turned from her mission of vengeance by her love for Vivaldo. But it is Eric Jones who represents the essence of love; the homosexual leaves his idyllic existence in France to teach the obtuse Americans how to love someone through mercy, compassion, and respect. Fortified by this knowledge, Vivaldo returns to Ida, prepared to accept her on her own terms. Jones is a redemptive figure who is superior to the other characters because of his unselfish devotion to a pure concept of love. His wisdom is not matched by Rufus or Ida, who have been blighted by discrimination. Vivaldo, on the other hand, is unable to comprehend the suffering of his black friends until he consults with Jones.

Another Country is not Baldwin's best literary effort. He is too concerned with expressing his views on homosexuality and racism to concentrate on his artistic talents. Baldwin attacks white society not only on racial grounds but for its sexual mores as well. The fact that Jones is an outcast because of his homosexuality is parallel to Rufus' role as an outsider because of his color. The emphasis on propaganda causes Baldwin to contrive the plot to such an extent that his artistic integrity is questionable. He leaves his objective stance to proclaim the superiority of the homosexual white man, and to condemn the society that fails to accept sexual rebels and blacks. Baldwin abandons his earlier rejection of protest literature in *Another Country* and enters the racial protest realm himself in his portrait of the blighted life of Rufus Scott. In a later novel, *Tell Me How Long the Train's Been Gone*, he joins the rank of the militant protest writers.

The desire for revenge, a major aspect in the lives of Baldwin's black characters, also plays an important role in William Gardner Smith's *The Stone Face* (1963). The protagonist, Simeon Brown, a black expatriate, escapes from America where he is hounded by racism. In France he falls in love with a Polish actress who is going blind; but when an operation proves successful, and she is no longer dependent on him, the protagonist discovers that his life is empty. Following the example of the Algerians, who are fighting for their freedom in France, he decides to return to the United States and wreak vengeance upon the stone face of white oppression that is etched in his memory.

Brown, a writer, flees to Paris to keep from going mad in the racist society of his native country. The white tormentors who are responsible for his flight have become solidified in his mind as a white face bearing the unaltering expression of hate. In France he discovers that Negroes are relatively well treated. It is the Algerians who are discriminated against. Brown pays little attention to this fact at first, for he is engrossed in an affair with Maria. Having a white person dependent on him is satisfying to his ego. However, when this condition ceases, Brown forces himself to look at the plight of the Algerians, especially that of his friend Ahmed, who is actively involved with the struggle for Algerian liberation. The Negro questions his motive for merely watching the world go by while the oppressed people of the world are staging revolutions. His recovery from his lethargy is indicated by his assault on a French policeman who is beating a helpless Algerian woman. Exhilarated by his attack on a symbol of white oppression, Brown decides to return to Philadelphia to take up the crusade for equal rights.

Brown, then, decides to combat the stone face that he previously had attempted to escape from. He is filled with the need for revenge against the white society that has alienated him

153

from his country. It is basically through his relationship with the white girl that he arrives at his final decision: he realizes that when the girl's affliction is taken care of, through an operation, she no longer needs him. He is merely a burden to her, as she is transformed into an independent woman. She becomes free while he is still afflicted with the stigma of his color. Thus Brown fills up the void of her loss with the cause of freedom. Given impetus by the Algerians, who occupy the role of "niggers" in France, he becomes actively involved in a battle against oppression.

Smith, the author of *Last of the Conquerors*, an early protest novel, and *South Street*, one of the first of the militant books, does not go entirely to the militant side in *The Stone Face*. While Brown is a potential militant figure, the author presents him only as a man who is awakened to the need to face the image of racism that follows him. Smith himself, though, wages war on racism through his verbal assaults. Much of the novel consists of dialogue in which American Negroes point out the faults of their native country with an undisguised bitterness. The protagonist is depicted as the victim of a catalog of physical and mental acts of discrimination in his early life in Philadelphia. This tendency to emphasize the Negro as a victim of racism to an inordinate degree, coupled with a crude romantic portrayal of the Polish actress, detracts from a novel that is essentially an extensive study of prejudice. Smith, who, like Baldwin, had attacked the protest novel during the period dominated by Richard Wright, is guilty of the same faults in *The Stone Face* that he earlier condemns as unartistic.

Smith tends to stress the point that blacks are treated with respect in France. However, when white Americans are present this is not necessarily the case. Smith himself pointed this out in *Last of the Conquerors*. Robert Boles' *The People One Knows* (1964) emphasizes the prejudice of Americans in a European setting. The corrupting elements of racism are shown to exist outside the borders of the United States not only in the physical sense but psychologically as well.

Saul Beckworth is a Negro who has been hospitalized in a French mental institution after a suicide attempt. Hypersensitive to racial references, he is bothered by the remarks of another patient, an acknowledged racist. The presence of the man sets off a series of past discriminations in the mind of Saul. He is cheered, though, by the arrival of two white friends, Heinz and Emilienne. Allowed to leave the hospital, Saul and the white girl spend an idyllic day together until he is racially insulted by an American who resents the sight of a Negro accompanying a white female. Although he is treated as a hero by the French people in a bistro following his rescue of a drowning duck, Saul is unable to forget the humiliation suffered by Emilienne because of the racial incident.

The People One Knows illustrates the devastating effects of racism on a sensitive young Negro. The fact that he has left the United States does not decrease the pressure that has forced him to try to commit suicide. The prospect of another attempt is implied at the end of the novel, for the protagonist is in a depressed state from being reminded of the American taboo against miscegenation. Boles, as in *Curling*, depends to a large degree on a stream of consciousness technique. Much of the novel takes place in the tormented mind of Saul Beckworth. Only in the atmosphere of the French countryside and in the streets of a small town is he able to climb out of his shell. There is a tension present between the French girl and Saul, though, that is climaxed by the racial scene, which prevents a further intimacy between the two for the remainder of the day. In concentrating on the insecurity of the protagonist, who is revealed to have been a young man of great potential, Boles maintains an aesthetic distance that allows him to explore the mind of the character without presenting a tract. The effects of racism are depicted subtly and from a psychological viewpoint. The author implies that it is not necessary to depict scenes of violence or a series of grievances to reveal the nature of prejudice. Although *The People One Knows* is a narrow novel it is stylistically superior to most of the apologetic protest novels.

Another version of the black expatriate and his struggle to escape or to come to terms with racism is presented in Frank Yerby's *Speak Now* (1969). In his first novel dealing specifically with a racial theme, Yerby, the producer of over twenty historical romances, depicts the adventures of an American musician, living in Paris to avoid racism. In France he is regarded as a great musician, not as a Negro, but he cannot escape racial prejudice as it exists in the form of a white girl from Georgia. While Yerby implies that racism can be overcome by love, he stresses the point that it could not happen in the United States.

155

Harry Forbes, a famous musician who was educated in Switzerland, is unable to live in America because he is too proud to accept the inferior status that is automatically assigned to him because of his color. At peace with himself, to a large degree, in Paris, Forbes comes to the rescue of Kathy Nichols, a white girl from a rich family. The girl is broke and pregnant, and Forbes gives her money, a place to stay, and thinks of a plot that will help her to escape from the fury of her father. He also educates the Southern girl in racial matters. Kathy, her inhibitions and fears destroyed by the persuasive powers of Forbes, falls in love with him. The Negro, against his better judgment, reciprocates, and they are eventually married. They realize that life would be impossible for a mixed couple in the United States. Even the French react unfavorably to a mixed couple, but Forbes decides that they will take the challenge of living as man and wife in Paris.

Yerby's accommodating conclusion is qualified by the fact that both Forbes and the girl agree to accept the racism they are sure to encounter in France. The musician refuses even to consider the possibility of returning to America, where he is familiar with the brutality of racism. Love can triumph, according to the author, but only at the cost of alienation from a racist world. Despite the use of melodrama, sensationalism, romance, and stereotypes to excessive degrees, Yerby catches the revolutionary temper of the late sixties in both France and the United States. The novel is set amid the student riots of Paris and the black characters relate this to the racial conflict in America. Against this dynamic background Yerby enacts a passionate story that also competently reflects the racist attitudes of white people, especially in regard to miscegenation; but in typical Yerby fashion, the romance and the melodrama are paramount.

Yerby, like Baldwin, indicates that under certain conditions interracial love can triumph over racism on an individual basis. White society in general, though, as depicted in both *Speak Now* and *Another Country*, is impervious to the problems and the agony of Negroes. The love affairs described in these novels, and in the others of the apologetic field, tend to alienate the participants from their society, and, in many cases, from their country. Whether racism tends to force the lovers closer together, causes them to crack under the pressure, or simply forces them to see that a mixed couple cannot function within white society, the affair is fated to be a source of pain. It tends to evoke the bigotry of people around them, and sometimes of the lovers themselves.

William Melvin Kelley's *A Drop of Patience* (1965) illustrates how the pressures of society cause a white woman to terminate her relationship with a Negro. Ludlow Washington, a blind musician, is protected to some extent from racism because of his limited contact with the world. He concentrates instead on his music and achieves fame. Washington accepts the love of a white woman and in time comes to depend on her. The woman discovers that her love is not as meaningful as the pressure applied by her parents and her friends, though, and she abandons the musician. Washington is shocked by the incident and drifts into a state of lethargy. Realizing the racial implications of the girl's action, his last public performance is a self-degrading minstrel act. He then retires to the rural South, refusing to return to New York and the public eye.

The racial shock of recognition is too much for the blind musician to overcome. His affliction and his talent have separated him from the typical black, and he is not psychologically prepared to accept overt racism. The white woman loves him perhaps more for his fame and talent than for deeper personal reasons and when her acquaintances begin to question her motives for becoming involved with a Negro, she capitulates to public opinion. Neither the woman nor her love is strong enough to withstand the taboo against interracial sexual relationships. Kelley does not quite match the stylistic effectiveness of Robert Boles' *The People One Knows*, but he presents a dispassionate portrait of the effects of prejudice and sexual racism. The novel is narrow in scope and perhaps overly contrived in an attempt to make a point, but within its limitations it is a quietly forceful book.

A somewhat more sensational version of star-crossed interracial love is *White Marble Lady* (1965). Roi Ottley's novel, published posthumously, also deals with a black who achieves fame in the music business and attracts the love of a white woman. Ottley is primarily concerned with showing that the racism of white society places a tremendous amount of pressure on mixed marriages. Jeff Kirby, the Tan Troubadour, and Deborah, the white friend of Kirby's agent, eventually fall in love. They decide to get married despite the objections raised by various people, including the white agent, who does not want any "nigger" to touch his former girl friend, and Deborah's parents, who call a meeting of all their relatives to discuss the catastrophe. The marriage does not last long as both Jeff and his wife begin to show the pressure of living among hostile people. Deborah finally has a mental breakdown.

Ottley attempts to include a panoramic view of American life and the varying degrees of racism that exist in the country. He loses control of his material, though, and tries to compensate by resorting to sensationalism to the extent that the last part of the book becomes a propagandistic diatribe. The novel lacks both originality and artistry, but the author is relatively successful in depicting the white response to miscegenation as he explores the psychological and social aspects of their fears. Providing a prophetic comment on the unsuccessful efforts of Jeff Kirby to crack the wall of prejudice around him, is the legendary story of Ditcher Kirby, an ancestor, who failed in a valiant attempt at a slave revolt.

The psychological pressures of racism are often as devastating as any overt action. In *Catherine Carmier* (1964) Ernest J. Gaines explores the racial situation in Louisiana, where the various mixtures of blood are responsible for the creation of a rigid caste system. Gaines shows how the influence of the Cajuns, who consider themselves white despite the presence of Indian blood in their genealogy, is used to destroy the Negroes. The latter category includes anyone who is known to have some black ancestry. This means that the whites are often discriminating against their own relatives. A drop of Negro blood, though, is enough to brand a person as a "nigger," which makes him an enemy of the whites.

The Cajuns are the dominant people in the section of Louisiana in which the novel is set. For years they have been forcing Negroes to leave their farms, retaining a few of them to work the land that the Cajuns steal from them. The only remaining landholder among the blacks is Raoul Carmier, who refuses to accept his racial status. He considers himself as white as the Cajuns who are trying to take his land away from him. It is rumored that he purposely killed his black son. His two daughters, however, are capable of passing for white, and one of them does. Catherine, though, stays home where her father can worship her, but where she is also regarded as a Negro by the whites. Raoul protects her from black suitors as he is afraid of further tainting the blood of his family. The Carmiers, then, are trapped in a strange sort of limbo in which they are hated by the whites and separated from the other people of colored blood by the perverse attitude of Raoul. An outcast, he expends his energy in working his land, in stubborn resistance to the economic pressures of the Cajuns, and in trying to keep Catherine happy.

Intruding into this situation is Jackson, a young black man who returns to visit his relatives after receiving a college education on the West Coast. Jackson soon discovers that his childhood home is no longer suitable for him and he makes plans to leave despite the objections of Charlotte, his ancient guardian, who expects him to stay in the area and educate the remaining Negroes. But Jackson is no longer a local Negro who is willing to subjugate himself to the Cajuns. Gaines describes his reaction to the Cajuns as he refuses to use the segregated facilities at the local general store.

> What fools. Just because he did not clown in front of them and drink in the sideroom with the other Negroes, they were suspicious of him. Already he had heard that they were asking whether or not he was a Freedom Rider. What a joke. He a Freedom Rider? And what would he try to integrate, this stupid grocery store? He felt like laughing in their stupid faces.[3]

An independent youth who is searching for something meaningful in a world that seems to be devoid of justice and sanity, Jackson decides to resume his friendship with Catherine Carmier, whom he had known as a child. He discusses the Carmier family with Madame Bayonne, a black prophetess who correctly analyzes his inability to adjust to the racist way of the South, and also predicts his troubles with Raoul. Indifferent to Catherine at first, he becomes enamored by the girl and the challenge she represents. The light-complexioned Catherine responds to the advances of the young man, who represents a welcome relief from the prison her father has created for her. After several meetings, unknown to Raoul, the couple decide to elope. Raoul, however, is informed of the plan by the Cajuns, who relish the opportunity to set Negroes against each other, and he discovers them in the act of departing. A furious fight follows from which Jackson emerges triumphant. But Catherine cannot leave until she attends to her fallen father, and the novel

159

ends as Jackson waits impatiently outside the house.

The implication is that the influence of Raoul Carmier will not easily be overcome. A victim of racism who reverts to racism himself, Raoul has kept his daughter in bondage all her life. While Jackson represents freedom, she is reluctant to take the step that will make her a part of the black world. But it is a step that she has to make if she wants to live, rather than merely exist in the utopian microcosm of her father, which extends only to the borders of the rapidly deteriorating Carmier property. The novel is an examination of the psychology of racial prejudice and Raoul Carmier is the primary case study. In his refusal to accept an inferior status, he emulates the white world, and surpasses it in many ways, to the point that he convinces himself that he is white. The last thing, of course, a typical Cajun wants to happen is to have his daughter marry a "nigger." It is ironic but prophetic, then, that Jackson attempts to win the hand of Catherine. In effect, he is "stealing" a white man's daughter. The fact that Catherine is as white as the Cajuns in complexion, emphasizes the absurdity of the caste system created by the people who are technically recognized as white. Yet, it is the whites who, from their perverted point of view, expect to gain by the defeat of Raoul. If he loses his daughter, he will probably lose his land too, as it is basically for Catherine's benefit that he works so hard.

Catherine Carmier is a rich novel that is presented objectively and skillfully by a young author. In a story set in a remote section of the South, Gaines manages to expose the temper of the modern era in regard to racism. In the figure of Jackson he symbolically depicts the invasion of the Old South by the emancipated Negro. Jackson admits that he is not a Freedom Rider, but he is regarded as a threat by the racists. He disappoints the Negroes who accommodate themselves to the oppression of the Cajuns, but Jackson, in his supreme independence, is merely a pawn in the hands of the Cajuns, who use him to combat the other unyielding black man, Raoul Carmier. The bait, of course, is Catherine, the beautiful Southern belle who is denied her humanity by the Cajuns and by her father. She is so indoctrinated to the tenets of racism that she is hesitant to leave Raoul. Regardless of her decision, it is the Cajuns who will emerge triumphant.

The racial aspects that are explored in depth in *Catherine Carmier* are treated further in *Of Love and Dust* (1967). In his second novel, Gaines deals with the plantation as it exists in the modern South. He reveals that economic and sexual exploitation of blacks has changed little from the days of slavery. The racism is so pervasive that any white man that is somewhat lenient in his attitude toward blacks is in danger of being ostracized, or worse. The major taboo, though, is still that of miscegenation as it involves a black man and a white woman.

Narrated by Jim Kelly, a black laborer on a plantation owned by Marshall Hebert, the novel revolves around the events that occur upon the arrival of Marcus. The latter, a young Negro who has killed another black in a knife fight, is saved from jail through the efforts of Hebert, who arranges to have him work on the plantation, supposedly as a favor to his former cook. Marcus is rebellious from the start, though, and Sidney Bonbon, the white overseer, drives him mercilessly. Bonbon runs the plantation with an iron hand and delights in breaking in new hands. When he is not in the field with his horse and his rifle, the big Cajun is usually down in the old slave quarters with his black mistress, Pauline, and their mulatto children.

This leaves Marcus free to observe Louise, Bonbon's blond wife who is virtually ignored by her husband. Marcus pays no attention to the taboo concerning white women and he eventually wins the affections of the girl, who is anxious to escape from her prison. The two decide to leave the plantation despite the threat of Bonbon. The latter catches them as they are preparing to depart, and the overseer kills the black youth. Louise is later committed to a mental institution, giving her husband an opportunity to abscond with Pauline. Kelly, the narrator, knowing the story behind the killing of Marcus, also leaves the plantation.

During the course of the book Kelly discovers that Marshall Hebert has ulterior motives in arranging for Marcus' release from jail. Bonbon has once killed a man for the white plantation owner and he wants to get rid of the overseer, who has been stealing from him ever since the murder. Hebert plans to have Marcus kill Bonbon, but the Negro refuses to do it on the white man's terms. He asks Hebert to arrange to have the charges against him dropped so that he can run away with Louise. Bonbon can be expected to follow but even if he catches them he will not be able to assume his former role on the plantation because of the disgrace. Hebert, who controls the county, complies with this plan and secures the legal release of Marcus. However,

161

before the plot can be carried out the plantation owner changes his mind. As a typical Southerner he is unable to face the idea of the Negro taking the wife of a white man. He informs his despised overseer of the affair, knowing that in the confrontation between Bonbon and Marcus one of them will die and the other will be forced to flee.

Kelly, as a trusted field hand, is a confidant of Bonbon. He realizes that the Cajun overseer is in love with his black mistress, but that he cannot acknowledge his affection in public. As a merely sexual liason, though, it is perfectly acceptable, as black women have traditionally been erotic receptacles of white men. Kelly also comes to know Marcus well. He expects the rebellious spirit of the youth to be broken by the demeaning conditions of the plantation. The narrator has accommodated himself to the racist system and is surprised to see someone challenge it. His dislike of Marcus gradually grows into respect, though, as he observes the activities of the Negro in his individual battle to overcome racism. Gaines indicates the thoughts of Kelly as he reflects on the imminent flight of the lovers.

> I admired Marcus. I admired his great courage. . . . I wanted to tell him how brave I thought he was. He was the bravest man I knew, the bravest man I had ever met. Yes, yes, I wanted to tell him that. And I wanted to tell Louise how I admired her bravery. I wanted to tell them that they were starting something—yes, that's what I would tell them; they were starting something that others would hear about, and understand, and would follow.[4]

Kelly is being optimistic about the chances to accomplish a change in the attitudes of the South. He knows that Marcus' challenge of the sexual taboo is likely to get him killed, yet the spirit of Marcus lives on in Kelly to some degree. Although he is forced to leave the plantation because neither Hebert nor Bonbon's relatives will now trust him, the narrator refuses to accept a recommendation from Hebert, preferring to start a new life on his own. This is a relatively bold step for a man who has passively accepted the commands of whites all his life. It is hardly a revolution, though, and Kelly leaves the plantation with Hebert completely in charge of his empire.

Kelly's narration is pieced together from his own experience and from the fragments he picks up from the people on the plantation. It is only towards the end of the novel that he begins to lose his objectivity and support the cause of Marcus. By then it is too late to do anything but report the action in his regular way since the forces at work are beyond his control. In his role as confidant and observer he discovers, with no particular effort, the ambitions and guilts of the plantation personnel. Gaines' disclosure of his story of love and bigotry in this manner gives it an added dimension of authenticity reminiscent of Faulkner in *Absalom, Absalom!* If the mythical qualities of Faulkner's great novel are not as evident in *Of Love and Dust* it is basically because Gaines is a more economical writer. His saga of the South is perhaps only slightly less cogent, and is one of the better books on racism, along with *Catherine Carmier*, to be produced in twentieth century America.

The two great works of Gaines, probably the best black novelist of the decade, stress the point that racism stems largely from sexual fears. While the white males consider the sexual exploitation of Negro women as their prerogative, the taboo against white women and black men mating is rigidly enforced—by the white men. Guilty of his own actions and fearful of the mythical sexual potency of blacks, the white males tend to place their women on a lofty pedestal. To the Negro males, then, she represents a challenge—a chance to prove their masculinity and to gain revenge on the white world. Meanwhile, the white women are curious about the sexuality of blacks and often willing to engage in amorous activities, especially if their husbands are doing the same. In this vicious sexual cycle everyone is hurt to some extent. If the Negro is discriminated against, it is the white woman who is often ignored, and who has to worry about the shame of bearing a black child if she does step over the color line. At the same time the fear of being cuckolded by a black man continually haunts the white male. This fear transcends the personal level as the white man, concerned with his possible sexual inferiority, tries to promote the problem to a level which encompasses the honor of the white race and the purity of white womanhood. Concomitant to this rationalization is the theory that the Negro is an animal who must be kept submissive at all costs. The concept of white superiority is in the balance.

While no novelist of the period explores sexual racism to the extent, or with the skill, that Gaines does, it is a topic that tends to dominate the apologetic novel. The violence depicted in *Of Love and Dust* is not a common occurrence in the sixties, though, since psychological pressures tend to be the primary weapon of whites. Violence is always a threat, however, to the Negro who becomes involved with a white woman. To some bigots the breaking of the taboo is a crime that calls for an extreme form of punishment. Although lynching is no longer a fashionable event, in the historical context of the nineteenth century it is the primary means of subjugating blacks. In *All God's Children* (1965) Alston Anderson illustrates this method of maintaining white superiority.

In the manner of Margaret Walker's *Jubilee*, Anderson's novel is centered on the Civil War and the effect of freedom on blacks who were raised in slavery. The protagonist, October Pruitt, is not a person to accept the dictates of whites. Related to the people who own the plantation on which he is enslaved through the typical sexual activities of the white master, October is at an early age seduced by Angela, his white cousin. He eventually escapes from slavery and becomes a free citizen of Philadelphia. However, he is recaptured when he returns to the South to preach his brand of positive thinking to the slaves. He considers slavery as merely a physical discomfort; no man is really enslaved if his mind is free. Neither the slaves nor the whites have much respect for this philosophy, though, and October decides to escape again so that he can participate in the Civil War as a member of the Union Army. During the conflict he is captured by the Confederates but escapes by using a plan based on the white man's refusal to recognize Negroes, even if their life depends on it. When he returns to the Union forces, his talents are recognized and he forsakes his Sambo role to take on a responsible position.

After the war October gets married and becomes a farmer in Virginia. Despite the racism of the surrounding whites, the black man prospers. With the help of a white friend he tries to improve the conditions of his fellow blacks through the organization of labor. At this point October's narrative ends and his wife tells the rest of the story. Her husband has been lynched by a white mob after refusing to terminate his love affair with a white woman.

An intelligent man who believes in nonviolent activism as the answer to racist practices, October Pruitt is ahead of his time. Yet he may have survived in the Reconstruction era if he had been willing to compromise with the bigots. In asserting his freedom by associating with a white woman, his fate is almost assured. Like a nineteenth century version of Martin Luther King, October relentlessly challenges the white power structure. His idealism in the face of his experience as a slave is as remarkable as it is imprudent. Anderson attempts to summarize the history of the black man in America in his novel, but the various roles assumed by the protagonist in conjunction with this concept are so obviously contrived that they are largely ineffective. The conclusion, too, is merely an appendix which stresses the inhumanity of the South, a point which has already been made in more efficient ways. The novel is basically a modern version of an antithesis to the plantation tradition which merely turns the propaganda in the other direction without an improvement in literary quality.

Frank Hercules' *I Want a Black Doll* (1967) also deals with the problem of miscegenation from the viewpoint of a Southern mentality. The novel depicts a mixed marriage involving a black doctor and a white girl from the South. The social pressures exerted upon them tend to produce a hatred in the girl that is beyond reason. She is so upset at her pregnancy that she has an abortion rather than give birth to a black baby. She dies from the crude operation, and a cousin from the South swears to revenge her death—on her husband rather than on the abortionist. The white man discovers that the Negro is his half brother, but the crime of miscegenation is too great not to be punished by death. Although the Southerner has a black mistress himself, he murders his brother.

The extreme melodrama of the novel, revolving around racism, is so dominant that any artistic elements that may be present are overshadowed. Hercules is concerned only with condemning racial bigots. The destructive forces inherent in prejudice, almost as deadly in the North as in the South, are stressed through sensationalism and violence. The book is almost completely opposite in tone and emphasis from the author's earlier novel, *Where the Hummingbird Flies*, and is also greatly inferior.

The violence used to intimidate black men is usually directed toward another purpose in regard to the women. Elizabeth Vroman, in *Esther* (1963), explores the life of a Negro girl who is raped and impregnated by a white man. While the novel reveals the enduring qualities of the protagonist, it also illustrates the mental agony that is suffered by both the woman and her illegitimate daughter. The author stresses the point that this is merely another facet of the black experience in America.

Esther Kennedy, reared by her grandmother in Alabama, has ambitions to become a nurse. To finance this plan she works as a servant for the rich Miller family. She is raped by her employer's son and as a result gives birth to a daughter, Hope. Esther does become a nurse, though, and eventually marries Joe Mead, the town's first black doctor. An enmity exists between Joe and Hope that is increased when the girl learns the truth about her white father. Partly to spite Joe, Hope has an affair with a white boy that ends in disaster when Esther discovers the young couple embracing, and, reminded of her own experience, physically attacks the youth.

Esther, much like Lutie Johnson in Ann Petry's *The Street*, temporarily loses her senses and strikes out at the white world represented by an innocent boy. Although Esther has a success-ful career as a nurse, the personal indignities she is forced to suffer have affected her mind. She preaches moderation and understanding in racial affairs, but subconsciously she is seeth-ing with hate against the white world that will not recognize her humanity. In her effort to indicate the effects of racism, though, the author presents a melodramatic story and a cast of characters that is drawn from the television "soap operas." Vroman emphasizes her point with power but not much artistry.

While the sexual theme is dominant in the apologetic protest novel it is not mandatory. In Paul Crump's *Burn Killer, Burn*, and Robert Deane Pharr's *The Book of Numbers*, the emphasis is simply on the exploitation and subjugation of blacks, primarily through violence. The special target of condemnation in both novels is the police department. The policemen are shown to be greedy, brutal, and insensitive. Their primary function is to kill any Negro who steps out of line.

Crump's *Burn Killer, Burn* (1961) is in many ways an imitation of Willard Motley's *Knock on Any Door*. The protagonist, Guy Morgan, is a young Negro of potential who is thwarted by his environment and the prejudice of whites. Despite the crime, the desertion of his father, and the existence of police brutality in the ghetto, Morgan remains essentially a fine young man, partly because of the devotion of his mother. While his friends are victimized by violence on the part of whites, or become dope addicts, the youth becomes a famed athlete in high school. However, he is eventually shot by policemen. Guy Morgan has committed no crime, but he is carrying a gun and he retaliates by killing one of them. When he recovers from his wounds, Morgan is convicted of murder. He refuses an appeal and then commits suicide in his cell.

From a sensitive study of a boy who is perhaps too dependent on his mother, Crump's novel tends to deteriorate into a tract. The oppressive environment becomes more of a jungle as the novel progresses and it is obvious that the protagonist is fated to be a victim. Like Motley's Nick Romano, he gives way to the atmosphere of the streets where violence is common. Also in the manner of Nick, in the end he refuses life, having seen enough of the cruel and indifferent world. Crump, of course, puts a racial emphasis in his book simply by making his protagonist black. The same cops that hate Romano because he is a tough and arrogant hoodlum, hate Guy Morgan because he is a Negro.

While *Burn Killer, Burn* never transcends its own bitterness and propagandistic tendencies, Pharr's novel is relatively successful. The story of Dave and Blueboy, Negro gamblers who organize their own numbers bank in a Southern city, *The Book of Numbers* (1969) depicts the struggle of black people to establish and maintain their self-respect in a racist society. It traces the careers of the two former waiters as they rise to prominence in an illegal business that is usually controlled by whites. In organizing and financing the numbers game instead of merely participating in it, the black men are challenging the white power structure. Their success is due largely to Blueboy's ability to play the proper submissive role in front of the white policemen. The latter decide to assert their power, though, when their payoff is a little late in arriving. They beat Blueboy to death as a reminder that, as whites, they are superior to even rich Negroes.

Pharr retains an objectivity and a humorous tone through much of his novel, which is filled with numerous colorful, if shallow, Negro characters who populate the bistros and gambling houses of the ghetto. His major point is that oppression and racism deny blacks an opportunity to be recognized as individuals. A college education enables a Negro to take a job as a dishwasher or porter. The accumulation of money allows him a life of luxury, but only within the narrow confines of the ghetto. Even then, as in the case of Blueboy, there is no guarantee of safety from violence. The author's tendency to overstate his case, in the unpolished naturalistic style of the early protest writers, diminishes the effectiveness of a novel that still manages to explore the depths of the black experience with vividness.

There are several protest novels of the period which are related to the apologetic tradition but that are not quite the same in the sense that they present protagonists who never have a chance to rise even to the first level of humanity. They are defeated by oppression before they have a taste of success. Thus they are unlike the apologetic characters who are able to make some attempt at establishing an identity, achieving a goal, or challenging the racist aspects of society. In the manner of the Wrightian protest novels of the forties, these people are destroyed before they develop as anything more than slaves to the system of economic and racial exploitation. As such they do not emerge as metaphysical rebels or revolutionaries. They do not accommodate themselves to oppression, but fight it on an emotional or a rational level—which in either case, amounts to being victimized.

It is ironic that one of the propagators of this minor type of protest fiction is Richard Wright. The author of *Native Son* died in Europe three years before *Lawd Today* (1963) appeared. Actually one of Wright's earlier works, the novel is designed to show the psychological torment suffered by a Negro and his wife as a result of discriminatory practices. It traces one day in the life of Jake Johnson, a postal clerk in Chicago. The day in question happens to be the birthday of Abraham Lincoln. Amidst radio and newspaper accounts of the life of the liberator, Jake ventures forth into a world which he despises. Burdened by a lack of money and a sick wife, he discusses the state of the nation with friends before reporting for work. The major topic is their resentment of the white society that is designed to keep them in the lowest economic and social positions. The frustration of living in this world is reflected in the events of the day.

Unable to borrow money from a respectable institution, Jake is forced to obtain a loan from an individual who charges an exorbitant rate of interest. He has already paid a large amount of cash to an influential person in order to maintain his low paying job. He needs the money for his sick wife, but Jake, angered by the vicious cycle in which he is trapped, decides to appease himself with a few drinks after work. However, he gets drunk and the borrowed money is stolen. To climax his pathetic day, Jake beats up his wife before passing out.

The protagonist, reduced to an animal by his environment and the frustrations of being continually exploited, is the prototype of the "nigger" which bigots enjoy seeing. His life is centered on the compensatory devices of brutality, alcohol and sex. Instead of taking out his anger on the white world, which he fears, Jake indulges in self-hatred without admitting it. Wright attempts to illustrate that white oppression is responsible for the depraved condition of the defeated creature, but he is much less successful in this respect than in *Native Son*. He tries too hard to suggest by repetitive dialogue the points that should be revealed in the action of the novel. The narrow and static plot and the crude stylistic devices do not enhance this grim story. Wright, however, makes it clear that Lincoln did not liberate the Negroes of the United States.

The psychological damages of racial discrimination that are revealed in *Lawd Today* are also stressed in Rosa Guy's *Bird at My Window* (1966). The book relates the experiences of Wade Williams, a Harlem youth who becomes a pawn in the hands of the people who are trying to integrate the schools. Once the integration is achieved, Wade is discriminated against to a degree that hardly makes the legal action seem worth it. It is only when he enters the army and serves in France that Wade feels free, and that experience disappears when he is forced to kill a white man in an argument over a French girl. He again feels unshackled, but when he returns to America he is depressed by the racist atmosphere. He is finally admitted to a mental institution when he attacks Faith, his sister, and the one person he loves. When he is finally released he attempts to kill his insensitive mother, but accidentally kills Faith instead.

Driven insane by the pressures of the white world, Wade attempts to destroy the people that are closest to him. It is a form of self-destruction that is finally consummated in the death of the sister. Too weak to either accept the world or to scorn it, the protagonist succumbs to the oppression and violence that have surrounded him all his life. The author adds little to the definition of the black experience that has not been done previously, and she is no more than a competent artist; but the book is saved from oblivion by its objective and analytical exploration of racism and its damages.

While *Lawd Today* and *Bird at My Window* concentrate on the psychology of prejudice, Junius Edwards, in *If We Must Die*

(1963), concentrates on the physical aspects. In his short tract he depicts an idealistic black youth who, in attempting to register to vote, is denied his rights, fired from his job, put on the blacklist of every employer in the country, and finally is kidnapped and beaten by a gang of whites. The price of stepping outside of the prescribed boundaries, as determined by white racists, is high for the young Negro, who, in his ignorance, does not realize that he is not accepted as an American citizen. Edwards has nothing to say above the level of propaganda, but on this plane his book is forceful.

Sarah Wright's *This Child's Gonna Live* (1969) presents a much deeper portrait of the use of violence. The novel also examines the sexual aspects of racism, as whites ignore the results of their interbreeding and discriminate against their own blood relatives, especially on an economic basis. On yet another level, the book is a study of the psychological effects of white oppression. In an unmitigated tone of dismay the author records the narrative of a young black family that tries to eke out a living in Maryland in the 1930's under conditions that are impossible to overcome.

Jacob and Mariah try to hold their land against the encroaching poverty. Since the mills do not hire Negroes, the only way for a black man to earn a living is to work the land and the sea. Jacob, though, is in danger of losing the land that has been in his family for years. In an attempt to earn some money Jacob gathers his wife and children and sets off on an expedition to some of the places that hire blacks. The trip ends in failure, though, as the family is barely able to meet its expenses, and one of the children dies. They return to what remains of their farm in Tangierneck, and Mariah attempts to drown herself. Jacob rescues her and together they face the bleak prospects of struggling to earn a living.

The horror of their existence involves more than economic hardships. The omnipresent lynching mob is also a major threat. Jacob's father is lynched following the death of a white woman although there is no evidence that a murder or rape took place. Jacob and his family are also visited by nightriders, and are saved from violence only through a coincidence. On a lesser scale, there are numerous incidents of discrimination that make life a little harder to bear. Contributing to the psychological pressure is the preponderance of interracial sexual activity. A major concern to Jacob is the fact that Mariah's latest baby turns out to be rather white. He cannot afford to support his own children and the thought that the child may have been fathered by a white man is almost more than he can endure. But perhaps the day-to-day existence, with the worry of having enough to eat, of the children being sick, and of struggling to retain the land, is the most trying experience. Even the threat of violence is of less significance than starvation.

This Child's Gonna Live is an impressive novel from a stylistic viewpoint. The stream-of-consciousness narrative, reflecting a fever pitch of emotional turmoil in the characters, is effective in communicating the depravity of Negro life in Tangierneck. The vivid portrayal of misery is unrelieved by a ray of optimism or hope. Although the protest elements of the novel tend to dominate, the author remains in control of her material and the novel does not revert into sheer propaganda. Sarah Wright, in her first novel, does not get below the surface of all of the racial aspects she presents, but she succeeds, on a minor level, in depicting artistically a private version of hell created by a cruel society.

The major emphasis in the protest fiction of the decade is, of course, the exposure of white racism, and its effects on blacks. The revival of the apologetic tradition, highlighted by the work of John A. Williams and Ernest J. Gaines, illustrates that the Negro is primarily a victim of a society that will not recognize him as a man, or as a woman. This thought is echoed in the militant protest novels of the period. There is a difference, though, in the sense that in the latter type of fiction the blacks organize and directly challenge the white power structure. The exemplary characters of the apologetic novels are transformed into militant revolutionaries and the individual rebellions are turned into coordinated insurrections.

CHAPTER IX

Militant Protest

Militant protest fiction reflects the tempestuous racial situation of the sixties. Racial pride, the insistence on the dignity of being an Afro-American in the face of continuing racism has created conflicts in which blacks will no longer play a passive role. The influence of Martin Luther King has often yielded to that of Malcolm X and other extremists. This phenomenon has led to the distinguishing feature of the militant protest novel: the organization of blacks for resistance to white oppression. This usually means only the reciprocation of violence, but in its extreme form militancy produces revolutionary activity designed to thwart or destroy military and law enforcement agencies in the United States. This extremism aims to accomplish the positive goals that the peaceful movements have failed to bring about. The basic idea is not to overthrow the entire country but, by a show of force, to persuade officials to meet the demands of blacks.

Such militancy had prototypes in the first Afro-American revolutions: the slave insurrections. Arna Bontemps fictionalized the revolt of Gabriel Prosser in *Black Thunder* (1936), and more recently William Styron, a white Southerner, produced *The Confessions of Nat Turner* (1967), a novel severely criticized by blacks for the unfavorable elements in its portrait of the slave leader. But major revolts were rare during slavery, and since that time change has been sought primarily through the peaceful channels of litigation and the non-violent movements popularized by King. Generally, violence has been limited to the spontaneous race riots of the ghetto in which the majority of the victims are

173

Negroes. There are indications that this pattern may change, though, as extremist groups like the Black Panthers become more active.

An indication of the increasing impatience of blacks about the racial policies of the country is presented in the 1965 essay by John Oliver Killens, "The Myth of Non-Violence." Killens, a black novelist, asks the question:

> How long America? How long, especially my friends of the liberal persuasion, how long in the light of this violence against me, can you continue to speak to me of non-violence? The chasm widens steadily. Soon it will no longer be possible for me to hear you.
> For your black brother is spoiling for a fight in affirmation of his manhood. This is the cold-blooded Gospel truth. The more violence perpetrated against him, with pious impunity, the more he becomes convinced that this thing cannot resolve itself non-violently, that only blood will wash away centuries of degradation. The burden is on White America to prove otherwise. But you had better get going in a hurry, for we are at the brink.[1]

Killens' sense of urgency is reflected in the novels he produced in the decade, but he is not alone in concern for a potentially catastrophic division between black and white America. William Melvin Kelley, in *A Different Drummer* (1962), presents an imaginary situation in which the entire Negro population of a Southern state, outraged by decades of discrimination, departs for the North. This exodus is a non-violent movement given impetus by the act of an individual, but it is an effective means of combating white oppression.

Tucker Caliban, the leader of this silent rebellion, is the descendant of a legendary African chief who refused to become a slave. Caliban perplexes the white people of the village of Sutton by abandoning his small farm. Shortly after he leaves, the neighboring blacks prepare to follow him in what becomes a state-wide movement. The confused white townspeople enjoy the action at first, but are eventually angered by the disappearance of their subservient blacks. To appease their frustration they lynch the Reverend B. T. Bradshaw, a black man who appears in Sutton at about the time the exodus begins, and who is assumed to be the real leader of the Negro abdication.

While the townspeople of Sutton do not understand what is happening, one white family is indirectly involved in the movement. David Willson, the deteriorating head of an aristocratic Southern family, had attended school in Massachusetts. Its liberal atmosphere helped to replace his racist views with an enlightened attitude. He became very friendly with Bennett Bradshaw, an ambitious young Negro who eventually became his roommate. Together they planned to combat racism—Bradshaw as an active member of the National Society for Colored Affairs and David as a liberal newspaper writer in the South. After their college education both men pursued their ambitions. David though, was fired from his newspaper position for his radical views on racial matters and he eventually surrendered to the Southern way of life, at the cost of his humanity.

In the present action of the novel, David is ineffectual and no longer communicates with his wife or his children. His son Dewey, returning home from his first year of college in the North, tries to understand why Tucker Caliban quit working for the Willsons, who had employed his family for years. Dewey grew up under the tutelage of Caliban without recognizing that the Negro had ambitions of his own. Dewey does not now realize the depth of Caliban's desire to be more than a sharecropper or servant. Caliban wants mostly to be free, and his first major step is to buy the land on which his family had lived for years. He prefers to work for himself rather than to work for the Willsons, but he finds that he is not yet free. In an attempt to avoid the exploitation which confronts a black man, he burns his home, and with his transportable items and his family, leaves for the North.

When Bradshaw, leader of an ineffective militant religious sect, learns of the exodus he goes to Sutton to examine the situation. He is impressed by the movement, and at the same time he feels obsolete because of the little that he has accomplished for his race through the use of menacing dialogue and threats, rather than by direct action. He realizes that a new day is dawning in which impatient Negroes are demanding their freedom immediately. Men like himself, who preach hatred for whites while they line their pockets with the contributions of their parishioners, are doomed to extinction. This observation becomes both ironic and prophetic when Bradshaw is lynched by the white mob. The violent act indicates that Bradshaw is right: his days of leadership are over primarily because the racial situation calls for leaders on the order of a Caliban, who are not afraid to initiate a dynamic action to win self-respect for blacks at the risk of personal loss.

The revolution that the novel advocates, then, demands sacrifice. Caliban and his followers give up their land and their property to pursue a dream. One of the departing blacks tells Bradshaw that he is leaving his home because of a conversation he had with a neighbor who informed him about

> '... this colored man up in Sutton who told the Negroes all about it, all about history and all that stuff, and that he said besides that the only way for things to be better was for all the colored folks to move out, to turn their backs on everything we knowed and start new.'[2]

Caliban does not teach violence and hate in the manner of Bradshaw. He prefers instead to take direct action against racism. That it is non-violent is not as important as that it openly challenges the white power structure. The murder of Bradshaw is a final act of desperation by the whites who have no other blacks left to serve as scapegoats. Bradshaw's major mistake, outside of his coincidental appearance in Sutton, is that he merely rode the crest of the militant tide to personal glory. Caliban, on the other hand, frees himself from his omnipotent tormentors by sacrificing his possessions and refusing to be a slave any longer. His act is the extreme application of the philosophy of Martin Luther King.

Tucker Caliban appears in the narrative only as he is seen through the eyes of the other characters. The novel consists basically of the narrations of white people who have known the legendary figure. The multiple viewpoints tend to add an extra dimension to Caliban. One of the Sutton townsmen relates the story of Caliban's ancestor, the mighty African who battled with General Dewey Willson rather than become a slave. This episode is reminiscent of the historical background device employed by George Washington Cable in his famous nineteenth century novel, *The Grandissimes*. Caliban lives up to the legend of his progenitor by staging his own revolt, which is representative of the mass movement of colonized peoples in the twentieth century to attain their freedom, especially the American Negro as he has struggled for independence on the soil which had formerly enslaved him. As the various anecdotes of Caliban are pieced together by the narrators, he begins to take on the mythical proportions of William Faulkner's Thomas Sutpen. Kelley's epic story of the South, which precedes Gaines' *Of Love and Dust*, is marred by the author's failure to take into consideration many of the practical aspects of the mass exodus, but it remains one of the minor classics of the era.

A Different Drummer is distinct from the other militant protest novels in that its revolution is non-violent. The mass movement begun by Tucker Caliban, though, is an extreme form of action that approaches militancy in its audaciousness. More typical of the fiction depicting organized resistance to white oppression is Ronald L. Fair's *Many Thousand Gone* (1965). This novel depicts a violent black revolution in Mississippi. Subtitled "An American Fable," Fair's book also deals with a hypothetical situation in which a remote county is purposely isolated from the rest of the country so that slavery can be maintained.

Sam Jacobs, the founder of Jacobsville in Jacobs County, Mississippi, decides to keep his empire intact after the Civil War by isolating it from the outside world. Until his death in 1892 Sam is able to make slavery a profitable enterprise and his son continues the tradition. In the middle of the twentieth century, then, the Negroes of Jacobs County are kept in bondage. Raping and lynching are common practices and the only alternative to submission is death or an escape to the North. Through the messages relayed by several of the blacks who are fortunate enough to make their way to freedom, the slaves learn about the outside world. Sheriff Pitch, however, works diligently to stifle all information that leaks in, at the same time producing his own counter-propaganda. He also trains Josh Black, a descendant of one of the escaped slaves, to be his special aid in keeping the blacks subjugated. When federal officials arrive to investigate the county, Pitch imprisons them and plans a lynching party. Josh surprises the sheriff by leading a bloody rebellion in which all the whites are killed, except the government inspectors who are magnanimously released by the rebel commander.

Fair's short novel is indicative of the temper of the times but it is not a particularly skillful production. The author depends too much on scenes of violence, which are repeated throughout the book, rather than exploring the psychological implications of his mythical county. The motivations of the characters are weak and the violent conclusion is not adequately prepared for in the preceding material. Fair concentrates on exploring the brutality of the South as it exists in the modern era and as it existed under slavery. This is the primary accomplishment of *Many Thousand Gone,* since the propagandistic elements tend to dominate.

The tendency to depict a militant revolution is common in

the sixties. John Oliver Killens, one of the instigators of the militant protest novel with his publication of *Youngblood* (1954), kept up the pace with *And Then We Heard the Thunder* (1962), Killens' second novel deals with black soldiers during World War II who revolt against discriminatory treatment. After participating in numerous invasions, the blacks discover that their status has not improved. Whether they are in basic training in Georgia, on an island in the South Pacific, or recuperating in Australia, racism is a part of the unofficial policy of the whites.

The black protagonist, Solly Saunders, enters the army with the idea of fighting for America rather than for racial equality. Under his wife's guidance, Solly is primarily interested in advancing his own cause through his loyal support of his country's military system, but he discovers that racism permeates the service so much that he must subjugate his personal plans to a racial cause. His patience finally wears thin when, after being fortunate enough to survive some of the bloodiest episodes of the war, he and his black friends are mistreated in Bainbridge, Australia. Solly, therefore, chooses to join the race war that erupts there. During a lull in the battle, he makes a vow to himself.

'If I get home my brothers, I'll tell the world about your battle in Bainbridge. Maybe it's not too late yet. If I tell it to the whole wide world, tell them if they don't solve this question, the whole damn world will be like Bainbridge is this morning! The whole damn world will be like Bainbridge!'[3]

Although some of his descriptive passages about the war are vivid, Killens is not particularly concerned with an artistic execution. His basic purpose is to warn the world that Afro-Americans will no longer remain docile in the face of white racism. The narrative is filled with racial incidents that eventually convince the protagonist that violence is the only answer to the problems of the black soldier. The battle that concludes the novel is representative of the author's view of what will happen in the United States unless conditions change. *And Then We Heard the Thunder* is not an artistic triumph, but it is prophetic in its advocacy of violence and organized resistance. Killens' pedestrian prose style and his obvious propagandistic intent weaken the novel, and yet its powerful message cannot be ignored.

The work of Killens is the kind that Mari Evans, in "Contemporary Black Literature," calls "Black writing," as distinguished from "Negro writing." Black writing dismisses white tradition and establishes its own conventions, which revolve around propagandistic purposes. Negro writing, on the other hand, has no specific audience and no purpose other than to be judged by an aesthetic system created by whites. A category of Evans's concept of Black literature is revolutionary writing, which

> serves a vital, threefold purpose: calling the people to view the nature of their oppressor, identifying the oppressor, and advocating freedom by whatever means necessary. Couched in the language of the people, demystified, it does all this with the equivalence of modern war drums. Revolutionary writing is usually alienating to those not involved in understanding the bases for revolution. Since its thrust is not toward such an audience, disavowal and denigration do not diminish its power and effectiveness.[4]

Such a definition tends to justify novels such as *Many Thousands Gone* and *And Then We Heard the Thunder* from a propagandistic viewpoint, but it also suggests that these novels are primarily for black people. The opposite is probably closer to the truth; they are essentially warnings to the white world. The social function is perhaps of more significance than art in this type of fiction, but that does not automatically give artistic stature to Killens' commentary on the racial climate. Later writers such as Williams and Greenlee illustrate that the effectiveness of a propagandistic novel is still largely dependent on its artistry.

A relatively ineffective follower of Killens is Hari Rhodes. In *A Chosen Few* (1965), he echoes the warning of *And Then We Heard the Thunder* as he traces the career of a black serviceman. A story of Negro marines based in Florida following the Korean war, the novel deals with a segregated black unit which is commanded by a white officer. Staff Sergeant Robert Burrell, the protagonist, who is better known as Blood because of his war record in Korea, is ordered to leave his New Jersey base to serve in Montford Point. On his arrival in the South he is arrested for talking to a white waitress. His problems increase as time goes on.

Blood's personal problems become secondary, though, when one of the marines kills the local sheriff in a fight over a black prostitute. The Negro is murdered and his body hung on a flag pole as a symbol of white superiority. The entire black company moves into town to confront the whites. When the townsmen refuse to allow the body to be removed, a race war breaks out. The author explains Blood's reaction to the situation during the heat of the battle.

179

> On Saipan it made some kind of sense, but not here on American
> soil. He took another look at the two dead kids to his left and told
> himself not to be fooled by the changed face of the enemy or the
> difference in color. It became necessary for Blood to believe that
> those white civilians down there were as hostile and as alien as
> any enemy this country had ever fought and had to be dealt with
> accordingly.[5]

That Blood is identifying himself with his country is significant.
He sees himself as a defender of the principles of justice against
the corruptive forces represented by the white racist. Rhodes,
more famous as an actor than a writer, is careful to illustrate
that Blood and his fellow black soldiers are in the right. Violence
is the only thing that the whites respect and the use of it is
necessary to uphold the honor of the United States. The Negroes
symbolize the idealistic principles on which the country is based.
In emphasizing this point, Rhodes, in the manner of Killens,
disregards artistic standards. His purpose is to produce propaganda, and *A Chosen Few* is the competent, but limited, result.
However, most of the militant protest novels are effective in this
respect.

The civil rights movement that was given impetus by the emergence of Martin Luther King provides a framework for several
militant writers to analyze the racial situation of America. Appearing a year before the outstanding novel of Kelley, *A Different
Drummer,* Julian Mayfield's *The Grand Parade* (1961) is a study
of the various factions of a city torn apart by racial strife. The
plot is about the integration of a school, but the author examines
the entire community in an attempt to reveal the nature of prejudice.

The city of Gainesboro is thrown into turmoil by the announce-
ment of plans to integrate Lee Junior High School. The mayor,
Douglas Taylor, hopes to make the integration a reality, partly
from his conviction and partly for the sake of political expediency.
His primary advisor, Alex Kochek, understands the white bigots
and is valuable in helping Taylor communicate with the various
factions. J. D. Carson, a rich white suburbanite, is a political
opponent of the mayor who wants to prevent the integration
of the school as a means of embarrassing Taylor. He therefore
financially supports Clarke Bryant, a professional racist who
fights integration wherever there is a chance for a profit. Bryant,
an outsider, finds local support also in Hank Dean and Lew
Harris. Dean takes up the cause of racism in the hope of achieving

recognition and glory. Harris is afraid of blacks primarily because of the economic threat they represent to him. Mary McCullough, a white prostitute, is only too glad to cooperate with the racists by falsely claiming she was raped by Negroes—thus becoming a living martyr for the cause of segregation.

Mayfield also presents a variety of black characters who become involved in the struggle. Randolph Banks is a young politician who fights for immediate integration, but his wife is primarily concerned with maintaining her social position. His brother, Lonnie, is a handicap to the ambitions of Randolph because of his former affiliation with Marxists. Harold Bishop is an old educator who prefers to accept the terms of the whites rather than to initiate positive action. Reeves Mathews is a young activist minister who believes in non-violent direct action. Chick Bolton is a bitter young militant who advocates violence. Patty Speed, a former mistress of Randolph Banks, is a pragmatist who will use any method to advance the cause of blacks. Mildred Lancaster is the innocent child who is trapped in the middle of the action.

The drama that is enacted in Gainesboro by these participants is typical of those in many American cities since the desegregation ruling in 1954. The White Protection Council, under the direction of Bryant, threatens to stop physically the integration of the school. In retaliation, Bolton organizes a number of black citizens into a militant group with the purpose of confronting the whites. Randolph Banks attempts to stop the militant blacks from interfering by appealing to the influential Patty Speed. She responds by stating that

> '. . . don't you see we aren't getting anywhere your way? There must be another way to fight. I don't want violence, but why turn our backs on it if it's necessary? Don't you see, we can't afford to be the best Christians in the country. We're too poor, too far behind. We've got to fight any way we can.'[6]

The propaganda campaign waged by the racists, the false accusation of rape, the bombing of Negro homes, and the threat of violence at the school, indicate to Patty, and her cohort, Bolton, that peaceful means will not work. Not even Reeves Mathews' plan to have the mayor lead the black children into the school, prevents the white mob from perpetrating violence. They are met by Bolton's contentious aggregation and a riot ensues. Before the police break up the melee, Mayor Taylor is shot to death by Hank Dean, the fanatic who is satisfied with the notoriety the deed will bring him despite the fact that he is arrested and will probably be on trial for his life. Meanwhile, Mildred Lancaster, one of the black students, vows to succeed scholastically as she enters her new school.

It is Chick Bolton and the militants, then, who prevail. The peaceful plans to integrate are ineffective against the white mob that assembles to prevent physically the black students from entering the school. Bolton, however, meets violence with violence and he succeeds in his mission. Mayfield, the author of two accommodationist novels in the fifties, makes it clear in *The Grand Parade* that organized militancy is a necessity in dealing with racism. He is essentially objective in his presentation of the various points of view, though, and even the white racists are described with understanding. None of the black characters is the exemplary type that appears in the apologetic tradition. They are simply people, of various stengths and weaknesses, who have a common goal. Not all of them want to integrate the school for the same reasons, but the integration does represent a form of victory over white oppression.

Chick Bolton and Patty Speed, who emerge as militant rebels, both have shady pasts and a desire for revenge on the white world that has branded them as outcasts. The battle over integration fits into their plans to advance the Negro cause at the expense of white bigots. In analyzing their decision to confront the White Protection Council, Mayfield exposes the wrongs that have been committed against the Negroes in Gainesboro. He demonstrates that violence, under the auspices of organized resistance, is a valid technique for blacks. Concurrently, he illustrates the measures that have been taken to correct the situtation by dedicated people of both races. The emphasis, then, is not just on racism but on the various political and personal motives that function within the community. Although Mayfield deals to a large degree wtih character types rather than with rounded personalities, he makes an effort to explore the complexities of the citizens of a typical American city. His thorough analysis of the various factions and motives is skillfully dramatized. Rising above mere propaganda, the novel stands as a modern landmark in the field of protest fiction.

Mayfield is among the first of the militant writers to illustrate that protest can be handled artistically. Killens, perhaps influenced by *The Grand Parade*, turned out his best novel in his third attempt. 'Sippi (1967) deals with the civil rights struggle in the South. It also depicts the internal struggle for black leadership between the militants and the pacifists. Killens pits the philosophy of King against that of Malcolm X, and the latter emerges as the victor. Militancy is needed to combat the racism that pervades the state of Mississippi, according to the observations of the young protagonist, Charles Chaney.

Charles grows up on the plantation of Colonel Wakefield, who considers himself an enlightened Southern gentleman. Steeped in the racial philosophy of Rudyard Kipling, the Colonel attempts to lessen his burden by sending the youth to a Negro college. Charles gets to know civil rights participants, including the popular David Woodson, who interests him in the non-violent philosophy of King. Charles finds that the movement has even reached Mississippi when he returns home for a visit. His friends are all involved in a drive for voter registration. Not even the violent tactics of the Ku Klux Klan can stop them. A militant organization, the Elders of Protection and Defense, is organized to combat the Klan, but Charles refuses to join until the pacifistic preacher, Woodson, is killed by whites. He then decides to become a militant.

As usual, Killens presents a catalog of injustices against blacks, but he is more subtle than in his earlier novels. The drama involved in the attempt to destroy the Old South, represented by Colonel Wakefield and the Klan, is emphasized in the person of Carrie Lou Wakefield, the Colonel's daughter. The blond girl grows up with Charles Chaney on the plantation. Although tradition demands that she must sever her relationship with the black youth by the time she reaches puberty, Carrie never does. The girl attempts to atone for the sins of her father by taking an active part in the civil rights movement, although she does not understand the crimes of people like the Colonel. Through her association with Charles and other blacks she eventually becomes educated enough to inform her father that Gunga Din and the concept of white superiority died with Kipling. A new era is developing in which blacks are no longer willing to be servants.

The Colonel, of course, does everything in his power to maintain the taboo against the mating of a black male and a white female. He fails in the case of his daughter, though, as she completely rebels from the ways of the Old South. Charles himself learns of the racism of Colonel Wakefield only after he has been away from the plantation for a time. When he learns of his benefactor's treachery, Charles severs all relationship with him, including the financial arrangement. He sets out on his own to face the world. One of his first decisions involves his shift to the side of the militants.

While Killens remains a crude stylist, his third novel is his best. He manages to reflect the racial mood of the sixties. What 'Sippi lacks in art it makes up for in its sociological and historical observations. Essential to the novel is the depiction of the rise of militancy among young blacks. The racism encountered in the South makes this phenomenon inevitable. Even before he is converted to militancy, the protagonist defends Malcolm X when he learns of his assassination. His complete acceptance of a philosophy of violence is inevitable in the Mississippi described by the author.

The influence of Malcolm X, who attempted to organize all of the black people of the world as a means of protection against racism, is summarized in an essay by James Boggs.

> Hundreds of thousands of black men and women who at the time of Malcolm's death . . . had not even reached the stage of reformist activity today consider themselves black revolutionists and regard every word uttered by Brother Malcolm following his break from the Muslims as the gospel truth. Young people from thirteen to thirty play and replay the records of his speeches, study his autobiography, and refuse to attend school or go to work on the anniversary of his birth and assassination. Such has been the tempo of revolutionary development in the United States since 1965.[7]

The kind of revolutionary activity, propagated by Malcolm X, that is depicted in 'Sippi is also an important part of William Mahoney's Black Jacob (1969). The novel probes the political and racial situation in Mississippi during the sixties. In the manner of Killens, the author builds a plot around the struggle of Negroes to obtain equality through voting rights. Again, white racism is shown to be so firmly entrenched that it can be combated only through force.

Jacob Blue, a black doctor in Matchez, Mississippi, astonishes the white population by running for Congress. His announced intention is at first ridiculed by the white leaders, but Blue, with the help of young black radicals who organize the voters, becomes a serious challenger for the political office. The white power structure, though, responds to this threat by springing into action. While a decoy is made by appointing a Negro to a sinecure, the police are instructed to instigate a riot in the ghetto in order to turn public opinion against blacks. The doctor, learning of the plot against him, decides to reciprocate. He joins forces with the militant leaders, Jesse and Raz X, who have their organizations prepared to wage war on the whites. Blue, however, is forced to hold the militants in check when he is caught in a political bind. Manipulated by both the whites and the complacent middle class blacks, the doctor eventually renounces his connection with the latter faction, and runs on a reform platform. Although he publicly identifies with the militants, he loses the election by a very close margin. Shortly after the election Blue is assassinated by a white racist, who is backed by the local white authorities.

Mahoney points out the necessity for a black man to "think black" rather than to try to emulate the corrupt white society. Blue discovers himself only when he denounces the racists and the black moderates, and identifies completely with the young militants. His murder merely emphasizes the validity of the black revolutionary forces. *Black Jacob* is a relatively thorough and objective study of the racial scene in the South. Mahoney, though, depends too much on melodrama, obvious propagandistic passages, and characters who tend to be types rather than individuals. These shortcomings do not allow him to escape entirely from the second rank of the protest novelists. His analytic comments are not completely objectified into art.

The increasing militancy of black writers in the sixties is emphasized by the career of James Baldwin. One of the leaders in the revolt against protest in the early fifties, Baldwin, with *Tell Me How Long the Train's Been Gone* (1968), has come full circle from the literary theory that underlies *Go Tell It on the Mountain*. From a concern with isolated segments of black life, he concentrates in his fourth novel on the problems associated with existence in a racist society. Writing of the reluctance of white people to respect the dignity of blacks, Baldwin, in "Down at the Cross," states that-

> Neither civilized reason nor Christian love would cause any of these people to treat you as they presumably wanted to be treated; only the fear of your power to retaliate would cause them to do that, or to seem to do it, which was (and is) good enough.[8]

The power to retaliate is a basic factor in *Tell Me How Long the Train's Been Gone*. This novel traces the career of Leo Proudhammer, a famous black actor, from his boyhood to his conversion to militancy. As the novel opens, Leo suffers a heart attack at the height of his career. While recuperating, he reflects on his past in a series of extensive flashbacks. The narrative shifts to the protagonist's boyhood and the reader discovers that his youthful days in Harlem are not happy ones. His father turns to alcohol after failing to find a respectable job. His mother tries to hold the family together without much success. Leo turns to Caleb, his older brother, to discover the secrets of life. Their adventures on the streets of Harlem educate the youth to the fact that he is a "nigger" in the eyes of whites, especially the policemen. Baldwin describes Leo's reactions to racism as the boy studies a white man sitting next to him on a bus.

> How could we fox them if we could neither bear to look at them, nor bear it when they looked at us? And who were they, anyway? which was the really terrible, the boomeranging question. And one always felt: maybe they're right. Maybe you are nothing but a nigger, and the life you lead, or the life they make you lead, is the only life you deserve. They say that God said so—and if God said so, then you mean about as much to God as you do to this red-faced, black-haired fat white man. . . .[9]

But Leo is strong enough to escape from the ghetto and the subservient role assigned to him. After Caleb is imprisoned for a crime he did not commit, Leo concentrates on becoming an actor. He eventually becomes associated with an actor's workshop, where he gets a chance to learn the trade. He also meets Barbara, a white girl, and a passionate romance develops. The pressures exerted by white society, though, cause them to separate periodically. As Leo's acting career begins to flourish, Barbara's place is taken by Black Christopher. A Malcolm X figure, Christopher possesses Leo both sexually and intellectually. The militant's attitude is explained to a large degree in a speech, delivered to a white, concerning American history and the idea that most black entertainers develop their talents in church activities because religion is the only thing that blacks are allowed to have.

> 'I'm not blaming you. . . . You had a good thing going for you. You'd done already killed off most of the Indians and you'd robbed them of their land and now you had all these blacks working for you for nothing. . . . . So you gave us Jesus. And told us it was the Lord's will that we should be toting the barges and lifting the bales while you all sat on your big, fat, white behinds and got rich. . . . . That's what happened and you all is still the same. You ain't changed at all, except to get worse. You want to tell me different?'[10]

Under the tutelage of the younger man, Leo gradually accepts the militant philosophy. Christopher convinces him that Afro-Americans are doomed to extinction in the United States unless they rise to the occasion and answer a call to arms. Leo, as he recovers from his illness, decides that he will forsake his profession to join Black Christopher and the militants when the word is given. He realizes that he has devoted his life to the achievement of personal success without considering the fact that his race is still the downtrodden in America. Convinced that the whites plan to keep them subjugated, or perhaps even exterminate all Negroes, Leo Proudhammer embraces militancy.

In Baldwin's fourth novel he rejects Christian religion as well as his early literary tenets. The protagonist's close relationship to his brother is finally terminated when Caleb becomes a minister. Leo's own experiences have shown him that religion is not the answer to the problems of the black man in the modern world. Feeling that he has been discarded by his father and by Caleb, and unable to stand the pressure of life with Barbara, Leo turns to Black Christopher, who is indeed a black savior from Leo's viewpoint. Christopher becomes, in essence, a combination lover-brother-father-minister to the protagonist. Fortified by the strength that Christopher supplies, Leo lives up to his name by becoming himself a proud black militant.

Although *Tell Me How Long the Train's Been Gone* is an overtly propagandistic novel, it is Baldwin's best since *Go Tell It on the Mountain*. The Harlem scenes especially are written with a poignancy that enables the reader to grasp the essence of the black man's existence in a white man's world. Baldwin tends to reveal his own search for security as the narrative progresses and Black Christopher, the redeemer, emerges as the dominant figure. Yet Baldwin manages to remain in control of his material to a greater extent than he does in *Another Country*. The conclusion marks a logical progression in the life of the protagonist, who finally matches his professional accomplishments with a spiritual triumph.

John A. Williams, who earlier in the decade had helped to popularize the apologetic protest novel, also turns to militant fiction in the late sixties. *The Man Who Cried I Am* (1967) reveals a government plan to exterminate the Negro population of the United States. The only hope of thwarting this plan lies in making the blacks aware of the danger and organizing them into a counteractive force. This job is relegated to the militant Minister Q, Williams' version of Malcolm X.

The protagonist, Max Reddick, is a black novelist who, at the age of forty-nine, is trying to discover the meaning of his life before his imminent death. Throughout his life Reddick has struggled to retain his patience in the face of racism. Becoming a successful writer opens up opportunities for him, but also reveals new ranges of bigotry and false promises made to blacks. This extends to the President of the United States himself, who employs Max for a time as a speechwriter. Disillusioned by America, Max travels to Holland to visit his estranged wife. While in Europe, the writer learns of the death of Harry Ames, a former compatriot, and novelist whose career resembles that of Richard Wright. In checking into the affairs of his friends, Max discovers King Alfred—a plan by the American government to rid itself of the threat to its security represented by the increasing militancy of blacks. Ames was murdered because of his knowledge of King Alfred and Max Reddick is also killed by government agents, but not before he informs Minister Q of King Alfred.

Reddick's final act is a matter of necessity in terms of his racial loyalty, but it is also the culmination of a developing militant philosophy. Before his discovery of King Alfred, he explains to his wife that

'The law . . . is for the privileged and if you're white in America, you are privileged. We hope for the law to protect us, but it doesn't. I've seen the White House break laws, and I am not about to console myself that if brought before the court for being in a street fight, I can count on a fair dispensation of justice. The other side has guns, . . . and power, everything serious killers should have to do their jobs. Without law on my side, I become the law, my guns are the law, and the only law people in any nation live by is the law of force or the threat of force.[11]

The plot to exterminate Negroes tends to validate the power concept of the protagonist. Weakened by his illness and shocked by King Alfred, Reddick lives long enough to assert himself, to call Minister Q, the Black Power leader. For years Minister Q has been preaching about the treachery of the white man and the need for armed revolt. Reddick had formerly regarded this kind of attitude as too radical, but in the end he realizes that the militant leader is the one person who can possibly save the Afro-Americans. Although his personal commitment of militancy occurs too late to allow him to organize effectively and warn his fellow blacks, he has time to recognize his mistake and to proclaim his new allegiance.

In Minister Q, Williams has created a militant black in the image of Malcolm X. In contrast to Reverend Paul Durrell who, in the manner of Martin Luther King, calls for economic boycotts as an assertion of black power, Minister Q preaches hatred and distrust of whites. According to the militant, they have stolen black history and everything else of value the black man has had. The black women have been raped and the men emasculated by the oppressive system under which they are forced to live. Minister Q does not want integration. Rather, he wants the land that he feels is owed to blacks, for the purpose of creating a separate black nation. Until this is accomplished, he advises Negroes to be proud of their heritage and warns them to be prepared to defend themselves against the barbarity of the whites.

Williams, who has since written a book devoted to the debunking of Martin Luther King, *The King That God Couldn't Save* (1970) makes a strong argument for the militant philosophy of Malcolm X in *The Man Who Cried I Am*. Although there is some attempt made to objectify the material, the propagandistic elements tend to dominate. Williams, supposedly for effect, overstates his case in the concluding part of the novel. In fact, as the reader travels through the fifties and early sixties from the vantage point of the protagonist, much of the history of the period is reinterpreted in racist terms. The disclosure of King Alfred, then, is not such a shock after all. Williams has been preparing for it all along, but Reddick, with his faith in the American system, is too blind to see the truth until it is too late. In presenting his pessimistic view of the racial situation Williams is fulfilling the role of the revolutionary writer to the hilt. Literature becomes, in a sense, secondary to propaganda. But Williams, like Baldwin in *Tell Me How Long the Train's Been Gone*, is endowed with enough talent to be at least partially successful from an aesthetic point of view. He is able to transform a racist view of history into an entertaining novel, which should not be ignored in terms of its veracity.

If Williams disturbed a few people with his version of American racism in *The Man Who Cried I Am*, his fifth novel of the decade is perhaps even more shocking. *Sons of Darkness, Sons of Light* (1969) presents violence not just as a means of protection, or as an outlet for frustration, but as a means of bringing about important changes in the policy of the government. Violence is used as both a retaliatory measure and as the primary aspect of a revolution.

Gene Browning, a member of the Institute for Racial Justice, a moderate civil rights organization, has reached a turning point in his life. He realizes that he has been a victim of the American way of life that, in reality, promotes organized racial discrimination. When Carrigan, a police detective, kills a black youth, Browning is assigned by the organization to raise money for the legal proceedings, thus giving him an opportunity to put into action an individual plan of revenge. He decides to embezzle a portion of the money he collects, to pay for the murder of Carrigan. Williams describes Browning's feelings by stating that he

> . . . wanted people to know that if they were willing to take black lives the way they had been, then they also ought to know that they had to forfeit their own. Once everyone understood that, things would improve.[12]

With this view in mind, the protagonist contacts an old friend who has connections in organized crime. After arranging for the murder, Browning departs on his fund raising excursion. In his travels around the country he learns of some of the revolutionary activity that is beginning to take shape. He is informed by Dr. Jessup of a training program for armed revolution that is under way in the hills of California. Jessup, a respected black doctor, insists that militancy is the answer.

> '. . . I've listened to all the arguments. We're on our way. We are going to accomplish in two weeks what IRJ hasn't been able to accomplish in fifteen years. We are going to nullify industry and police power in the Southland. Then we'll get what we want, which is jobs, a clear untempered political maneuverability, and a few other things that'll come later. . . . .'[13]

Jessup is only one of the militants with ambitious plans. Morris Greene and Leonard Trotman devise a number of demands that they hope to see enforced as the result of a series of explosions that are due to take place in New York on Labor Day. The police, meanwhile, angered by the murder of Carrigan, move in on the ghettos with the idea of attacking any Negro who is left unprotected. Their Operation Black Out, however, is met with organized resistance on the part of blacks who have been trained by militant leaders. With the police occupied by snipers and guerilla warfare, the strategic bridges and buildings in the New York area are blown up. The result is a race war, as white mobs retaliate against Negroes. In this chaotic atmosphere, the family of Gene Browning prepares to defend itself, fortified by the presence and weapons of Woody Chance, a white youth who dates Browning's daughter.

The single violent act initiated by Gene Browning, who thinks of himself as a racial moderate, sets off a series of violent events that is climaxed by the bombings and the race war on the Labor Day Weekend of 1973. Browning discovers enough about the revolution, though, to realize that his act is of little significance in the large scale operation that is developing throughout the country. He assumes the role of a metaphysical rebel who consciously tries to change the injustice of society by an individual deed of violence. Browning is outdated in his approach to the solution of racial problems, however, for it is the revolutionaries who are in vogue. It is only through organization that racism can be effectively combated.

The novel, set in the explosive America of 1973, portrays with vivid realism the hatred that results in mass violence. The emotional tension that exists between white bigots and black militants is contrasted to the professional attitude taken towards violence by Mantini, the former Mafia chieftain, and Itzhak Hod, the hired killer. To Mantini, murder is strictly a matter of business. To Hod, the murder of Carrigan is a means of earning money to get back to Israel. He rationalizes his action by considering that as a Jew, he, too, has been persecuted by people like Carrigan. In fact, to complete his objective form of revenge, he decides to kill Herman Mahler, a white man who had been freed from a charge of murder in connection with the death of three Negro girls. While Hod decides to make his own laws and exterminate a guilty person, in the manner of Gene Browning, his decree is dispassionate and based only on a curious desire to see justice discharged. Browning's decision is more emotional and is also based on the vague hope of producing a change. To the black militants, however, the death of whites is a means of channeling their hatred into a constructive action which is itself a means of producing the change in the racial policies of the country—the change that Browning optimistically expects the whites to initiate.

Williams, in advocating the militant action of the revolutionaries, is nevertheless relatively successful from an artistic viewpoint. He has the ability to reflect the racial mood of the times in a style that is fast-paced and that skillfully exploits the sensational elements without deteriorating into bitter melodrama. Williams manages to reveal the human elements involved in the catastrophic events, so that even the minor characters, such as Mantini, Hod, and Carrigan, are presented with enough compassion and profundity to make them come alive. While the cause of the militants is justified, they are shown to be individuals with unique problems and weaknesses. It is only through an organized effort to defeat the oppressive society that black strength is created. In the case of Gene Browning, his personal problems are resolved only when he decides to work against the racist policies of America without the backing of the conciliatory Institute of Racial Justice. Recognition of his own ineffectiveness in racial matters is the first step in the process of self-discovery.

Sons of Darkness, Sons of Light is a prophetic novel that is being enacted on a small scale in the years following its publication. It illustrates a theory propounded by Frantz Fanon which suggests that violence tends to unify an oppressed people. From an individual point of view, it acts as a cleansing force which frees a person from his despair at watching the world go by without doing anything to stop the oppressive forces that work against him. Violence in the face of oppression restores self-respect.[14]

This idea is one of the basic assumptions of Sam Greenlee's *The Spook Who Sat by the Door* (1969). While violence on an organized basis is shown to be an effective force against white oppression, the author also demonstrates James Baldwin's thesis that most whites in America do not recognize the existence of Negroes, except when they are an inconvenience, because they are afraid of what a knowledge of blacks will reveal about themselves. By clinging to myths of their own generosity and superiority, they are able to justify their ignorance of black psychology. Blacks, on the other hand, know much more about the nature of whites, simply because their existence often depends on this knowledge.[15]

Greenlee's novel depicts an organized revolution initiated by a black man who is hired by the Central Intelligence Agency merely as a showpiece. His job is to sit by the door of a top official to indicate that the agency is integrated. From this sinecure, Dan Freeman, capitalizing on the blindness and stereotyped opinions of whites, is able to gather the information necessary to launch a major revolution.

The CIA, forced to integrate because of political pressure, intends to make it merely a token integration—but only after embarking on a program designed to eliminate all blacks from the agency. It is only when Freeman proves his remarkable capabilities that he is assigned to his public relations position. He is nevertheless regarded as a mere figurehead, a "house nigger," by the organization, and the general who directs the agency adopts Freeman as a personal servant. Playing to perfection the role of a faithful retainer, the former social worker takes advantage of his invisibility to learn the secrets of the agency. Greenlee indicates Freeman's easy task of conforming to the role expected by whites as he listens to one of the general's typical speeches.

> 'Honest sweat and toil. Pull yourself up by the bootstraps like the immigrants. These demonstrations and sit-ins stir up needless emotion. Your people must demonstrate a respect for law and order, earn the respect and affection of whites. Take yourself as an example: a fine natural athlete; no denying your people are great athletes.'
> 'Yes,' said Freeman,'and we can sing and dance, too.'[16]

The general, in his obtuseness, agrees, but admits to an intellectual and cultural gap that will take years to close. Freeman stifles his anger and thinks ahead to the day when whites will be forced to recognize blacks as individuals—even if it is from behind a gun barrel.

After several years of role playing in the CIA, Freeman returns to Chicago presumably to resume his former job as a social worker, but he uses this position for other purposes. By winning the confidence of the Cobras, a militant black gang from the ghetto, Freeman is able to organize them into an efficient army. He teaches them black history and culture, guerilla tactics, and the effective use of propaganda. He instills in them pride and self-respect, and channels their energies toward the goal of combating the police and armed forces of the white power structure. The Cobras, converted into Freedom Fighters, many with talents that need only the direction and encouragement of a strong leader to be put to use, respond with ideas and plans of their own. In the meantime, Freeman plays a passive role among his white compatriots, waiting for the chance to spring his troops into action.

The spark is supplied in a typical fashion when a white policeman kills a black youth. In the ensuing riot, Freeman plays the role of a peacemaker. When the National Guard is brought into the ghetto, Freedom Fighters go into action, as their leader watches with satisfaction. Guerilla tactics are used effectively to immobilize the troops. With the success of the Chicago encounter, Freeman spreads his revolution to other major cities. Members of the underground army are sent to train the street gangs in the same way that the former intelligence agent had organized the Cobras. White officials continue to look for the white person who is responsible for the planning of the revolution, refusing to suspect Freeman or any other Negro of having the knowledge and intelligence to put such an effective operation in motion. Freeman is finally betrayed, though, by a former girl friend, who aspires to be a member of the black bourgeoisie, and a black detective who is satisfied with being a part of the white power system. But even as Freeman is dying from a bullet wound, he realizes that the revolutionary movement no longer needs him in order to be successful.

While violence is a major aspect of the revolution, Freeman's object, as revealed in his conversations with some of his cohorts, is not necessarily to defeat whites in combat but to force them to make a choice between playing political games on an international level or in doing something about racism on the home front. He is not interested in integration as much as he is in getting the whites to let down the gates surrounding the ghetto and give the blacks an equal opportunity to make it on their own. In order to succeed, he is willing to keep his forces busy with their guerilla tactics in every major city in the country. In the meantime, in his role as a social worker, he remains behind the mask of passivity, watching the whites try to solve the problems of the ghetto in their usual inefficacious manner. Their last resort is always to bring in the police and the troops to keep the disturbances within the black neighborhood, but that is when the Freedom Fighters do their job of neutralizing the force of the white military-industrial complex.

Dan Freeman is the prototype of a Bigger Thomas who has progressed from an ineffectual metaphysical rebel to an efficient militant revolutionary who has the power of throwing the entire country into a panic. The figure of Bigger has developed from a man driven mad by frustration and hate, as in Offord's *The White Face*, to the student rebels of *'Sippi*, the non-violent activists of *A Different Drummer*, the individual rebels, as in *Of Love and Dust*, the embryonic militants of *The Grand Parade*, and, finally, to the revolutionaries of *Tell Me How Long the Train's Been Gone*, *Sons of Darkness*, *Sons of Light*, and *The Spook Who Sat By the Door*. Sam Greenlee moves beyond the militancy of a Malcolm X in his creation of Dan Freeman, who does not just attempt to organize blacks but who is able to produce underground armies capable of holding their own against white military and police power.

Greenlee's novel may be considered an outline of action for black militants, or a warning to white America about what the future holds if the general trends in the country continue. It may be regarded as merely an "entertainment" in the tradition of Graham Greene, Ian Fleming, or Len Deighton; but basically *The Spook Who Sat By the Door* is a relatively successful book on both a propagandistic and an artistic level, although with more emphasis on the former. Greenlee epitomizes the racial attitudes of the country in a style that is, for the most part, objective and almost comic in tone. The novel is somewhat reminiscent of Ellison's *Invisible Man* in its portrayal of the invisibility of Negroes. Greenlee does not maintain control of his material at all times; his bitterness is revealed in verbal tirades, and, on occasion, in authorial comments that tend to detract from the objective framework of the novel. Perhaps the weakest aspect, though, is the shallow stereotyping of the white characters. The superman exploits of the hero are made ridiculously easy because of the fact that he is dealing with intellectually and morally blind people. Although the book is generally inferior to the later work of John A. Williams, it is destined to be more popular merely because of its simplicity. Greenlee tends to reduce his characters to comic book caricatures. The result, though, is a book that may take its place with *Uncle Tom's Cabin* and *Native Son* as an effective exposé of American racial attitudes and practices.

The militant protest novels of the sixties indicate that the social implications of black literature are of prime importance, but that within the propagandistic context there is room for art. Kelley, Mayfield, Baldwin, Williams, and Greenlee illustrate that significant novels can be produced within the genre, but it is mainly the message of these books that American society cannot afford to ignore. The contents are a reflection of what is happening in the country and what may occur in the future. The fact that the majority of the best black novelists of the decade expressed themselves in a militant vein is an indication that racial conditions will have to change. One can only hope, in considering *Sons of Darkness*, *Sons of Light* or *The Spook Who Sat By the Door*, that life does not follow art.

Conclusion

The Negro novel, from *Native Son* to the militant protest of Williams and Greenlee, places a major emphasis on social criticism, primarily from a racial standpoint. Whether by the blatant propagandistic tactics of Wright or the subtle condemnations of Ellison, white American society is the primary target. Wright, in *Native Son*, introduced the psychological aspects of racism and since 1940 black novelists have modified or elaborated on this basic theme. The emphasis in these novels, generally, is the response of blacks to the racism they encounter. Some of the characters react violently, some with deliberation and organization, and others merely accept it as a part of their heritage. There are distinct behavioral patterns in each fictional category, as well as concomitant motifs.

The major element of the Wrightian protest novel is the violence committed by a metaphysical rebel. The seemingly purposeless acts of these social misfits are replaced in later protest fiction by violence that is directed at the white oppressor. The rebels, in essence, tend to mature over the years into militants who represent a threat to white society. Thus Wright's Bigger Thomas develops into Greenlee's Dan Freeman. The psychological condition of the protagonist changes from that of a subhuman environmental product to an angry radical who is representative of the deprived but awakened masses of the modern world. The familiar flight motif of the Wrightian fiction gives way to the confrontation between the races. In the later protest novels the protagonists no longer flee from the white mob. They meet force with force, and often are the perpetrators of violence. A remaining aspect of Wrightian protest, though, is the guilt of the white society of America—a society that allows racism to deprive Negroes of their human rights.

While the Wrightian protest novel technically disappeared, it lived on in altered forms. Assimilationism, however, after becoming relatively popular from about 1945-1956, played almost no part in later fictional trends. During its era of prominence, when Willard Motley, Ann Petry, William Gardner Smith, Chester Himes, James Baldwin and Richard Wright all worked in the field, assimilationism stressed the psychological dilemmas of whites who were trapped by the stifling conventions of society. In this sense it mirrored the plight of the Negro masses. The trend was largely an attempt to expose the shortcomings of a society in which even white people are repressed. Novels like Motley's *Knock on Any Door* (1947), Petry's *Country Place* (1947), and Smith's *Anger at Innocence* (1950), illustrated the depravity that existed in the white world as a result of ignorance, poverty, and narrow-mindedness. However, this kind of social criticism was forsaken in the late fifties when black authors joined the renewed struggle for civil rights and black pride. The same writers who previously wrote about white characters turned to racial protest fiction in the sixties.

One of the areas that prospered by the movement toward racial equality, originally sparked by Martin Luther King, was apologetic protest. The formula featuring an idealized black hero who is victimized by a white mob, an overworked motif of the trend, eventually became obsolete in apologetic fiction. In the fifties and sixties the protagonist develops different dimensions, and becomes essentially an average individual who rebels against white authority. Violence remains an important element but it is secondary to the psychological effects of discrimination. Negroes are victims of mental anguish and economic exploitation more often than of lynch mobs. Perhaps the most common aspect is the sexual conflict between the races. The racial mythology concerning blacks, and the concomitant fears it awakens in whites, is a major theme of the vast majority of apologetic protest novels, including Wright's *The Long Dream* (1958), Williams' *Night Song* (1960), Gaines' *Of Love and Dust* (1967), Baldwin's *Another Country* (1962), and Yerby's *Speak Now* (1969). The exploitation of black females by white males is stressed in novels such as Savoy's *Alien Land* (1949), Vroman's *Esther* (1963), Sarah Wright's *This Child's Gonna Live* (1969), as well as *Of Love and Dust*. The psychological pressures surrounding a black and white sexual relationship is the most popular motif of apologetic fiction. The basic conflicts evoked by miscegenation are at the root of much of the country's racial problems, and black novelists have continually attempted to prove it.

Accommodationism, which came into popularity in the early fifties, also has had a tendency to concentrate on the psychological aspects of racism. However, the sexual theme is stressed less than the quest for a racial identity in a society that proclaims that "white is right." From the protagonist of Ellison's *Invisible Man* (1952) to Paule Marshall's intriguing portrait of Merle Kinbona in *The Chosen Place, the Timeless People* (1969), the emphasis has been on the necessity of maintaining or establishing dignity in the face of corroding discriminatory practices that tend to mold Negroes into stereotyped inferiors. As early as Dorothy West's *The Living Is Easy* (1948) the psychological problem of adjusting to white society was shown to be a self-effacing process. Cleo Judson is the prototype of the black woman who is so enamored of the white world that, in her attempt to imitate it, she learns to detest people with black skins. A similar theme is portrayed in Redding's *Stranger and Alone* (1950), and Himes' *The Third Generation* (1954). Novels such as *Invisible Man* and Wright's *Lawd Today* (1963) demonstrate that self-effacement is implicit in playing the roles designated by white authority.

In the sixties the trend was continued in somewhat altered form by the existential novelists. Cecil Brown, Bill Gunn, Carlene Hatcher Polite, Robert Boles, and Charles Wright are among the writers who concentrate on depicting a protagonist who is hopelessly lost in the maze of the complicated modern world. The characters drift aimlessly through life with only a vague idea of somehow attaining a satisfactory place in society—without being fully aware of what such a position would consist. A major factor in these novels, though, is a concern for racial pride. If the protagonists are lost they are also conscious of a desire to identify with other black people in their common heritage. While this impulse remains uncertain in some of the fiction it is a major concern in such accommodationist works as Demby's *The Catacombs* (1962), Simmons' *Man Walking on*

199

Eggshells (1962), and Marshall's *The Chosen Place, the Timeless People*. The latter especially is representative of a striving towards identification with African ancestry, without embracing the militant philosophy that often accompanies black nationalism. In the later accommodationist novels, though, militancy is shown to be an active force in the black community. The fact that the protagonists reject extremism is not representative of a total victory for a moderate or conservative approach to racial problems, since the decisions grow increasingly more difficult in the fiction of the sixties.

More typical of the period is the militant protest novel, which centers basically on armed confrontation between the races. The first wave of militant fiction depicted violence as a necessary means of defense against the violent actions of whites. Smith's *South Street* (1954), Killens' *Youngblood* (1954), *And Then We Heard the Thunder* (1962), *'Sippi* (1967), and Mayfield's *Grand Parade* (1961) attempt to reveal that retaliatory force is essential to the protection of black people. The trend in more recent years, though, has been the portrayal of revolution climaxed by Greenlee's *The Spook Who Sat by the Door* (1969) and Williams' *Sons of Darkness, Sons of Light* (1969). The stress in these novels is not primarily the overthrow of American cities in a full-scale war, but on the use of force as a bargaining factor in demands for the immediate enactment of civil rights and the delivery of substantial material possessions to Negroes.

Greenlee and Williams have been leaders in a militant literary movement that has capitalized on the social atmosphere of the time. Books in a similar vein by white novelists include *Horn* by D. Keith Mano (1969), Edwin Corley's *Siege* (1969), Fletcher Knebel's *Trespass* (1969), Hank Lopez' *Afro-6* (1969), Dan Brennan's *Insurrection* (1970), Richard Gallagher's *Doomsday Committee* (1970), and Bruce Douglas Reeve's *Man on Fire* (1971). The message communicated by militant protest fiction is that time has run out for America. For too long it has legislated only token measures against racism while concentrating on policing the world. The young black activists are not content to display the patience of most of their forbears. The only way to get immediate response from the white establishment, to the militant protagonists, is to shock it into recognition through violence. The militant protest novel, then, reflects the explosive racial situation in the country and serves as a warning to what the future may hold.

The social function of the modern Negro novel, inaugurated by *Native Son,* is dominant in the militant novels of the sixties, as well as in most of the other fiction since 1940. There is little to indicate that this emphasis will be changed in the future.

The novel has traditionally been used as a vehicle for social criticism. Black novelists, especially in the sixties, have illustrated that the tradition can still be effective for propagandistic purposes. They have demonstrated also that literature does not necessarily have to be measured by some arbitrary demarcation between propaganda and art. The two elements can be merged effectively into a novel. The major test for a black writer at the present is how well he can blend social protest into an objective narrative. No novel by an Afro-American has eclipsed *Invisible Man,* but several have neared the same level in recent years.

Notes Chapter I

[1]Sterling Brown, *The Negro in American Fiction* (New York: Antheneum, 1969), p. 28.

[2]William Wells Brown, *Clotel, or the President's Daughter* (New York: Collier Books, 1970), p. 177.

[3]Lorenzo Dow Turner, *Anti-Slavery Sentiment in American Literature Prior to 1865* (Port Washington, New York: Kennikat Press, 1966), p. 78.

[4]Theodore L. Gross, "The Negro in Literature of the Reconstruction," *Images of the Negro in American Literature*, ed. by Seymour L. Gross and John Edward Hardy (University of Chicago Press, 1960), p. 57.

[5]Hugh M. Gloster, *Negro Voices in American Fiction* (Chapel Hill: University of North Carolina Press, 1965), p. 31.

[6]Gloster, p. 33.

[7]S. Brown, p. 106.

[8]J. Saunders Redding, "The Negro in Relation to His Roots," *The American Negro Writer and His Roots* (New York: American Society of African Culture, 1960), p. 4.

[9]David Littlejohn, *Black on White* (New York: The Viking Press, 1966), p. 35.

[10]James Weldon Johnson, *The Autobiography of an Ex-Coloured Man, Three Negro Classics* (New York: Avon, 1969), p. 403.

[11]Johnson, p. 485.

[12]Johnson, p. 486.

[13]Gloster, p. 160.

[14]Robert A. Bone, *The Negro Novel in America* (revised ed., New Haven: Yale University Press, 1965), p. 98.

[15]Walter White, *The Fire in the Flint* (New York: The New American Library, 1969), p. 126.

Notes Chapter II

[1]Dan McCall, *The Example of Richard Wright* (New York: Harcourt, Brace and World, 1969), p. 41.

[2]Irving Howe, *A World More Attractive* (New York: Horizon Press, 1963), p. 100.

[3]Richard Wright, *White Man, Listen!* (Garden City, New York: Anchor, 1964), p. 105.

[4]Richard Wright, *Native Son* (New York: Harper, 1966), pp. 13-14.

[5]Horace R. Cayton, "Ideological Forces in the Work of Negro Writers," *Anger and Beyond: The Negro Writer in the United States*, ed. Herbert Hill (New York: Harper and Row, 1966), pp. 42-43.

[6]Wright, *Native Son*, pp. 22-23.

[7]Wright, *Native Son*, pp. 224-225.

[8]Wright, *Native Son*, p. 367.

[9]Wright, *Native Son*, p. 370.

[10]Wright, *Native Son*, p. 392.

[11]Edward Margolies, *Native Son: A Critical Study of Twentieth Century Negro American Authors* (Philadelphia: J. B. Lippincott, 1968), pp. 81-82.

[12]Albert Camus, *The Rebel: An Essay on Man in Revolt*, trans. Anthony Bower (New York: Vintage, 1956), pp. 23-24.

[13]Wright, *Native Son,* p. 368.

[14]James Baldwin, *Notes of a Native Son* (New York: Bantam, 1964), p. 31.

[15]Richard Wright, "How Bigger Was Born," *Black Voices: An Anthology of Afro-American Literature,* ed. Abraham Chapman (New York: Mentor, 1968), p. 560.

Notes Chapter III

[1]Carl Offord, *The White Face* (New York: Robert M. McBridge, 1943), p. 175.

[2]Offord, pp. 312-313.

[3]Chester Himes, *If He Hollers Let Him Go* (New York: Berkley, 1964), p. 7.

[4]Margolies, *Native Son*, p. 90.

[5]Himes, *If He Hollers Let Him Go*, p. 122.

[6]Himes, p. 177.

[7]Ann Petry, *The Street* (Boston: Houghton Mifflin, 1946), pp. 168-169.

[8]Nancy M. Tischler, *Black Masks: Negro Characters in Modern Southern Fiction* (University Park: Pennsylvania State University Press, 1969), p. 65.

[9]Willard Motley, *Knock on Any Door* (New York: Signet, 1962), p. 460.

Notes Chapter IV

[1]Will Thomas, *God is for White Folks* (New York: Creative Age, 1947), p. 227.

[2]Lionel Trilling, *The Liberal Imagination: Essays on Literature and Society*, (Garden City, New York: Doubleday Anchor, 1950), pp. 208-215.

[3]Bone, *The Negro Novel in America*, p. 167.

Notes Chapter V

[1]Baldwin, *Notes of a Native Son*, p. 17.

[2]William Gardner Smith, "The Negro Writer: Pitfalls and Compensations," *Phylon*, Vol. XI, No. 4 (1950), p. 298.

[3]J. Saunders Redding, *On Being Negro in America* (New York: Bantam, 1964), p. 14.

[4]Redding, *Stranger and Alone* (New York: Harcourt Brace, 1950), p. 197.

[5]Alain Locke, "Inventory at Mid-Century: A Review of the Literature of the Negro for 1950." *Phylon*, Vol. XII, No. 1 (1951), p. 6.

[6]Bone, *The Negro Novel in America*, p. 195.

[7]Owen Dodson, *When Trees Were Green* (New York: Popular Library, 1964), p. 118.

[8]Ralph Ellison, *Invisible Man* (New York: Signet, 1963), pp. 19-20.

[9]Ellison, p. 35.

[10]Ellison, p. 86-88.

[11]Ellison, p. 440.

[12]James Baldwin, *Go Tell It on the Mountain* (New York: Dell, 1969), p. 33.

[13]Margolies, *Native Sons*, p. 106.

[14]Marcus Klein, *After Alienation: American Novels in Mid-Century* (Cleveland, Meridian, 1965), p. 179.

[15]Richard Wright, *The Outsider* (New York: Perennial Library, 1965), p. 143.

[16]Russell Carl Brignano, *Richard Wright: An Introduction to the Man and His Work* (University of Pittsburgh Press, 1970), pp. 163-164.

[17]Gwendolyn Brooks, *Maud Martha* (New York: Harper, 1953), p. 163.

[18]Chester Himes, *The Third Generation* (New York: Signet, 1964), p. 233.

[19]Julian Mayfield, *The Hit* (New York: Vanguard Press, 1957), p. 146.

Notes Chapter VI

[1]Margolies, *Native Sons*, p. 116.

[2]Ann Petry, *The Narrows* (Boston: Houghton Mifflin, 1953), p. 145.

[3]Richard Wright, *The Long Dream* (New York: Ace Books, 1958), p. 62.

[4]John Oliver Killens, *Youngblood* (New York: Trident Press, 1966), p. 475.

[5]William Gardner Smith, *South Street* (New York: Farrar, Straus and Young, 1954), p. 195.

Notes Chapter VII

[1]Charles Wright, *The Messenger* (New York: Crest, 1964), p. 125.

[2]C. Wright, p. 122.

[3]Bill Gunn, *All The Rest Have Died* (New York: Delacorte Press, 1964), p. 212.

[4]Carlene Hatcher Polite, *The Flagellants* (New York: Farrar, Straus, and Giroux, 1967), p. 188.

[5]Frantz Fanon, *The Wretched of the Earth*, trans. Constance Farrington (New York: Grove Press, 1968), p. 69.

[6]Kristin Hunter, *God Bless the Child* (New York: Bantam, 1967), p. 277.

[7]Hunter, *God Bless the Child*, p. 268.

[8]Hunter, *The Landlord* (New York: Avon, 1969), p. 152.

[9]Hunter, *The Landlord*, p. 271.

Notes Chapter VIII

[1]Calvin G. Hernton, *Sex and Racism in America* (New York: Grove Press, 1966), p. 176.

[2]John A. Williams, *Night Song* (New York: Dell, 1963), pp. 142-143.

[3]Ernest J. Gaines, *Catherine Carmier* (New York: Atheneum, 1967), p. 175.

[4]Gaines, *Of Love and Dust* (New York: Bantam, 1969), p. 264.

Notes Chapter IX

[1]John Oliver Killens, *Black Man's Burden* (New York: Pocket Books, 1969), pp. 120-121.

[2]William Melvin Kelley, *A Different Drummer* (New York: Bantam, 1964). p. 117.

[3]Killens, *And Then We Heard the Thunder* (New York: Pocket Cardinal, 1964), p. 497.

[4]Mari Evans, "Contemporary Black Literature," *Black World*, No. 8 (June 1970), p. 93.

[5]Hari Rhodes, *A Chosen Few* (New York: Bantam, 1969), p. 243.

[6]Julian Mayfield, *The Grand Parade* (New York: Paperback Library, 1963), p. 274.

[7]James Boggs, "The Influence of Malcolm X on the Political Consciousness of Black Americans," *Malcolm X: The Man and His Times*, ed. John Henrick Clarke (Toronto: Collier-Macmillan, 1969), p. 43.

[8]Baldwin, *The Fire Next Time* (New York: Dell, 1964), p. 34.

[9]Baldwin, *Tell Me How Long The Train's Been Gone* (New York: Dell, 1969), pp. 172-173.

[10]Baldwin, *Tell Me How Long The Train's Been Gone*, p. 355.

[11]John A. Williams, *The Man Who Cried I Am* (New York: Signet, 1968), p. 294.

[12]Williams, *Sons of Darkness, Sons of Light* (Boston: Little, Brown, 1969), p. 23.

[13]Williams, *Sons of Darkness, Sons of Light*, p. 81.

[14]Fanon, *The Wretched of the Earth*, p. 94.

[15]Baldwin, *The Fire Next Time*, pp. 135-136.

[16]Sam Greenlee, *The Spook Who Sat By the Door* (New York: Bantam, 1970), p. 32.

Bibliography

Baldwin, James. *The Fire Next Time*. New York: Dell, 1964.

_____. *Go Tell It on the Mountain*. New York: Dell, 1969.

_____. *Notes of a Native Son*. New York: Bantam, 1964.

_____. *Tell Me How Long the Train's Been Gone*. New York, Dell, 1969.

Boggs, James. "The Influence of Malcolm X on the Political Consciousness of Black Americans." *Malcolm X: The Man and His Times*. ed. John Henrick Clarke. Toronto: Collier-Macmillan, 1969. 50-55.

Bone, Robert A. *The Negro Novel in America*. rev. ed. New Haven: Yale University Press, 1965.

Brignano, Russell Carl. *Richard Wright: An Introduction to the Man and His Work*. University of Pittsburgh Press, 1970.

Brooks, Gwendolyn. *Maud Martha*. New York: Harper, 1953.

Brown, Sterling. *The Negro in American Fiction*. New York: Atheneum, 1969.

Brown, William Wells. *Clotel, or the President's Daughter*, New York: Collier Books, 1970.

Camus, Albert. *The Rebel: An Essay on Man in Revolt*. trans. Anthony Bower. New York: Vantage, 1956.

Cayton, Horace R. "Ideological Forces in the Work of Negro Writers." *Anger and Beyond: The Negro Writer in the United States*. ed. Herbert Hill. New York: Harper & Row, 1966. 37-50.

Dodson, Owen. *When Trees Were Green*. New York: Popular Library, 1964.

Ellison Ralph. *Invisible Man*. New York: Signet, 1963.

Evans, Mari. "Contemporary Black Literature." *Black World*. No. 8, (June, 1970), 4.

Fanon, Frantz. *The Wretched of the Earth*. trans. Constance Farrington, New York: Grove Press, 1968.

Gaines, Ernest J. *Catherine Carmier*. New York: Atheneum, 1967.

_____. *Of Love and Dust*. New York: Bantam, 1969.

Glouster, Hugh M. *Negro Voices in American Fiction*. Chapel Hill: University of North Carolina Press, 1965.

Greenlee, Sam. *The Spook Who Sat by the Door*. New York: Bantam, 1970.

213

Gross, Theodore L. "The Negro in the Literature of the Reconstruction. *Images of the Negro in American Literature*. ed. Seymour L. Gross and John Edward Hardy. University of Chicago Press, 1966. 71-83.

Gunn, Bill. *All the Rest Have Died*. New York: Delacorte Press, 1964.

Hernton, Calvin C. *Sex and Racism in America*. New York: Grove Press, 1966.

Himes, Chester. *If He Hollers Let Him Go*. New York: Berkley, 1964.

_____. *The Third Generation*. New York: Signet, 1964.

Howe, Irving. *A World More Attractive*. New York: Horizon Press, 1963.

Hunter, Kristin. *God Bless the Child*. New York: Bantam, 1967.

_____. *The Landlord*. New York: Avon, 1969.

Johnson, James Weldon. *The Autobiography of an Ex-Coloured Man, Three Negro Classics*. New York: Avon, 1969.

Kelley, William Melvin. *A Different Drummer*. New York: Bantam, 1964.

Killens, John Oliver. *And Then We Heard the Thunder*. New York: Pocket Cardinal, 1964.

_____. *Black Man's Burden*. New York: Pocket Books, 1969.

_____. "Youngblood." New York: Trident Press, 1966.

Klein, Marcus. *After Alienation: American Novels in Mid-Century*. Cleveland: Meridian, 1965.

Littlejohn, David. *Black on White*. New York: Viking Press, 1966.

Locke, Alain. "Inventory at Mid-Century: A Review of the Literature of the Negro for 1950." *Phylon*, Vol. XII, No. 1, 1951. 5-12.

Margolies, Edward. *Native Sons: A Critical Study of Twentieth Century Negro American Authors*. Philadelphia: Lippincott, 1968.

Mayfield, Julian. *The Grand Parade*. New York: Paperback Library, 1963.

_____. *The Hit*. New York: Vanguard Press, 1957.

McCall, Dan. *The Example of Richard Wright*. New York: Harcourt, Brace and World, 1969.

Motley, Willard. *Knock on Any Door*. New York: Signet, 1962.

Offord, Carl. *The White Face*. New York: Robert M. McBride, 1943.

Petry, Ann. *The Narrows*. Boston: Houghton Mifflin, 1946.

_____. *The Street*. Boston: Houghton Mifflin, 1946.

Polite, Carlene Hatcher. *The Flagellants*. New York: Farrar, Straus, and Giroux, 1967.

Redding, J. Saunders. "The Negro Writer in Relation to his Roots." *The American Negro Writer and His Roots*. New York: American Society of African Culture, 1960. 1-8.

_____. *On Being Negro in America*. New York: Bantam, 1964.

_____. *Stranger and Alone*. New York: Harcourt, Brace, 1950.

Rhodes, Hari. *A Chosen Few*. New York: Bantam, 1969.

Smith, William Gardner. "The Negro Writer: Pitfalls and Compensations." *Phylon*, Vol. XI, No. 4, 1950. 297-303.

_____. *South Street*. New York: Farrar, Straus and Young, 1954.

Thomas, Will. *God Is for White Folks*. New York: Creative Age, 1947.

Tischler, Nancy M. *Black Masks: Negro Characters in Modern Southern Fiction*. University Park: Pennsylvania State University Press, 1969.

Trilling, Lionel. *The Liberal Imagination: Essays on Literature and Society*. Garden City, New York: Doubleday Anchor, 1950.

Turner, Lorenzo Dow. *Antislavery Sentiment in American Literature Prior to 1865*. Port Washington, New York: Kennikat Press, 1966.

White, Walter. *The Fire in the Flint*. New York: The New American Library, 1969.

Williams, John A. *The Man Who Cried I Am*. New York: Signet, 1968.

_____. *Night Song*. New York: Dell, 1963.

_____. *Sons of Darkness, Sons of Light*. Boston: Little, Brown, 1969.

Wright, Charles. *The Messenger*. New York: Crest, 1964.

Wright, Richard. "How Bigger Was Born." *Black Voices: An Anthology of Afro-American Literature*. ed. Abraham Chapman. New York: Mentor, 1968.

_____. *The Long Dream*. New York: Ace Books, 1958.

_____. *Native Son*. New York: Harper, 1966.

_____. *The Outsider*. New York: Perennial Library, 1965.

_____. *White Man, Listen*. Garden City, New York: Anchor, 1964.

215

Supplementary Bibliography

(Date of original publication in parenthesis)

Anderson, Alston. *All God's Children*. Indianapolis: Bobbs Merrill, 1965. Ch. 8.

Attaway, William. *Blood on the Forge*. New York: Doubleday, Doran, 1941. Ch. 4.

_____. *Let Me Breathe Thunder*. New York: Doubleday, Doran, 1939. Ch. 1.

Austin, Edmund. *The Black Challenge*. New York: Vantage, 1958. Ch. 6.

Baldwin, James. *Another Country*. New York: Dell, 1962, Ch. 8.

_____. *Giovanni's Room*. New York: Dell, 1956. Ch. 6.

_____. *Go Tell It on the Mountain*. New York: Dell, 1969. (1956). Ch. 5.

_____. *Tell Me How Long the Train's Been Gone*. New York: Dell, 1969. Ch. 9.

Bland, Alden. *Behold a Cry*. New York: Scribners, 1947. Ch. 4.

Boles, Robert. *Curling*. Boston: Houghton Mifflin, 1968. (1967). Ch. 7.

_____ *The People One Knows*. Boston: Houghton Mifflin, 1964. Ch. 8.

Bontemps, Arna. *Black Thunder*. New York: Macmillan, 1936. Ch. 1.

_____. *Drums at Dusk*. New York: Macmillan, 1939. Ch. 1.

_____. *God Sends Sunday*. New York: Harcourt, Brace, 1931. Ch. 1.

Brooks, Gwendolyn. *Maud Martha*. New York: Harper, 1953. Ch. 5.

Brown, Cecil. *The Life and Loves of Mr. Jiveass Nigger*. New York: Farrar, Straus and Giroux, 1969. Ch. 7.

Brown, Frank London, *Trumbull Park*. Chicago: Henry Regnery Co., 1959. Ch. 6.

Brown, Lloyd. *Iron City*. New York: Masses and Mainstream, 1951. Ch. 6.

Brown, William Wells. *Clotel, or the President's Daughter*. New York: Collier Books, 1970. (1853). Ch. 1.

Caldwell, Lewis. *The Policy King*. Chicago: New Vistas, 1945. Ch. 4.

Chesnutt, Charles W. *Colonel's Dream*. New York: Doubleday, 1905. Ch. 1.

——————. *House Behind the Cedars*. Boston: Houghton Mifflin, 1900. Ch. 1.

——————. *Marrow of Tradition*. Boston: Houghton Mifflin, 1901. Ch. 1.

Crump, Paul. *Burn Killer, Burn*. Chicago: Johnson's, 1962. Ch. 8.

Cullen, Countee. *One Way to Heaven*. New York: Harper, 1932. Ch. 1.

Daly, Victor. *Not Only War*. Boston: Christopher, 1932. Ch. 1.

Delany, Martin R. *Blake, or the Huts of America. Anglo-African Magazine*, 1 (Jan-July), 1859. Ch. 1.

Demby, William. *Beetlecreek*. New York: Avon, 1950. Ch. 5.

——————. *The Catacombs*. New York: Pantheon Books, 1965. Ch. 7.

Dodson, Owen. *Boy at the Window*. New York: Farrar, Straus, and Giroux, 1951. (later released as *When Trees Were Green*, Popular Library). Ch. 5.

DuBois, W. E. B. *Dark Princess: A Romance*. New York: Harcourt, Brace, 1928. Ch. 1.

——————. *Mansart Builds a School*. New York: Mainstream, 1959. Ch. 6.

——————. *The Ordeal of Mansart*. New York: Mainstream, 1957. Ch. 6.

——————. *Quest of the Silver Fleece*. Chicago: McClurg, 1911. Ch. 1.

——————. *Worlds of Color*. New York: Mainstream, 1961. Ch. 6.

Dunbar, Paul Laurence. *The Fanatics*. New York: Dodd, Mead, 1901. Ch. 1.

——————. *The Love of Landry*. New York: Dodd, Mead, 1900. Ch. 1.

——————. *The Sport of the Gods*. New York: Dodd, Mead, 1902. Ch. 1.

——————. *The Uncalled*. New York: Dodd, Mead, 1898. Ch. 1.

Edwards, Junius. *If We Must Die*. Garden City, New York: Doubleday, 1963. Ch. 8.

Ellison, Ralph. *Invisible Man*. New York: Signet, 1963. (1952) Ch. 5.

Fair, Ronald L. *Hog Butcher*. New York: Harcourt, Brace, 1966. Ch. 7.

——————. *Many Thousands Gone: An American Fable*. New York: Harcourt, Brace, 1965. Ch. 9.

Fauset, Jessie. *Comedy American Style*. New York: Stokes, 1933. Ch. 1.

_____. *Plum Bun*. New York: Stokes, 1928. Ch. 1.

_____. *There Is Confusion*. New York: Boni and Liveright, 1924. Ch. 1.

Fisher, Rudolph. *Walls of Jericho*. New York: Knopf, 1928. Ch. 1.

Gaines, Ernest J. *Catherine Carmier*. New York: Atheneum, 1967. (1964). Ch. 8.

_____. *Of Love and Dust*. New York: Bantam, 1969. (1967). Ch. 8.

Gilbert, Mercedes. *Aunt Sara's Wooden God*. Boston: Christopher, 1938. Ch. 1.

Greenlee, Sam. *The Spook Who Sat by the Door*. New York: Bantam, 1970. (1969). Ch. 9.

Griggs, Sutton E. *The Hindered Hand*. Nashville, Tennessee: Orion, 1905. Ch. 1.

_____. *Imperium In Imperio*. Cincinnati, Ohio, Editor Publishing, 1899. Ch. 1.

_____. *Overshadowed*. Nashville, Tennessee: Orion, 1901. Ch. 1.

_____. *Pointing the Way*. Nashville, Tennessee: Orion, 1908. Ch. 1.

_____. *Unfettered*. Nashville, Tennessee: Orion, 1902. Ch. 1.

Gunn, Bill. *All the Rest Have Died*. New York: Delacorte Press, 1964. Ch. 7.

Guy, Rosa. *Bird At My Window*. Philadelphia: Lippincott, 1966. Ch. 8.

Harper, Frances E. W. *Iola Leroy*. Boston: James H. Earle, 1892. Ch. 1.

Heard, Nathan C. *Howard Street*. New York: Dial, 1968. Ch. 7.

Henderson, George Wylie. *Jule*. New York: Creative Age, 1946. Ch. 4.

_____. *Ollie Miss*. New York: Stokes, 1935. Ch. 1.

Hercules, Frank. *I Want a Black Doll*. New York: Simon and Schuster, 1967. Ch. 8.

_____. *Where the Humming Bird Flies*. New York: Harcourt, Brace, 1961. Ch. 7.

Hill, John H. *Princess Malah*. Washington, D.C.: Associated Publishers, 1933. Ch. 1.

Himes, Chester. *Cast The First Stone*. New York: Coward McCann, 1952. Ch. 6.

_____. *If He Hollers Let Him Go*. New York: Berkley, 1964. (1945). Ch. 3.

_____. *Lonely Crusade*. New York: Knopf, 1947. Ch. 4.

_____. *The Primitive*. New York: New American Library, 1955. Ch. 6.

_____. *The Third Generation*. New York: Signet, 1964. (1954). Ch. 5.

Hughes, Langston. *Not Without Laughter*. New York: Knopf, 1930. Ch. 1.

_____. *Tambourines to Glory*. New York: Hill and Wang, 1958. Ch. 5.

Hunter, Kristin. *God Bless the Child*. New York: Bantam, 1967. (1964). Ch. 7.

_____. *The Landlord*. New York: Avon, 1969. (1966). Ch. 7.

_____. *The Soul Brothers and Sister Lou*. New York: Avon, 1968. Ch. 7.

Hurston, Zora Neale. *Jonah's Gourd Vine*. Philadelphia: Lippincott, 1934. Ch. 1.

_____. *Seraph on the Suwanee*. New York: Scribners, 1948. Ch. 4.

_____. *Their Eyes Were Watching God*. Philadelphia: Lippincott, 1937. Ch. 1.

Jarrette, A. Q. *Beneath the Sky*. New York: Weinberg, 1949. Ch. 4.

Johnson, James Weldon. *The Autobiography of an Ex-Coloured Man, Three Negro Classics*. New York: Avon, 1969. (1912). Ch. 1.

Jones, J. McHenry. *Hearts of Gold*. Wheeling, West Virginia: Daily Intelligencer Steam Job Press. 1896. Ch. 1.

Jones, LeRoi. *The System of Dante's Hell*. New York: Grove Press, 1965. Ch. 7.

Kaye, Philip B. *Taffy*. New York: Crown, 1950. Ch. 5.

Kelley, William Melvin. *A Different Drummer*. New York: Bantam, 1964. (1962). Ch. 9.

_____. *Drop of Patience*. Garden City, New York: Doubleday, 1965. Ch. 8.

Killens, John Oliver. *And Then We Heard the Thunder*. New York: Pocket Cardinal, 1964. (1962). Ch. 9.

_____. *'Sippi*. New York: Trident Press, 1967. Ch. 9.

_____. *Youngblood*. New York: Trident Press, 1966. (1954). Ch. 6.

Larsen, Nella. *Passing*. New York: Knopf, 1929. Ch. 1.

_____. *Quicksand*. New York: Knopf, 1928. Ch. 1.

Lee, George. *River George*. New York: Macaulay, 1937. Ch. 1.

Lucas, Curtis. *Third Ward Newark*. New York: Ziff Davis, 1946. Ch. 3.

Mahoney, William. *Black Jacob*. London Macmillan, 1969. Ch. 9.

Marshall, Paule. *The Chosen Place, the Timeless People*. New York: Harcourt, 1969. Ch. 7.

Mayfield, Julian. *The Grand Parade*. New York: Paperback Library, 1963. (1961). Ch. 9.

_____. *The Hit*. New York: Vanguard Press, 1957. Ch. 5.

_____. *The Long Night*. New York: Vanguard Press, 1958. Ch. 5.

McKay, Claude. *Banjo*. New York: Harper, 1929. Ch. 1.

_____. *Home to Harlem*. New York: Harper, 1928. Ch. 1.

Meriwether, Louise. *Daddy was a Numbers Runner*. Englewood Cliffs, New Jersey: Prentice Hall, 1970. Ch. 7.

Motley, Willard. *Knock on Any Door*. New York: Signet, 1962. (1947). Ch. 3.

_____. *Let No Man Write My Epitaph*. New York: Random, 1958. Ch. 6.

_____. *We Fished All Night*. New York: Appleton, 1951. Ch. 6.

Offord, Carl. *The White Face*. New York: Robert M. McBride, 1943. Ch. 3.

Ottley, Roi. *White Marble Lady*. New York: Farrar, Straus and Giroux, 1965. Ch. 8.

Parks, Gordon. *The Learning Tree*. New York: Fawcett Crest, 1963. Ch. 7.

Paynter, John H. *Fugitives of the Pearl*. Washington, D.C.: Associated Press, 1930. Ch. 1.

Petry, Ann. *Country Place*. Boston: Houghton Mifflin, 1947. Ch. 4.

_____. *The Narrows*. Boston: Houghton Mifflin, 1953. Ch. 6.

_____. *The Street*. Boston: Houghton Mifflin, 1946. Ch. 3.

Pharr, Robert Deane. *The Book of Numbers*. New York: Avon, 1969. Ch. 8.

Polite, Carlene Hatcher. *The Flagellants*. New York: Farrar, Straus and Giroux, 1967. Ch. 7.

Powell, Adam Clayton, Sr. *Picketting Hell*. New York: Wendell Malliet, 1942. Ch. 4.

Redding, J. Saunders. *Stranger and Alone*. New York: Harcourt, Brace, 1950. Ch. 5.

Rhodes, Hari. *A Chosen Few*. New York: Bantam, 1969. (1965). Ch. 9.

Savoy, Willard. *Alien Land*. New York: Dutton, 1949. Ch. 3.

Schuyler, George. *Black No More*. New York: Macaulay, 1931. Ch. 1.

_____. *Slaves Today*. New York: Brewer, Warren and Putnam, 1931. Ch. 1.

Shaw, O'Wendell. *Greater Need Below*. Columbus, Ohio: Bi Monthly Negro Book Club, 1936. Ch. 1.

Simmons, Herbert. *Corner Boy*. Boston: Houghton Mifflin, 1957. Ch. 6.

_____. *Man Walking on Eggshells*. Boston: Houghton Mifflin, 1962. Ch. 7.

Smith, William Gardner. *Anger at Innocence*. New York: Farrar, Straus, 1950. Ch. 6.

_____. *The Last of the Conquerors*. New York: Farrar, Straus, 1948. Ch. 3.

_____. *South Street*. New York: Farrar, Straus, and Young, 1954. Ch. 6.

_____. *The Stone Face*. New York: Pocket Books, 1963. Ch. 8.

Stowers, Walter H. and Anderson, William H. *Appointed*. Detroit: Detroit Law Printing, 1894. Ch. 1.

Thomas, Will. *God Is for White Folks*. New York: Creative Age, 1947. Ch. 4.

Thurman, Wallace. *The Blacker the Berry*. New York: Macaulay, 1929. Ch. 1.

Toomer, Jean. *Cane*. New York: Harper, 1923. Ch. 1.

Turpin, Walter Edward. *O Canaan!* New York: Doubleday, Doran, 1939. Ch. 1.

_____. *These Low Grounds.* New York: Harper and Brothers, 1937. Ch. 1.

Van Peebles, Melvin. *A Bear for the FBI.* New York: Pocket Books, 1968. Ch. 7.

Vroman, Mary Elizabeth. *Esther.* New York: Bantam, 1963. Ch. 8.

Walker, Margaret. *Jubilee.* Boxton: Houghton Mifflin, 1966. Ch. 7.

Webb, Frank. *The Garies and their Friends.* London: G. Routledge, 1857. Ch. 1.

West, Dorothy. *The Living Is Easy.* Boston: Houghton Mifflin, 1948. Ch. 4.

White, Walter. *Fire in the Flint.* New York: The New American Library, 1969. (1924). Ch. 1.

_____. *Flight.* New York: Grosset and Dunlap, 1926. Ch. 1.

Williams, John A. *The Angry Ones.* New York: Pocket Books, 1960. Ch. 8.

_____. *The Man Who Cried I Am.* New York: Signet, 1968. (1967). Ch. 9.

_____. *Night Song.* New York: Dell, 1963. (1961). Ch. 8.

_____. *Sissie.* New York: Farrar, Straus and Cudahy, 1963. Ch. 8.

_____. *Sons of Darkness, Sons of Light.* Boston: Little, Brown, 1969. Ch. 9.

Wright, Charles. *The Messenger.* New York: Crest, 1964. (1963). Ch. 7.

Wright, Richard. *Eight Men.* New York: Pyramid Books, 1961.

_____. *Lawd Today.* New York: Avon, 1963. Ch. 8.

_____. *The Long Dream.* New York: Ace Books, 1958. Ch. 6.

_____. *Native Son.* New York: Harper, 1966. (1940). Ch. 2.

_____. *The Outsider.* New York: Perennial Library, 1965. (1953). Ch. 5.

_____. *Savage Holiday.* New York: Award Books, 1954. Ch. 6.

Wright, Sarah E. *This Child's Gonna Live.* New York: Delaorte Press, 1969. Ch. 8.

Yerby, Frank. *Speak Now.* New York: Dial, 1969. Ch. 8.

Young, Al. *Snakes.* New York: Holt, 1970. Ch. 8.

Index

DATE DUE

DEC 15 '78			
APR 8 '85			
GAYLORD			PRINTED IN U.S.A.